The House on the Mountain

Jewish spiritual teachings about nature, the environment, the earth, the heavens and humanity's role and responsibility for the welfare of the entire Universe

by

Rabbi Avraham Greenbaum

Edited by Nachum Shaw

Promised Land

JERUSALEM   LONDON   NEW YORK

For further information:

Promised Land Publishers

Apt. 8, 5 Gimmel Alroyi St.

Jerusalem 9210808

ISRAEL

or

Promised Land Publishers

8 Woodville Road

London NW11 9TN

ENGLAND

or

Promised Land Publishers

67 Wood Hollow Lane

New Rochelle

NY 10804

USA

Email: info@promisedlandpublishers.com

www.promisedlandpublishers.com

The House on the Mountain

OVERVIEW

The House on the Mountain consists of an Introduction, "In the beginning…" followed by three main parts: "The Mountain", "The Field" and "The House". Each of these three main parts is centered on a major facet of man's relationship with nature and each is associated with one of the founding fathers, Abraham, Isaac and Jacob. Each part consists of a number of individual segments presenting authentic sources from the Bible, Talmud, Midrash, Kabbalah and Chassidut in English translation together with discussion and commentary.

WHY THE "MOUNTAIN", THE "FIELD" AND THE "HOUSE"?

A mountain is a purely natural phenomenon. The "mountain" therefore represents "raw nature", the God-given natural environment in which we find ourselves. At the opposite extreme is the "house", a structure made entirely by man, albeit with materials all of which ultimately derive from nature. Intermediate between the God-given natural "mountain" and the man-made "house" stands the "field" –land or some other natural resource that man has to work and manipulate in order to produce his food and other needs.

In the contemporary world, the "house" – symbolizing the man-made urban civilization in which we live – is seriously out of harmony with the wider natural environment.

Present-day patterns of production and consumption are causing appalling damage to the environment.

But the Torah teaches that this can be rectified and that mankind will attain a new and lasting harmony with nature just as soon as we realize that the key lies in constructing the Sacred House, namely the Temple of God in Jerusalem.

The Talmud tells us that the three founding fathers, Abraham, Isaac and Jacob, were all engaged in laying the foundations for this Temple. Each made his own unique contribution – and conceived it in a different way: Abraham as a "Mountain": Isaac as a "Field" and Jacob as a "House". And it is as a "House" that it is destined to be built in Jerusalem in the near future.

Said Rabbi Elazar: What does Isaiah mean when he says, "And many peoples will go and say, 'Come let us go up to the Mountain of God, to the House of the God of Jacob!'"? The answer is: not like Abraham who saw it as a Mountain (as it is said this day, On the Mountain HaVaYaH is seen" – Genesis 22:14). And not like Isaac, for whom it was a Field ("And Isaac went out to meditate in the Field" – Genesis 24:63). But like Jacob, who called it a House: "And he called the name of that place *Beth El,* the House of God" (Genesis 28:19).

Pesachim 88a.

(See "In the beginning…" for further discussion)

CONTENTS

Dreaming the Dream
where Heaven and Earth Kiss

In a certain place on top of a certain mountain, Heaven and Earth kiss.

On the mountain is a field.

In the field is a house.

Do you want to come and see?

But you can't!

Not yet.

The house is still waiting to be built.

Right now we can only dream it!

It's the most beautiful place in the whole world.

And as we learn to dream the dream together, it will become real in front of our very eyes!

Look up at the Sky!

Rebbe Nachman of Breslov had a follower who was poor but very pious.

Taking advantage of some business opportunities he started becoming more prosperous. But the more his business commitments multiplied, the less time he had for his spiritual pursuits. Eventually he even stopped visiting Rebbe Nachman.

The Rebbe's window overlooked the main street in the town. Once he looked out and saw this man hurrying to the market. He called him. The man was ashamed and could not pretend he had not heard.

"Did you look up at the sky today?" asked the Rebbe.

"No."

Rebbe Nachman pointed to the market-place and asked him what he could see. "Horses, wagons, merchandise, lots of busy people..."

"Fifty years from now," said Rebbe Nachman, "there'll be a totally different market with different people, different wagons and different goods. You won't be here and I won't be here. So let me ask you: Why are you *in such a hurry that you don't even have time to look up at the sky?"*

Rebbe Nachman told the man to take at least a few moments every day to look up at the sky in order to remember that worldly life passes all too quickly and only the heavens endure.

This is something everyone should do. The mundane world can be so absorbing, but very soon it will be gone. Look up often at the sky in order to put things in their proper perspective.

The first lesson...

...is to look up at the sky often.

For today's man-made environment of products, buildings, roads, cars, planes, shops, work, entertainment, media, flashing signs and messages can be so totally absorbing that we may become quite oblivious to the magnificent world of nature that serves as the grand setting for our self-obsessed civilization, providing us with everything needed to make the lives we lead possible.

So forgetful has mankind become that contemporary civilization is seriously out of harmony with the world of nature. Human greed and wastefulness are rapidly depleting natural resources and causing significant environmental deterioration -- to a degree that threatens our very survival.

Long-term human survival will only be possible if we develop a new respect for the natural environment and adopt ways that will preserve and enhance it.

THE HOUSE ON THE MOUNTAIN is a journey into wisdom about nature and how to relate to it as found in the world's oldest living spiritual teaching, the Torah.

With its very first words the Torah guides our eyes straight up to the skies and beyond: "In the beginning, God created the heavens and the earth" (Genesis 1:1).

For if we will have the courage to raise our eyes above and beyond the obsessive man-made cocoon in which we live, we will not fail to be amazed and stirred by the wonder of the universe. Contemplating this tiny speck of earth amidst the vastness of the universe, we crave to know where we have come from and where we are going.

"Lift up your eyes on high and know: Who created these?" (Isaiah 40:26).

Think of the sun in all its brilliance and glory -- vital source of all plant life and every other life-form on earth. Think of the haunting beauty of the moon, the mystery of its ever-changing phases. Think of the planets and stars... their evocative configurations... the endless expanses of the milky way...

Where did they come from? Why are they there?

"Who created these?"

In the original Hebrew, the words are: "*MI* (Who) *BARA* (created) *ELEH* (these)?"

The Hebrew letters of the two key words, *MI ELeH*, when rearranged, spell out *ELoHIM*.

ELOHIM could literally be translated as "the Powers".

But the Torah teaches that all of the various different powers manifested in the endless multiplicity of objects and beings in the heavens above and here on earth ultimately have only one Source. The nature of this Source is quite unknowable. We give the Source a name: God. But no-one can penetrate the mystery.

Still, something in us yearns to know more. "Who created these?" *MI BARA ELEH?*

The question itself contains the answer. *MI ... ELeH? = ELoHIM.*

ELOHIM is one of the principal Hebrew names of God. [To avoid profaning the name of God, this is traditionally pronounced as *ELOKIM* except when addressing God directly in prayer.]

Every Hebrew letter is also a number. The numerical value of the sum of all the letters that make up a word is integral to the power of the word. When two separate words have different letters but the same total numerical value, this often points to a profound connection between the two words.

Significantly, the numerical value of the Hebrew letters of the divine name *ELoHIM* (86) is the same as that of the letters of the word *HaTeVA*, which means "Nature". [In Hebrew, the vowels are not part of the alphabet and therefore only the consonants are counted.]

Aleph (1) + *Lamed* (30) + *Heh* (5) + *Yud* (10) + *Mem* (40) = 86.

Heh (5) + *Tet* (9) + *Bet* (2) + *Ayin* (70) = 86.

The root of the word *HaTeVA* is *TaVA*. This means to "sink". It can also mean to "stamp with".

Thus when minting coins, the form of the mold *sinks into* the molten metal poured into it, leaving its *stamp* on the coin (the Hebrew word for coin is *maT'BeA*).

And so various divinely-constructed forms are "sunken into", mold and give shape to the primordial substance of creation so as to produce the multiplicity and variety of nature, with its laws and regularities. *HaTeVA.*

Yet within -- and at the same time above and beyond the world of nature, *HaTeVA*, stamped as it is with its laws and processes -- stands *ELOHIM*, the Source, Creator of those laws and processes.

"Lift up your eyes on high and know: Who created these?" *MI bara ELEH*? *MI...ELEH = ELOHIM!*

Looking up often at the skies helps us to direct our thoughts and our yearnings to the One Who (*MI*) is the Source and Creator of "all these" (*ELeH*). This is *ELOKIM* -- God -- the mystery of Whose being we can seek out within and through Nature.

INTRODUCTION

In the beginning...

---

*The beginning of the beginning * In the beginning * Where is that Garden? * Contemporary City Civilization * The effect on the Earth * The effect on the human spirit * Alienation from Nature * Taking Responsibility * So what are we supposed to do? * The Torah * The Mountain, the Field & the House*

The beginning of the beginning...

We must start at the very beginning. Even before the creation of the skies, the heavens and the earth.

Bereyshit. "In the beginning..." (Genesis 1:1).

The six Hebrew letters making up the opening word of the Bible, *BeReYShiT*, can be rearranged to spell out the words *RoSh BaYiT*, "the Head of the House".

Because first in mind -- even before the creation of the actual universe -- there was a vision of a House. Long before humans started building houses for themselves, as God began building worlds, there was already a vision of the ultimate House: the House of God, the Holy Temple on the Temple Mount in Jerusalem. In the words of Jacob, speaking of this place: "This is the House of God and this is the Gate of Heaven" (Genesis 28:17).

This House is the summit of all creation. The purpose of the entire creation is to reveal the beauty and perfection of God to His creatures. The Temple raises our eyes to that perfection. For the Temple directs our eyes beyond transient worldliness towards heavenly truth. This House comes to join Earth back to Heaven. The Temple is the place where Earth meets Heaven. It is the very Gate of Heaven.

The Holy Temple in Jerusalem comes to show and reveal that the loving God is the Head of the House, *RoSh BaYiT*, Ruler over the Universe. And that the whole world is a "House" -- a planned, ordered, intelligently-built structure -- in and through which God's divinity is revealed to all the inhabitants of the world.

It was from the earth of this place in Jerusalem that Adam was formed. For it is the destiny of his children -- all humanity -- to worship at this House.

After Noah was saved from the flood, it was in this place that he sacrificed.

This is the mountain where Abraham came to sacrifice Isaac.

This is the "field" to which Isaac returned to meditate.

This is the place where Jacob lay down and dreamed of a ladder stretching up to heaven. This is the place he called "the House of God".

This place King David knew to be the place of the Temple, and he prepared for its construction by King Solomon.

The Temple of Solomon stood there for 410 years until it was destroyed.

The Second Temple stood there for 420 years until it was destroyed.

For almost 2000 years since the destruction of the Second Temple, Jews have yearned and prayed daily for the rebuilding of the Temple.

Here on this exact same spot, the Third Temple is destined to be rebuilt.

We are waiting for it. We need it. "If the nations of the world had understood how valuable the Holy Temple was for them they would have surrounded it with troops and fortifications to guard it" (*Bemidbar Rabbah* 1:3). For only when all mankind will unite to worship God at this Temple will it be possible to join the earth back to heaven. And only then will mankind be able to live in harmony with the environment.

In the beginning...

BeReYShiT. That vision of the House was the beginning of creation. And then came the actual creation of all that is required to make it possible to build that House: the heavens and the earth: the sun, the moon, the stars; the land, the sea, the plants and trees, the fish, the birds and animals...

And finally, God said: "Let us make man in our form and likeness, and they will rule over the fish of the sea, over the birds of the skies, over the animals and over all the earth and every creature on it."

And God created man in His own likeness. He created them male and female. And God blessed them and said to them: "Be fruitful and multiply. Fill the earth and conquer it. Rule over the fish of the sea and the birds of the sky and all the living creatures that swarm over the earth."

And God planted a garden of delight. He caused the earth to sprout forth every kind of lovely tree. And the tree of life in the midst of the garden. And the tree of knowledge of good and evil.

God took Adam and Eve and placed them in this Garden of Eden to tend it and keep it. And God ordered the man: "You may eat freely from every tree in the garden. Except for the Tree of Knowledge of Good and Evil. For on the day you eat from it, you will certainly die."

But Adam and Eve ate from the tree....

And God said to Adam: "Because you ate from the tree from which I ordered you not to eat, the ground is cursed for you. You will have to toil in order to eat from it all the days of your life. The earth will bring up thorns and thistles, and you will eat the herb of the field. With the sweat of your face you will eat bread, until you go back to the ground. Because that is where you were taken from: you are dust, and to dust you will return."

And God said: "See, the man has become like one of us to know good and evil. And now, so that he should not put his hand out and also take from the Tree of Life and eat and live for ever...."

God drove man out from the Garden of Eden to tend the earth from which he was taken. And God placed angels and a fiery sword to guard the way to the Tree of Life. (Genesis ch's 1-3).

Where is that Garden?

Where is that enchanted garden? Will we ever see it again? In this world? Or in some other?

In Eden, everything Adam needed was instantly available. All he had to do was pick the fruit off the trees. But having been driven out of Eden, he was forced to fend for himself.

Ever since then, men have writhed and struggled to find easier ways of making a living so as to circumvent the curse and enjoy this world a little before dying and returning to the dust.

One of the things that most distinguishes man from God's other creatures is the intelligence with which he is able to make and use tools and artifacts that can aid him in this goal. Over the millennia, as human technology has become ever more ambitious, so the corresponding forms of economic and social organization have become more and more complex.

No matter how complex the technology and social organization, everything required to sustain human life ultimately derives from the surrounding God-given natural environment. Yet the more advanced our technology and society, the more man-made our surroundings become -- and the more cut-off we seem to be from nature.

For thousands of years the great majority of the population lived on the land, close to nature -- many of them quite literally fulfilling the curse of Adam, toiling and sweating to extract food from the ground. But the ever-accelerating technological revolution of the last few hundred years has caused a corresponding revolution in socioeconomic organization that has totally shifted the focus from the country to the city.

Today's urban agglomerations not only provide homes for their enormous concentrations of population. They also serve as the location for most of the industrial and economic activity that provides the goods and services, the educational infrastructure that produces the manpower and know-how, the communications media that keep everyone informed and involved in the system, and the governmental and other bodies charged with overall coordination and control.

Urbanization is a major global trend. Of the more than 7 billion people currently living on this earth, just over half still live away from cities. But the other half are now urbanized. It is expected that within twenty-five years, two thirds of the world's population may be living in cities. Three quarters of the population of the United States already live in cities.

Contemporary city civilization

Our contemporary urban technology and media based civilization transcends traditional geographic, political, racial and cultural boundaries. It has established itself as the dominant civilization throughout the world. Few if any aboriginal or pre-industrial people remain who are not under the rule of some city-based government and subject to modern urban technological and cultural influences. No matter where in the world you are -- even on a desert island, even in outer space -- all you have to do is turn on your radio and you are in instant touch with the latest news, stock prices, fashions, sports, entertainment, books, albums, websites and anything else you want.

The claim of this civilization to world ascendancy is based first and foremost on its amazing capacity to generate wealth. The success of countries and their governments is measured by their ability to ensure this abundance for everyone -- or at least for enough of the population not to let the have-nots get out of hand. Material consumption is a goal that unites people of all nations, races, beliefs and cultures: east, west, north and south.

Contemporary city civilization is a unique solution to Adam's predicament of how to survive and enjoy, providing ever more refined ways of satisfying an infinite array of secondary whims and desires. With a pampered palate, all modern comforts, technology beeping and flashing all around you, entertainment at the press of a button, endless opportunities for shopping, amusement, education, culture, sports and more and more... you could easily imagine this IS paradise!

The effect on the earth

It is surely a desirable goal to seek to satisfy everyone's basic needs and provide them with as many true comforts and conveniences as possible. Indeed, with wise organization and self-restraint, the whole world could be amply provided for without any danger to the environment.

But our current methods of trying to satisfy the world population's basic needs and sustain the sophisticated lifestyle of the more prosperous are causing the depletion of natural resources and degradation of the global environment at a rate that will make it impossible for humanity to carry on in the same way for more than a generation or two. The danger to the environment is clear to anyone willing to take even a brief glance at some of the information gathered by environmental monitoring agencies.

- With about 80 million people added to the world population each year, food security -- measured in the level of carryover stocks of grain -- has dropped to an all-time low.

- Uncontaminated water is now a scarce resource even in countries once considered rich in water resources.
- Deforestation continues unabated.
- Thousands and thousands of plant, fish, bird and animal species have become or are becoming extinct.
- Record levels of carbon emissions from fossil fuel burning are thought to be one of the main factors in overall global warming that has already caused billions of dollars' worth of losses in the last few years because of weather-related disasters, and could lead to major worldwide economic, social and environment dislocations in the future.
- Mortality is on the rise in many countries, and more and more people are suffering from pollution-related diseases.

("Vital Signs" and "State of the World" published by Worldwatch Institute, Washington).

Thousands of years after Adam's expulsion from paradise, mankind is more out of harmony with the environment than ever.

It is an ironic twist to a continuing saga. Adam was expelled from paradise for an act of excess, uncontrolled consumption, eating the extra fruit he was not allowed. And it is the excess, uncontrolled production and consumption habits of his sophisticated present-day descendants that are destroying the very earth we are entrusted to guard.

The effect on the human spirit

Quite apart from what contemporary civilization is doing to the physical environment, its effect on the minds and souls of those who live in it are just as devastating if harder to measure.

Charlie Chaplin in "Modern Times" graphically portrayed the crushing effects of industrialization on human dignity. That was back in the 1920's -- before people had been subjected to the full intensity of the contemporary city experience: unremitting heavy traffic, constant overhead aircraft, bulldozers, drilling, blaring sirens, alarms, amplifiers, phones, beepers, flashing lights, information overflow....

Contemporary civilization is the most technologically sophisticated and economically prosperous that ever was. Never before have so many people enjoyed such comforts and conveniences. Yet the commonest problems brought today to doctors and psychiatrists are depression, fatigue, hypertension, fear and anxiety!

The incidence of murder, violence, crime, sexual immorality, drug abuse and the like in the world's major cities is appalling. Subtler problems like the hyperactivity, attention-deficit and other behavioral problems so widespread among youth may seem less horrifying. Yet they could be signs of overall mental degeneration in our civilization.

It is hardly surprising that so many people in our culture show signs of wanting to escape. Some travel the globe in search of a different world, one that is more humane and serene. Others try to escape by turning inwards, or by blasting themselves with frenetic music, mind-altering drugs, muscle pumping and other forms of intensity. Among the most persistent themes in many present-day sub-cultures are anger, defiance and nihilism. But the majority seek solace from the pressures of modern life through the compulsive pursuit of material gratification, resulting in the food, sex, shopping, smoking, drinking, gambling and other addictions rife in our societies.

Alienation from Nature

All the resources required to maintain our contemporary consumerist civilization ultimately derive from the natural environment. Yet this selfsame culture tends to foster a myopic lack of awareness of nature that is one of the major factors causing people not only to ignore the continuing destruction of the environment but actively to contribute to it.

Urban living and contemporary technology cut people off from nature physically and mentally. The physical spaces where most of the urban population spend their lives -- houses, apartment blocks, roads, shops, offices, factories, schools, public facilities, cars, buses, trains, planes -- are all man-made. People are surrounded by man-made objects, artifacts and equipment of all kinds.

Even more enveloping are the man-made communications media, which for most of the population are the main source of information about the wider world as well as entertainment and culture. TV's, radios, papers, magazines, promotion and advertising surround us from childhood to old age. We may not be obliged to pay attention to them. But the sophistication with which they capture people's attention make them the determining influence molding the outlook and consciousness of the overwhelming majority of the population.

For many people, watching images on a screen is far more compelling than looking directly at their actual surroundings (which they may in any case find uninteresting or depressing). Audio output from speakers or headphones is far more involving than the real, live sounds all around (which may include a high proportion of meaningless technology-generated noise.) Media hypnosis thus engenders in people a glazed detachment from their own direct experience of the actual world around them through their eyes, ears and other senses, making them all but unaware of the sky, the trees and plants, birds, insects and other living creatures found even in cities.

The scale and economics of the media ensure that they remain the mouthpiece of entrenched interests in a system geared not so much to satisfying people's true needs as to arousing their material appetites. This is what makes the sales that create the profits that oil the system. The implicit message of the promotion that bombards us everywhere is: "You, the consumer, are king. The entire world is a giant smorgasbord of thrilling products, services and opportunities of every kind, all laid on for *your* pleasure and delight. Just take and enjoy! Don't wait! Have it *now*! Buy! Special offer! Better value! More for less! Free gifts! Eat, drink and be merry, for tomorrow we die!"

The majority of the population are swept along by the general tide of consumerism, sparing little thought for the collective effect of their own and everyone else's individual acts of excess and waste on the wider global environment.

At least this mindless folly is slightly more forgivable than the frantic pollution of the environment and destruction of irreplaceable resources perpetrated by profit-hungry businessmen, major corporations and indeed some of the very governments that talk about the need for greater public awareness and stricter controls.

Taking responsibility

A civilization hell-bent on a lifestyle that is environmentally unsustainable and destructive is sick.

We must therefore thank God that more and more sensitive, thoughtful and responsible people are profoundly disturbed and pained at the spectacle of contemporary man destroying himself and the world, and are asking what we should do about it.

Perhaps there are animals that eat their fill and then move on leaving a trail of filth and waste behind them. But man has a higher destiny. We are the recipients of God's special blessing: "Be fruitful and multiply. Fill the earth and conquer it. Rule over the fish of the sea and the birds of the sky and all the living creatures that swarm over the earth."

"Be fruitful and multiply. Fill the earth and conquer it." God *wants* a large human population, for such a multitude of souls -- each one different, each unique -- attests to the glory of the Creator. But only if the population is made up of truly dignified, refined human beings who not only take from the world and consume but also *give*. Man's mission is to conquer his selfish, animal instincts so as to develop his innate divinity and *serve* -- give and contribute of himself in order to bring this world to perfection and turn it back into the beautiful, harmonious garden it was created to be.

"Rule over the fish of the sea and the birds of the sky and all the living creatures that swarm over the earth." The blessing applies to all of Adam's descendants. It applies to *us*. We are the guardians of the Earth and all the different life-forms and species it contains.

As we witness the destruction of the environment and see thousands of species of plants and animals becoming extinct, we must ask ourselves: How are we fulfilling our role? How are we discharging our responsibility?

One could easily be discouraged from even starting to think about what to do to improve the world. The odds against succeeding seem so great. True, more and more people are waking up to the responsibility we bear. But we are numerically few compared to the great majority of the world population who don't seem to care at all. What power do we have against the massive forces that are destroying the world? How can we have any significant effect?

Yet we are not at liberty to cast off our responsibility. The Talmud teaches: "Every single person is a whole unique world. And therefore, every person is obliged to say, The entire world was created only for me" (*Sanhedrin* 37a). "If so," said Rebbe Nachman of Breslov, "then it is up to me to consider carefully

at all times what I must do in order to improve the world..."

(Likutey Moharan Pt I, 5:1).

The way we discharge our responsibility will determine the kind of world we will live in when we are older and the kind of world we will leave to our children and children's children.

So, what are we supposed to do?

Experts are crying out about the destruction of the environment. Pressure groups lobby. International organizations pass resolutions. Governments introduce legislation. Corporations speak piously about their commitment to the environment. Yet the practical measures being taken have hardly begun to turn the tide of abuse and destruction.

Why should this be? If we are so sophisticated and intelligent, why are we unable to solve our problems?

Could it be because the problems are caused by our very intelligence itself, which has outstripped our ability to control and direct it for good and not evil?

It is not our technology that is bringing us to grief so much as the short-sightedness and greed with which it is applied. Man has created a formidable technological and socio-economic apparatus to satisfy his needs. But so far, he has not had the sense to keep it under the proper control in order not to destroy himself and the world in the process.

It is an old, old problem. It goes right back to Adam, who through a failure of self-control ate from the forbidden tree of knowledge and was driven out of paradise.

It was because Adam took the fruit for himself against God's command that he was cursed with having to go out into the world and fend for himself.

"You want to be so clever? You don't want to submit to a higher wisdom that says thus far but no further? Then go out and learn for yourself! Try to do everything by yourself. Rely only on your own human intelligence. Make all the mistakes you want. Until in the end you will come to grief. And then you will realize that, wise as you are, you are still not wise enough to work everything out by yourself....

"The whole world is a gift to you. But it comes with God's book of instructions. Without them, nothing will work properly. Go back and do things the way God advises -- and then you will see that everything will work out!"

The Torah

If we truly desire to discharge our responsibility for the world, we have an obligation to search out what God advises for its welfare, as prescribed in His teaching to mankind, the Torah.

However, we should not expect to find there a point-by-point scheme for saving the environment along the lines of some human-devised plan. For the issue is not merely how to stave off the destruction of the environment for just that little bit longer so that humanity can simply continue pursuing exactly the same materialistic aims as today with only a modicum of extra prudence.

Man's materialistic preoccupations keep him from his true destiny. The Torah therefore comes to wean us from them, leading us on a higher, spiritual pathway where the question is not "What can I get out of the world for myself?" but "What are my obligations? How can I contribute? What can I give?"

As more and more people cultivate an attitude of responsibility and giving instead of only grabbing and taking, it will automatically become easier to introduce the economic and social changes necessary to preserve the environment and ensure long-term human survival.

By talking to each other about such an attitude and encouraging as many people as we have the power to influence to adopt it, we are contributing to and strengthening a new current that is already spreading more and more widely, and has the power to bring the entire world to greater sanity.

Let us therefore put the question of environmental responsibility in a broader perspective by asking: What does the Torah teach about how mankind should relate to the God-given world of nature that provides the grand setting for our civilization as a whole and for the lives of every one of us in it?

How does the Torah teach us to relate to nature?

The only way we can gain a proper perspective on this vital question from our standpoint within an ailing civilization is by endeavoring to step outside.

Let us therefore turn for insight to a band of teachers very different from the urbane experts and specialists of today. They were sky-gazers, meditators, daveners, dreamers, story-tellers, singers, sages, saints, mystics, prophets, founding fathers and leaders of humanity. Some may be famous and familiar from history and literature. Yet however much we know about them, we really do not know them at all.

The extensive Torah library provides a rich treasury of teachings about nature from many different saints and sages from Biblical, Mishnaic and Talmudic times until today. We will draw from very many of them, and especially from the Master Sage, Rebbe Nachman, who is the soul breathing life into this whole excursion. Rebbe Nachman will be close by during the whole journey from beginning to end.

But the journey will be a long one if we are to cover the ground thoroughly. We will have to take it in stages. There will be four main stages of this journey, and in each one we will look for special insight to one leading guide. Of the four main guides, three are the three founding fathers, Abraham, Isaac and Jacob, while the fourth is David, Sweet Singer of Israel.

The common tie binding them together is that all four sought to rectify the sin that drove Adam out of the Garden. In order to restore harmony between man and God, between Earth and Heaven. Only this way can man live in harmony with the world around him. Only this way can mankind survive. Only this way can we get back into the Garden.

All four knew that the success of the entire venture ultimately depends upon one thing: the actualization of the House that was the first thought of the entire creation, "In the beginning" -- *BeReYShiT* -- *RoSh BaYiT*, the "Head House": a single place of worship to which all of mankind will turn in unity.

The Mountain, the Field and the House

Said Rabbi Elazar: What does Isaiah mean when he says, "And many peoples will go and say, 'Come let us go up to the Mountain of God to the House of the God of Jacob!'" ? Why the God of Jacob and not the God of Abraham and Isaac? The answer is: Not like Abraham, who saw it as a Mountain ("as it is said this day, On the *Mountain* HaVaYaH is seen" -- Genesis 22:14). And not like Isaac, for whom it was a Field ("And Isaac went out to meditate in the *Field*" -- Genesis 24:63). But like

Jacob, who called it a House: "And he called the name of that place *Beth El*, the *House* of God" (Genesis 28:19).

(Pesachim 88a)

It was to this focus of worship for all mankind that Abraham aspired when he journeyed to the mountain to sacrifice Isaac. Only for Abraham, it was and remained a mountain -- a high, forbidding place out of the reach of most people.

Having been bound at that spot, Isaac went back there again and again to meditate, pray and plan for the realization of the dream. Isaac made it a habit. He brought it nearer. For Isaac it was a field, a place in which to labor and work towards the vision. Fields are more useful to most people than mountains. The concept of a field is one people can more easily grasp than that of a mountain.

Yet a field is still not a place of human habitation to the same extent that a house is. Everybody needs a house to live in. Everyone can understand the idea of a house.

It was as a House that Jacob conceived the Temple: a House of Prayer. And it is as a House of Prayer that it will become graspable and meaningful to all humanity.

"I will bring them to My Holy Mountain and make them rejoice in My House of Prayer. Their sacrifices and peace-offerings will find favor on My altar. For My House will be called the House of Prayer for all the nations" (Isaiah 56,7).

David's messianic mission was to spread the teaching of prayer to all mankind. Thus, it was Jacob's concept of a House that David sought to actualize and build in his city of Jerusalem.

And it is this House that will be built quickly in the near future when Mashiach, son of David, leads the building of the third, final, eternal House, the Holy Temple in Jerusalem. And then all mankind will unite in the service of God and the world will come to perfection.

The progression from the concept of an entirely natural Mountain to that of a human-cultivated Field and finally that of a totally man-constructed House corresponds to mankind's progression from the time Adam first stepped out into the unspoiled God-given world of nature through thousands of years of agrarian living to the super-sophisticated man-constructed scientific-technological-urban civilization we live in today.

The Mountain is symbolic of the raw, God-given, natural environment. The Field represents the primary place of interaction between man and his environment: man has to dig, sow and manipulate the Earth in other ways in order to exploit the God-given resources so as to feed himself and provide his other needs.

But when it comes to actually eating, drinking, resting, relaxing and enjoying, people's first choice is the "House" -- whether their own homes or the other man-made buildings and structures in which we go about our various daily activities.

Men have built houses and more houses and more houses... until the Earth is filling up with bigger and bigger cities, the urban agglomerations that constitute the main centers of contemporary civilization.

The paradox is that this man-made civilization is now destroying the natural environment that is the very basis of its life. This is a civilization that is out of harmony with the environment.

Only through the sacred House that Jacob saw and the Son of David will build soon in Jerusalem, the Holy City, will it become possible to make peace and restore harmony between man and his human-constructed, technology-based, house-centered, citified world on the one hand, and the surrounding God-created, God-given world of nature on the other.

May this House be built quickly in our time. Amen.

"I lift up my eyes to the mountains. From where will my help come? My help is from HaVaYaH, *Maker of Heaven and Earth"*

(Psalms 121:1-2).

PART I

The Mountain

ABRAHAM

MOTIFS: The Mountain / Sunrise, Morning / Life, Youth, Regeneration / Element: Water / Color: White, Silver / Mother Letter: *Mem* / Divine Name: *EL* / Attributes: The Right Column -- Wisdom (*Chochmah*), Kindness and Charity (*Gedulah, Chessed*) Victory (*Netzach*) / Prayer / The Priest (*Cohen*) / Prayer of the Day: Morning (*Shacharit*) / Festival: Passover (*Pesach*), Redemption, Freedom, overcoming the desire for wealth

Abraham was totally unique. He was a revolutionary, a rebel against a world that had fallen into worship of the planets and stars as the ultimate powers in the universe.

Abraham -- himself a master astrologer -- saw that worship of the stars was none other than a guise for man's worship of his own selfish lusts. Abraham smashed the idols -- the man-made images with which people blind themselves to the truth about this world. Rejecting the sophisticated city-culture of his time, Abraham set off on a life-long quest for the Land -- a country whose inhabitants would live a life of perfect harmony with God, among themselves and with nature.

Abraham grasped that the entire universe is a single holistic system. His life-mission was to teach all humanity this truth and explain its practical implications for our lives. Yet at the outset of his journey, Abraham was alone. He had no-one to teach or guide him since everyone else in the world was swept up by the prevailing orthodoxies. For Abraham, the only option was to go to his own self.

When a person is willing to let go of conceit and self-centeredness and observe and think about nature without any ideological or other preconceived notions, nature itself becomes man's greatest teacher about his true place in the universe.

Through observation of the external universe combined with profound introspection and contemplation, Abraham laid the foundations for the view of the world that he expressed in his Sefer Yetzira (the "Book of Creation"). This is the underlying worldview of later talmudic, midrashic, kabbalistic and other Judaic writings.

Abraham realized that man, as the recipient of God's never-ending generosity, is under an obligation to give something in return. Perceiving that the underlying principle of the entire universe is love and kindness, Abraham therefore cultivated these qualities to perfection. Not only did he emphasize the importance of showing practical kindness and charity to all (essential foundation for any truly civilized society). Abraham also taught that man's highest "kindness" is when he uses his unique human faculty of speech to thank God and pray for the welfare of the world. This in itself draws blessing into the world.

The climax of Abraham's spiritual quest was when God told him to sacrifice his beloved son Isaac on "the mountain that I will show you"-- Mount Moriah, the Temple Mount (Genesis 22, 1-19). Abraham showed himself ready and willing to sacrifice his all for God. This in itself was enough, and a heavenly voice told him not to go through with the sacrifice.

Abraham is the supreme exemplar of the willingness to sacrifice ego and self-interest for the greater good. This is the precondition for peace among men, between man and the natural environment and between man and God. The mountain symbolizes God's daunting challenge to man to climb to the greatest heights of spiritual perfection.

Mountains and other natural surroundings were and are the preferred environment in which many spiritual seekers in the Jewish tradition have sought to pursue this goal.

Abraham Was Unique!

*H*ow is it possible to evoke Avraham Avinu -- our father, Abraham?

Many people may have an image of Abraham -- perhaps as a kindly old man with a flowing white beard, or some other. Such pictures are derived from legends, picture bibles and the like. But to begin to approach the authentic Abraham -- or at least try to get some faint understanding of this, totally unique figure in world history -- it is necessary to expose and discard false images, just as Abraham himself smashed the idols and forged ahead on a completely original path.

Abraham was the first human being to take full responsibility for the Earth and indeed for the entire Universe. He said: "It's entirely up to me!" He devoted every fiber of his being to his goal: to bring everyone to know God and live in harmony with His law. Abraham was willing to sacrifice everything for God, even his very son. His reward is that his soul lives on forever in the eternal Jewish People that he founded. His name and teachings have been carried to the entire world through the Christian and Moslem religions, both of which proudly trace themselves to him.

Rebbe Nachman of Breslov points out that Abraham drew strength and power from the very fact that he was unique and alone in the world:

The prophet Ezekiel says, "Abraham was one, and he inherited the land" (Ezekiel 33:24). What does Ezekiel mean by stressing that Abraham was *one*? Abraham based his whole service of God on the fact that he was alone. He looked on himself as the only person in the world who was serving God -- as if everything was up to him -- and he paid no attention whatever to all the other people who were on the wrong track and who were putting obstacles in his way. Abraham paid no attention to his father or any of the other people who tried to prevent him from doing what he knew to be true. He carried on as if he was the only one in the world, as if everything depended on him. That is the meaning of Ezekiel's statement: "Abraham was one."

Rebbe Nachman draws out from this a lesson for everyone:

And so too anyone who wants to serve God can only start if he takes the view that there is no-one else in the world except himself, and everything is up to him. He should not pay attention to anyone trying to put obstacles in his way -- not even his own father and mother, wife and children, nor obstacles from other people who laugh at him, try to persuade him to give up or otherwise stand in his way. One must pay no attention whatever to them, just like Abraham. "Abraham was one." He looked upon himself as if he was the only one in the world and as if everything depended on him.

(Likutey Moharan II, beginning)

The Stars and Planets

One of the greatest tragedies of contemporary civilization is that millions and millions of people in urban agglomerations and even in rural areas live out their lives in total unawareness of the glory and wonder of the sky.

Most people sleep through the sunrise. Sunset is hidden from them by the man-made urban landscape. For many, the light of the sun is simply an annoying glare best removed with the help of sunglasses, or better still by going inside a building.

The true glory of the night sky is hardly ever visible to city dwellers since its subtle lights are simply obscured by the ubiquitous glow of city lights and pollution, even when weather conditions are relatively clear.

But seeing the night-sky in a desert or some other remote, uninhabited area, no-one can fail to be staggered by the awesome majesty of the celestial canopy of stars and planets and the haunting beauty of the moon.... The wonder and mystery become ever deeper as one begins to recognize and make friends with the different stars and planets and to understand their nightly, monthly and yearly pathways.

Long before modern astronomy gave us a sense of the mind-boggling immensity of the universe and the sheer intensity of the energy involved in bodies like the sun, people instinctively understood that the heavenly bodies radiate power on a scale out of all proportion to anything mere human beings are capable of producing.

No matter how many billions of lights are turned on in a city at night, the effect is puny compared to the sun lighting up the day. All life on earth depends on the sun.

Despite the tremendous advances in science since the invention of the telescope, our knowledge about the sun and the rest of the universe is still very limited. In some ways, we may know less than our ancestors thousands of years ago.

Many people today cannot identify the twelve constellations of the zodiac or the positions of the major planets. Many do not even know where to find the moon in the sky at different times of the month.

It is ironic that in the contemporary world, people's lives are more than ever dominated by radiations of light -- from TV and computer screens, traffic lights and the like. Flashing lights are one of the major media of communication and social control. With the advances in laser technology, people have begun to appreciate the immense power that can be wielded through the accurate focusing of light.

Yet people have no idea that the magnificent celestial lightshow means anything or does anything. Scientists continue to speak as if the millions and millions of stars lighting up the sky are all shining purely by chance, as if their radiations have no significance whatever. Most people assume they must be right.

But wise men in most other times and cultures have known better. As Rebbe Nachman related:

> There was once a king who devised a plan to conquer the entire world without war. Since the world is divided into seven areas, it contains seven parts. There are also seven planets: each planet shines on one part of the world. Likewise, there are seven metals, and one planet shines on each type of metal.
>
> The king gathered together all seven types of metal. He also ordered that he be brought the golden portraits of the kings which hung in their palaces. Out of these he made a man. The head was made of gold, the body of silver and the other parts of the body of other metals. The man thus contained all seven types of metal. The king placed the figure on top of a high mountain, so that all seven planets would shine on it.
>
> Whenever a person needed advice as to whether to engage in a venture or not, he would stand in front of the part of the body made of the metal corresponding to the part of the world from which he came. He would then meditate on his question. If it was something that he should do, that part of

the statue's body would glow and shine. If not, that part of the body would remain dark. With this statue, the king conquered the entire world and amassed great wealth....

From "The Bull and the Ram", Rabbi Nachman's Stories, pp. 109ff.

Most ancient civilizations, including those in the time of Abraham, believed the planets and stars to be the ultimate powers of the universe and worshipped them accordingly. Many of the gods and goddesses of ancient cultures were associated with particular planets or constellations of stars, which were believed to rule over the days of the week and months of the year as well as over fertility, prosperity, power and other aspects of life. Traces of such beliefs can be seen, for example, in the English and French names of the days of the week, which are derived from the Germanic and Roman names of the planet gods thought to rule over them.

Rabbi Moshe ben Maimon -- known as Rambam or Maimonides (1135-1204) -- explains how humanity lapsed into actual worship of the planets and stars in the generations after Adam:

> It was in the days of Enosh, the grandson of Adam. The wise men of the time understood that the One God had created these stars and planets to control the workings of the world. They saw that He had

placed them on high and given them such glory, for they are His officers and attending ministers.

Accordingly, they thought it would be appropriate to praise and honor them, imagining that it must be God's will to show respect to beings He Himself had made so great, just as an earthly king wants people to show respect for his servants and officers. Having reached this conclusion, they started building temples to the stars and planets and brought them sacrifices and offerings. They praised and glorified them with words and prostrated before them in order -- as they imagined -- to fulfill the will of the Creator...

With the passage of time, there arose false prophets who claimed that God had commanded them to worship a particular planet or all of the different constellations, to bring them specific offerings and libations, to build them temples and to make statues of the "form" of the star or planet in order that the common people, women and children would be able to worship it. These prophets informed the people that a particular planet had a certain form dreamed up by the prophet himself. He would say that this form had been revealed to him in prophecy.

In this way people started making statues which were placed in temples or under trees and on mountain and hill-tops. People would gather there to worship. The priests used to tell the simple people that this statue had the power to benefit or harm people and that they should worship and revere it. The priests told people what to do and what not to do in order to elicit favor and succeed in their various enterprises. Other deceivers arose claiming that the planet or constellation or angel itself had spoken to them and told them how to serve it. Cults of various kinds began to spread throughout the entire world.

As time went on the entire world became totally unaware of God. Men, women and children knew only about the wood or stone statues and temples with which they had been brought up from childhood and which they had been taught to bow to, worship and swear by. Their wise men imagined there was no other God besides the stars and constellations on whose account these statues had been made. With the exception of a few individuals, such as Enoch, Noah, Shem and Ever, no one knew or recognized the Creator of all the worlds…This was the way the world was until the birth of the pillar of the world: our father Abraham.

Rambam, *Mishneh Torah*, Laws of Idolatry, 1:1-2

Abraham Smashes
the Idols

*A*braham was born and brought up in the magnificent city civilization of Babylon -- Iraq. This was the civilization that tried to produce the ultimate man-constructed "house", the Tower of Babel. It was supposed to reach to the very heavens, but then it collapsed and sank into the ground (Genesis 11). Abraham traveled widely throughout the Fertile Crescent and Egypt, where he had intimate dealings with a court that viewed itself as the very last word in sophistication and saw fit to kidnap his wife for Pharaoh's pleasure (Genesis 12:14-20). The same happened when Abraham visited the Philistine kingdom of Gerar (*ibid.* 20:1-18). Abraham personally witnessed the awesome physical catastrophe that befell the decadent, degenerate city culture of the once lush, now barren, salty plain of Sodom just north of Israel's Yam HaMelach ("Dead" Sea) (*ibid.* chapters 18-19).

The technology in Abraham's time may have been primitive compared with what we have now. Yet the cultures of the time produced impressive buildings and artifacts, and people's practical know-how was often far greater than that of the majority in our automated civilization. The human social and cultural environment was no less elaborate than today's. People were surrounded by man-made objects and images just as we are today. Wise men and priests attained levels of astronomical, mathematical, botanical, pharmaceutical and other kinds of knowledge that would put many contemporary "experts" and "specialists" to shame. Their theological and philosophical systems appear to have been no less subtle and complex than any today.

Abraham rejected the entire belief system of his contemporaries, despite the fact that he himself came from the very cream of the elite. His father, Terach, was, according to tradition, favorite of the then most powerful man in the world, Nimrod. Today Nimrod would be called a tyrant or control freak or perhaps the first superman. The Bible says of Nimrod: "He began to be a mighty one in the earth. He was a mighty hunter before God, which is why it is said: Like Nimrod, a mighty hunter before God" (Genesis 10:8-9) The classic Bible commentator Rashi explains: "He ensnared the minds of people with his talk and deceived them into rebelling against God" (Rashi ad loc.)

Nimrod's line was that man is entitled to do whatever he pleases. This was a philosophy that gave especially wide scope to Nimrod himself since he himself was the biggest strongman. No one would dare do anything against his whims and desires. I.e. *Nimrod* is god!

It appears that by nature Abraham too was always looking to where the power lies. (The Divine name associated with Abraham's spiritual quality of Chessed, Love and Kindness, is *EL*, which literally signifies Power.) But from his earliest childhood, Abraham had the sense to realize that ultimate power cannot possibly lie in a mere human being, no matter how strong and influential, since he is here today and dead tomorrow.

From the time of Abraham's first spiritual awakening he searched tirelessly to discover the true source of the various manifestations of power and strength found in the world. A famous Midrash shared by Judaism and other traditions depicts Abraham as a little infant abandoned in a cave by his parents. They were afraid that Nimrod would kill their little child since Nimrod's astrologers had told him a baby had been born who was destined to shine to the entire world.

> Abraham cried and cried because he was so hungry. God sent the angel Gabriel, who gave him milk to drink until Abraham grew and was three years old. One night he decided to leave the cave. When he went out, the world was dark. He looked up at the skies and saw the twinkling stars. He was amazed by so many millions of little lights. He said, "These must certainly be the most powerful forces in the whole universe. These must be the gods."

> But then came the dawn and the stars disappeared.

"No," said Abraham, "those little lights can't be gods because they have disappeared. Something else has outshone them. I won't worship them anymore."

Then the sun rose and shone in all its glory. Abraham said, "This is the most powerful force. This is God. I will worship this." But towards evening, as the sun set, Abraham understood that the sun is also not God. Out of the darkness, the moon rose and shone its light, and Abraham thought: "Yes, this time I have found God".

At that moment, the Angel Gabriel came down and took Abraham to a fountain of pure water. "Immerse and purify yourself," said the Angel. Afterwards the Angel revealed to him that *HaVaYaH*, the One God, holds power and dominion over the Heavens above and the Earth below. God created the entire world."

When Abraham heard the words of the angel, he prostrated and prayed to *HaVaYaH*, Creator of Heaven and Earth.

(Midrash)

Abraham understood that a subordinate power has no option but to submit to a higher power. What he sought all his life was the highest Power of all -- in the knowledge that if he could discover the secret of ultimate power, he himself would be able to channel it and wield it for good.

Abraham understood that people's worship of the stars and planets and other subordinate powers was actually a guise for worshipping themselves, i.e. endeavoring to gratify their own selfish appetites for wealth, sex, food, drink, power, honor, etc. Even when people bow down to and "serve" gods of prosperity, love, war and the like, they are actually trying to abandon themselves to deep instinctual desires for personal gratification. [The veneration displayed by many today for the products of contemporary technology and the energy devoted to their acquisition may also be viewed as a form of idolatrous service of the self. Why do those same people not put similar energy into venerating and serving *HaVaYaH*, ultimate Source all the resources upon which human life depends?]

The world-famous story about Abraham's breaking the idols shows the wit and wisdom with which he exposed man's folly and self-deception when he worships idols and other products of his own activity.

Abraham's father, Terach was an idol-manufacturer. Once he had to travel, so he left Abraham to manage the shop. People would come in and ask to buy idols. Abraham would say, "How old are you?" The person would say, "Fifty," or "Sixty". Abraham would say, "Isn't it pathetic that a man of sixty wants to bow down to a one-day-old idol?" The man would feel ashamed and leave.

One time a woman came with a basket of bread. She said to Abraham, "Take this and offer it to the gods".

Abraham got up, took a hammer in his hand, broke all the idols to pieces, and then put the hammer in the hand of the biggest idol among them.

When his father came back and saw the broken idols, he was appalled. "Who did this?" he cried. "How can I hide anything from you?" replied Abraham calmly. "A woman came with a basket of bread and told me to offer it to them. I brought it in front of them, and each one said, "I'm going to eat first." Then the biggest one got up, took the hammer and broke all the others to pieces."

"What are you trying to pull on me?" asked Terach, "Do they have minds?"

Said Abraham: "Listen to what your own mouth is saying? They have no power at all! Why worship idols?"

Midrash Bereishit 38:13)

Calling Terach an idol-manufacturer suggests that he was a major ideologist and opinion-molder in the society in which he lived. When Abraham would ask how a person of sixty could bow down to a newly-made idol, he was pointing out that if you are searching for the ultimate power, it's no use looking at ephemeral, man-made objects, no matter how impressive. Items constructed today to satisfy some whim or fancy will be abandoned or destroyed tomorrow.

Abraham was saying: Why do you worship modernity just because it glitters and glisters temporarily. If you really want to find the source of power, you must work backwards to the cause of the cause of the cause... To find the source of creation you have to go back in time. Far, far back: years and years. Thousands and thousands and millions and millions of years. (Rebbe Nachman often quoted a popular song that included the words "The old, old, old, old God" -- *Tzaddik* #413).

The women coming with her basket of bread for the gods was expressing a profound human need to pacify and please the higher power.

If Abraham refused to offer the bread, it was not because he did not believe in the principle of sacrifice. When the time came for him to worship the One God, he sacrificed his very self. He was prepared to offer up his precious, most beloved son, Isaac. But only to the true God, never to some subordinate power that is itself dependent upon a higher power.

Abraham's comic trick of putting the hammer in the hands of the biggest idol and telling his father how each of the idols wanted to eat first lays bare the selfish desire for personal gratification that lies at the root of most idolatry. The woman brought the offering of bread in the hope that this would placate the gods so they would provide food for *her* to eat. Feeling vulnerable herself, she tried to pacify the powers she felt to be above her. But Abraham showed that her gods were as self-centered and greedy as she was.

The essence of Abraham's later teaching was that the foundation of true religion and spirituality is to practice the reverse of selfishness and personal gratification -- i.e. kindness and charity. *HaVaYaH*, as the supreme Power over all other powers, can afford to show love and kindness to all. When man overcomes his own instinctive selfishness and cultivates these divine traits, he himself experiences and becomes connected with God.

This teaching of kindness and altruism was a direct contradiction to the philosophy and outlook of the ruling tyrant, Nimrod, who was the epitome of self-seeking. Nimrod's god was Fire, the power that consumes and destroys everything.

The same Midrash continues:

> Nimrod called Abraham and commanded him to worship Fire.

> Abraham said to him, "So let's worship water since water has the power to extinguish fire."

"Right," said Nimrod, "We should worship water."

"In that case, we should worship the clouds, since they carry water."

"Yes, we should worship the clouds."

"Then we should worship the wind, since it drives the clouds across the sky."

"Yes, we should worship the wind (*ru'ach*) -- air, spirit."

"But," said Abraham, "humans have the power to rule over the spirit. Should we worship human beings?"

"You're playing with words," cried Nimrod. "I worship only fire, and I am going to throw you into a huge furnace. Let the God you worship come along and save you from it!"

(*Midrash Bereishit ibid.*)

Abraham took Nimrod step by step through the fundamental elements of creation as seen in most pre-modern thought systems: Fire, Water and Air, all of which are expressed in and through the Earth element. Fire is indeed a most powerful force. Yet water (the element with which Abraham is particularly associated) has the power to extinguish fire. Water -- flowing humbly from the heights of mountains ever downwards, soaking into the earth, vitalizing dry seeds, causing vegetation to sprout, giving life to fish, animals, birds and all other creatures -- expresses the unstinting, ever-flowing kindness and love of Abraham. This indeed is more powerful than the fire of Nimrod's selfish cravings.

Abraham's relentless logic brought Nimrod to the brink of having to admit that man can indeed control his own spirit and instincts. If he fails to control himself and surrenders to the fire of his lower instincts, then his "religion" is basically about self-worship. Nimrod's veneration of fire was merely an expression of his own burning passion to consume and destroy.

The insight was one Nimrod could not accept, and he decided to throw Abraham to his god of fire.

Nimrod gave orders to construct an enormous furnace into which Abraham was then catapulted. But God miraculously saved Abraham from the furnace.

The Midrash concludes that all the burning logs turned into blossoming trees that produced beautiful fruits. Man can consume and destroy, but God alone has the power to create life and bring about growth and regeneration.

To the Land

And God said to Abram, "Go out from your country, from the place of your birth and upbringing and from your father's house to the Land that I will show you" (Genesis 12:1)

To the Land / The House and the Mountain / The Master of Prayer

Abraham could no longer remain in Nimrod's kingdom. He was being called. How exactly Abraham experienced God's call we cannot know. But it was an experience that had the absolute certainty that is the mark of true prophecy.

To attain his destiny, Abraham had to abandon not only his physical place of birth but the entire civilization and culture he had grown up in. He had to leave his father Terach's house. For as the house of an idolater -- one who worshipped intermediate powers and man-made objects -- this house could not serve as a model for the House whose foundations Abraham now had to lay in order to rectify creation, namely the Holy Temple that would be built as the centerpiece of the Land to which he was journeying.

Abraham was not merely moving to a more congenial alternative location. "And God said to Abram, Go -- *Lech Lecha*": the Hebrew phrase literally means: "Go to *yourself*". Abraham's journey was into *inner space* -- the world of spirit.

Yet it was at the same time most definitely a journey to an actual physical territory -- the Land of Israel. For the spiritual teaching that Abraham brought to the world was not to retreat to some fantasy heaven detached from eating and drinking, making a living, having a family and other earthly realities. Abraham's mission was to show that the Living God is found in and through the practical details of everyday life just as much as in the outer reaches of the cosmos and the heights of the spirit.

Abraham's teaching had to be *lived* in an actual country where real people with practical needs and problems would submit to a set of rules and guidelines that would be applied in real, everyday life. This would demonstrate to the world that when we strive to bring God and spirit into the tiniest practical details of our lives, this brings the highest blessings to ourselves and to the entire world. Abraham would "command his children and his household after him to keep the way of *HaVaYaH*, to practice charity and justice" (Genesis 18:16).

The House and the Mountain

It would be inappropriate to categorize Abraham and the other founding fathers, Isaac and Jacob, as "nature-lovers," "environmentalists" and the like. Yet their lives and example are of profound significance as we seek to understand Judaic teachings about how to relate to nature and the environment.

The essential mission of Abraham, Isaac and Jacob was to rectify Adam's sin of "eating the fruit of the tree of the knowledge of good and evil". This had left in humanity a deeply-ingrained attitudinal flaw that makes people view this world as merely a playground for pleasure and enjoyment rather than as the springboard for spiritual ascent. Reckless pursuit of personal gratification leads to the relentless self-seeking of a Nimrod. This must lead sooner or later to the destruction of human life on earth. Today we indeed see that our future is threatened precisely because of the environmental destruction being wrought through greed, excess and waste.

In order for humanity to survive and attain our exalted spiritual destiny, this attitudinal flaw has to be rectified in the actual lives of real people. In order to live, we have no option but to eat and consume other natural resources provided by the earth. The question is how we will do this: wisely and carefully, or greedily and foolishly? It is human nature to join together socially and organize cooperatively in order better to exploit the environment and provide more effectively for our needs and desires. How can our societies go about satisfying everyone's needs without letting people's greed destroy us all?

Human life centers on houses -- the buildings, buildings and more buildings that make up our cities. It is therefore primarily within the house, the home and our other buildings that we -- as individuals and as members of families and other social groups -- have to rectify the basic flaw of putting all the focus on material consumption rather than on spiritual growth.

Accordingly, it was Jacob who completed the founding fathers' preparations for the ultimate rectification of this basic attitudinal flaw. For it was Jacob who taught the world the concept of the Temple as a House. The Holy Temple is to serve as the prototype of the rectified, sanctified house -- the house that will be a healthy unit in a viable urban civilization -- a place in which people's activities are organized in a way that enables them to fulfil themselves and satisfy their various needs in full harmony with God, with nature and with each other.

Various aspects of the Holy Temple correspond to a human house and home. The sacrificial altar upon which animal and we eat our meals. The inner chambers of the Temple and especially vegetable offerings are brought corresponds to the table at which the Holy of Holies correspond to the intimate spaces in our homes that we use for interacting with each other or being by ourselves.

The Temple -- the rectified, holy House -- was and is thus destined to be the showpiece of the country promised to Abraham and his descendants in order to establish an exemplary society of humans living in perfect harmony with God, nature and each other.

Yet for Abraham the vision was still a Mountain. In order to lay the foundation for the rectified House that Jacob was to build, Abraham first had to go *out* of the house -- away from civilization -- to the Mountain.

"And he moved from there *towards the mountain* -- this was east of [literally 'before'] *Beit El*, the 'House of God'... and he built there an altar to *HaVaYaH* and he prayed in the name of *HaVaYaH*" (Genesis 12:8).

All his life, Abraham was constantly journeying steadily closer to his Mountain -- the summit of personal spiritual perfection. And this very journey was quite literally a journey towards the actual Temple Mount. It was there that Abraham was to face the supreme test of his life when God told him to sacrifice his son. There he instituted for all time the concept of sacrifice -- setting aside personal gratification in order to serve a higher spiritual purpose.

But in order to reach this Mountain where the rectified House -- the Holy Temple -- would be built, Abraham first had to go *away* from houses, towns and cities. Abraham left his father's house, rejecting the city civilization of his time with its accompanying vice and corruption.

For most of his long life, Abraham was very much an outdoor person. He lived in tents. Even when recovering from circumcision at the age of ninety-nine, Abraham wanted to be outside: he sits at the door of his tent in the heat of the day (Genesis 18:1). He entertains his angelic guests outside under a tree. Abraham's preferred place to live was out in the wilderness -- the place of vision-quest and prophecy. Abraham's prophecies clearly came to him out in the open -- in deserts, on mountains, under the canopy of the stars, in wild places where birds of prey would swoop down trying to snatch his sacrifices.

Of necessity Abraham had first to separate himself from human society and retreat to raw nature in order to rediscover the Creator. Only by first reconnecting with the Creator in and through nature would it be possible to establish a true foundation upon which to build a rectified man-made society through which humanity will attain its destiny.

As a traveler, a tent-dweller and a sojourner, Abraham well knew that essentially all of us are strangers and travelers in this world. We are visitors, dependent upon the hospitality and kindness of God. The visitor understands that not everything in the world is mine to use or destroy just as I please. Things have owners. The stranger is grateful when people share what they have with him. He appreciates the importance of doing the same for others, thereby participating in the divine quality of kindness and generosity that flows through the entire creation.

Thus, Abraham provided for others. He dug wells in order to provide pure waters to quench people's thirst (Genesis 21:25-32; ibid. 26:15ff.). He "planted the *ESheL* [a tree or an orchard] in Beer Sheva, and he called there on the Name of *HaVaYaH, El Olam*, God, Power of the Universe" (Genesis 21:23). Abraham's efforts in environmental maintenance -- developing water resources and planting trees -- were part of his teaching to humanity that nature and its resources are gifts of God. We are responsible to develop and cultivate them.

And these are gifts over which it is fitting to call upon His Name and pray!

The Master of Prayer

Abraham sought to draw others after him out of false-consciousness associated with life in the man-made environment of the city. In the words of Rebbe Nachman:

> Abraham would come into a city and run about crying, "Woe! Woe!" and people would run after him the way they chase a madman. He would argue with them at length, trying to show them they were all caught up in a profoundly mistaken way of thinking. He was quite familiar with all the arguments and rationalizations they used to justify their idolatry. He used to demonstrate the falsity of their ideas and reveal the truths of faith. Some of the young people were attracted to him. He never even tried to draw older people closer because they were already firmly entrenched in their false beliefs and it would have been very hard to get them to change. It was the younger people who were drawn after him: they ran after him. He would go from city to city and they would run after him....

(Tzaddik #395)

The picture of Abraham presented here by Rebbe Nachman is reminiscent of the hero of the Rebbe's story of "The Master of Prayer". The Master of Prayer was a mystic who deliberately took himself away from cities and other places of human habitation in order to commune with God.

Once there was a Master of Prayer. He was constantly engaged in prayer and singing songs and praises to God. He lived away from civilization. But he would visit inhabited areas regularly and spend time with people -- usually those of low status, such as the poor. He would have heart to heart discussions with them, speaking about the purpose of life. He would explain that the only true goal is to serve God every day of your life, spending your days praising and singing to God.

He would speak to someone at great length, motivating him. His words entered the other's heart, and the person would join him. As soon as the person agreed with him, he would take him and bring him to his place away from civilization.

For the Master of Prayer had chosen for himself a place far from human habitation. A river flowed there, and there were fruit trees whose fruit he and his followers would eat. He was not at all concerned about the clothes people wore.

The Master of Prayer's way was to visit inhabited areas and spread his ideas, convincing people to emulate him, serving God and constantly praying. Whenever people wanted to join him, he would take them to his place away from civilization, where their only activities would be praying, singing praise to God, confession, fasting, self-mortification, repentance and similar occupations. He would give them his books of meditations, prayers, songs, praises and confessions, and they would occupy themselves with them at all times.

Among the people he brought there, he would find some who had the ability to lead others to serve God. He would allow such individuals to visit inhabited places and also bring people to serve God. This way the Master of Prayer constantly spread his teachings. He constantly attracted people and took them away from civilization....

The Master of Prayer and his men lived far away from civilization. They would spend their time engaged only in prayer, song, praise to God, confession, fasting, self-mortification and repentance. For the people he attracted to God, fasting and self-discipline were better and more precious than all worldly enjoyment. They would have greater pleasure from fasting or self-discipline than from all worldly pleasures.

"The Master of Prayer", *Rabbi Nachman's Stories* pp. 279ff.

The ensuing lengthy story of how the Master of Prayer set about rectifying the "Country of Wealth" can be seen as Rebbe Nachman's parable about the overall rectification of human society that started when Abraham abandoned the city civilization of his day and set off on his journey to the Land.

It is noteworthy that for the Master of Prayer, as we have seen in the above brief extract, one of the first steps in redeeming people from the false consciousness engendered by the city was to take them out to his place amidst nature. For it can be easier to find God amidst natural, God-created surroundings than in the man-constructed city environment.

Go to Your Self

*I*s it necessary to be an advanced sage and mystic in order to find God in nature and enter into a relationship with Him? Not according to Rebbe Nachman. Most important of all is to have a powerful *yearning* for God.

> A person may be totally unable to study, if he is ignorant, for example, or if he does not have a book to learn from, or if he is out in a desert. Even so, if his heart burns within him, yearning and longing to find God and serve Him, then his heartfelt longing to learn is itself a form of study from a book...

Likutey Moharan I:142

Abraham had nothing but his own yearning. As the only one in his generation who was searching for the truth about the world, Abraham had no guides or teachers. There was no existing tradition for him to turn to. He had no alternative but to follow the prompting of his own heart and rely on his own observations and reasoning. The only way to succeed in such a venture is with the utmost sincerity and honesty.

This sincerity is beautifully depicted in the figure of another individual who also found God in nature all by himself -- a simple young shepherd boy once seen by the saintly Rabbi Israel, the Baal Shem Tov ("Master of the Good Name", 1698-1760), founder of the Chassidic movement):

Once the Baal Shem Tov was shown from Heaven that a certain shepherd boy was serving God better than he was. The Baal Shem Tov had a powerful longing to see this shepherd, and he set off in his carriage with a group of his disciples. They finally came to a mountainside. There on the mountain stood the shepherd. He blew his horn to gather the flock. When all the sheep were gathered, the shepherd took them to a stream to drink. As the sheep stood there drinking, the shepherd opened his mouth and cried out in a loud voice:

"Master of the World: You created the Heavens and the Earth, this mountain and the flock, the owner of the flock, me and your Jewish People. You provide for all your creatures and you give me my food as well. I am ignorant and unlearned. I am simple. I don't know how I can serve you and what praise I can give you, for I was orphaned at an early age and I grew up among non-Jews. I don't know any Torah... But I do have my shepherd's horn! And I'm going to blow it as hard as I can in Your honor!"

The shepherd blew and blew with all his strength until he collapsed exhausted onto the ground. He lay there quite still for a time. Then he got up and said:

"Master of the Universe: You created the Heavens and the Earth, and you give food to all. You created all the flocks and You created me. Just as You are One, so You have one People who are always studying Your Torah and praying to You. But I am a young shepherd. I don't know any Torah or any prayers. My father and mother abandoned me as a child and I grew up among non-Jews. All I know is shepherds' songs."

Immediately he started singing at the top of his voice. He sang and sang until he again fell to the ground totally exhausted. When he finally came back to himself, he said: "Master of the Universe, I've played You my horn and sung for You. But how can anything like this begin to do justice to Your real greatness, God of all the Worlds, Who gives life and food to all? How can I serve You, our Father, our King? But there is one thing that I can do, and I'll do it in Your honor!"

As soon as he finished speaking, he threw himself down into a handstand and waved his legs furiously in the air for as long as he could. Again and again, he stood on his hands and waved his legs in the air for as long as he could ... until he was totally exhausted and he collapsed on the ground. He lay quite still for a long time.

When at last he came back to himself, he got up and said: "Master of the World: I have blown my horn for You; I have sung You songs; I have done handstands in Your honor. But what is any of this worth compared to Your greatness, awesome Father in Heaven? What more can I do to serve You?

"Last night the squire who owns the flock, made a party for all his attendants. At the end, he gave everyone a silver coin as a gift. He also gave me one. And this coin I am giving You as a gift -- to You, God, Creator of the World who created the Heavens and the Earth and the mountain and the water and the flock and me, the little shepherd..."

As he said this, he threw the coin upwards... and at that moment the Baal Shem Tov saw a hand stretched out from the Heaven to accept the coin.

The Baal Shem Tov said to his students: "This young shepherd has fulfilled the commandment to "love God with all your heart, all your soul and all your might" (Deuteronomy 6:5).

from *Sichos Yekarim* printed in *Kol Sipurey Besht* by R. Israel Yaakov Klapholtz, pp. 253-5

Greatness

"In every place where you find the greatness of the Holy One, blessed-be-He, there you find His humility" (*Megillah* 31a)

The story of this shepherd is a teaching about true "greatness". In Hebrew, this is "gedulah", kabbalistically the quality particularly associated with Abraham (the same quality is also often called *chessed*, expansive kindness.)

The Baal Shem Tov was already a "great" man: a towering Tzaddik and sage, a cherished, respected leader with a coach and horses and a flock of disciples. Yet he saw that this shepherd was "greater" than himself: the shepherd served God better. The greatness of the shepherd lay in the fact that he was totally without pretensions. He just did what he himself could do best with the utmost simplicity.

Doing your own thing in the best possible way is the greatest praise there could be of God. God is great beyond great beyond great... It is impossible to begin to measure or fathom the true greatness of the Creator of the entire universe. It would be impossible for a puny human -- a tiny speck on a planet that is itself a tiny speck in the vast, infinite universe -- to do anything to serve God in proportion to God's true greatness.

Yet the greatness of God is revealed more than anything in the endless variety displayed throughout the creation. It is the uniqueness of every single detail of creation -- with God simultaneously and equally present in each one, from the highest to the lowest -- that is the most powerful possible testimony to the endless greatness of God.

When a person develops the unique goodness within himself and does his own thing in the best way he can, this itself is the greatest praise he could give God. For when each unique detail in creation shines to perfection, it shows the endless power of God to create every possible variety of beauty.

This shepherd knew that God is infinitely great. But that did not deter him from blowing his horn, singing and doing handstands with all his strength. For he instinctively understood that God, being so great, has the power to be directly and intimately involved in every detail of His creation. He takes equal joy and delight in each one. The shepherd knew that when he did what he could do best, that was precious to God. The shepherd surely enjoyed doing what he did. But he offered it easily and sincerely as his gift of love and praise to God.

This shepherd must have been very familiar with nature from spending all his days out in the hills with his flock. He must have known every nook and cranny of the surrounding areas, all the streams and watering spots, all the different types of vegetation and wildlife. He surely knew about the different times of the day and seasons of the year and how to take care of the flock under different weather conditions. He did not need a watch or a calendar. By day he could tell the time from the position of the sun; by night from the stars. Years of experience and observation give the simplest shepherds profound sensitivity to and understanding of the natural environment.

The scientific mind seeks to "know," "analyze" and "understand" the various phenomena in the world. The scientist observes coldly and dispassionately and asks "What? What do we have here?" But this shepherd looked up at the heavens and his heart prompted him to ask "*Who*?" -- "Who created these?" (Isaiah 40:26) -- Who is the Power that stands behind all the wonder and glory revealed in the skies and on the earth? This shepherd knew instinctively that God cannot be a cold, impassive Being. Such a supreme artist and craftsman is surely more alive, aware, sensitive and involved than any person. Therefore, it is possible to make contact with God. This shepherd wanted to make direct *contact* with God and to talk to Him in the only way he knew -- in his own words. He wanted to express the love he felt for God in his own unique, simple direct way.

The most natural way to initiate a connection with anyone is to give them something, whether it be a smile, a kind word or an actual gift. But what can anyone give to the infinite God?

When the shepherd threw up his silver coin, he showed he was willing to give up his own self! The coin represents a person's desire for self-gratification. People cling to their money because it is money that enables them to satisfy their needs and desires. But when we are too preoccupied with our own needs and interests, this can prevent us from seeing

God's glory and greatness even though it surrounds us all the time.

Only when a person is willing to put aside his self-preoccupation for a while will he become sensitive to what God is communicating to him whether through natural phenomena or indeed in any other aspect of life.

In the words of Rebbe Nachman:

> If you take a little coin and hold it in front of your eyes, it will stop you from being able to see a great mountain even though the mountain may actually be thousands and thousands of times bigger than the little coin. But because the coin is positioned in front of your eyes, it stops you seeing something that is actually far larger.
>
> So too, when a person comes into this world he becomes so involved in worldly vanity that he comes to imagine there could be nothing better. This tiny little material world stands in the way and prevents him seeing the awesome spiritual light of the Torah, even though it is actually thousands and thousands of times greater than all the world!
>
> *Likutey Moharan* I:133

Observing Nature

*W*asps will to tend to gravitate towards an open pot of jam even though it may be only one small object among many others in the room. But since the wasps are interested in the jam, that is what they notice.

A similar principle governs the way many of us tend to perceive the surrounding world much of the time. We notice the things that have some meaning and relevance within our personal orbit of interest and understanding. Yet all kinds of other facets of the surrounding environment may escape our attention completely.

To experience the presence of God in nature (and indeed anywhere), one must be willing to detach oneself from the pull of worldly ego-interest so as to become open to higher levels of awareness.

When a person physically leaves the man-made world of buildings, highways, technology and culture and gets out into natural surroundings -- wide, open meadows, mountains, forests, lakes, seas, deserts -- the first reactions may be joy and relief ("It's so beautiful, so tranquil..."). Then, as one relaxes and puts aside thoughts of the everyday world, one begins to notice that a whole complex universe of plants, insects, animals and birds is in a state of busy activity all around....

Careful observation and thoughtful contemplation of nature soon teaches us how little we know and understand about life and the world. This in itself engenders the humility that is necessary in order to begin to experience the divine.

This quality of humility is really the summit of the Mountain that Abraham was traveling towards all his life. "Who shall go up the mountain of *HaVaYaH* and who will stand in the place of His holiness? The person with clean hands and a pure heart...." (Psalms 24:3-4)

At the climax of the Book of Job, one of the most eloquent passages in the whole Bible teaches us how detailed observation and contemplation of the natural world has the power to instill in us a profound sense of our own smallness and our ignorance about the amazing world in which God has placed us. The Book of Job describes how the righteous, pious Job is suddenly struck with terrible personal tragedy and painful diseases. Job cannot accept that there is any justice in his suffering, despite lengthy speeches delivered by friends who have come to visit him attempting to persuade him that there must be justice in it since suffering is sent by God, and God is just.

After all the arguments and counter-arguments, God Himself answers Job "out of the whirlwind" (Job ch's 38ff.). God's "answer" is a series of challenges to Job as to whether he understands the meaning of all kinds of phenomena in the natural world. If Job's understanding of the surrounding world is so limited, why should he expect to be able to comprehend the deep mysteries involved in why people go through pain and suffering?

Then *HaVaYaH* answered Job out of the whirlwind and said: Who is this that darkens counsel by words without knowledge? Gird up your loins like a man, and I will ask you questions, and you tell Me!

Where were you when I laid the foundations of the earth? Declare, if you have the understanding. Who determined its measurements -- if you know -- or who stretched out the measuring line over it? On what were its foundations fixed? Who laid its cornerstone, when the morning stars sang together and all the angels shouted for joy?

Or who shut up the sea with doors when it broke forth and came from the womb? When I made it a garment of cloud and wrapped it in thick darkness and imposed My decree on it and set bars and doors and said, "This far you may come but no further, and here your proud waves must stop."

Have you commanded the morning since your days began or told the dawn its place, that it might take hold of the ends of the earth and the wicked will be shaken out of it?...

Have you entered into the wellsprings of the sea, or have you walked in the recesses of the deep?

Have the gates of death been revealed to you, or have you seen the gates of the shadow of death? Have you surveyed the very breadths of the earth? Declare, if you know it all.

What is the way to the dwelling of light, and where is the place of darkness, that you should follow it to its bounds and know the paths to its house?

You know it, for you were born then and the number of your days is great!

Have you entered the treasures of the snow, or have you seen the treasuries of the hail that I have saved for a time of trouble, the day of battle and war?

By which way is the light parted or the east wind scattered on the earth? Who has broken a channel for the waterflood or a way for lightning and thunder, to make it rain on a land where there is no man, on the wilderness where there is no man, in order to satisfy the desolate and waste ground and to cause the bud of the tender herb to spring forth? Does the rain have a father? Who has given birth to the drops of dew. From whose womb came the ice? Who gave birth to the hoar-frost of heaven? The waters are congealed like stone, and the face of the deep is frozen.

Can you bind the chains of the stars of the Pleiades or loosen the bands of Orion? Can you lead forth the Mazarot in their season? Or can you guide the Bear with her sons? Do you know the ordinances of the heavens? Can you establish its rule over the earth?

Can you lift up your voice to the clouds so that abundant waters will cover you? Can you send forth lightning flashes so that they will go forth and say to you "Here we are"?

Who has put wisdom in the inward parts? Or who has given understanding to the mind? Who can number the clouds by wisdom and lay down the expanses of the heavens when the dust runs into a mass and the clods stick together?

Will you hunt for prey for the lioness or satisfy the appetite of the young cubs when they couch in their dens and lie in wait in the hidden places? Who provides the raven his prey when his young ones cry to God and wander for lack of food?

Do you know the time when the wild goats of the rock give birth or can you mark when the hinds calve? Can you count how many months they are pregnant? Do you know the time when they give birth? They bow themselves, they bring forth their young, they cast out their fruit. Their young ones grow strong and grow up in the open field. They go forth and do not come back again.

Who has sent the wild ass out free? Who has loosed the straps of the wild ass? His house is in the wilderness and his dwelling-place is in the salt-land. He scorns the tumult of the city and does not listen to the shouting of the driver. The range of the mountains is his pasture and he searches for everything green.

Will the wild-ox be willing to serve you or wait for you by the stall? Can you bind the wild-ox with straps in the furrow? Will he plough the valleys after you? Will you trust him because of his great strength, or will you leave your work to him? Will you rely on him to bring your produce home and gather the corn of your threshing-floor?

The wing of the ostrich beats joyously, but are her wings and feathers those of the kindly stork? For she leaves her eggs on the ground and warms them in the dust, and forgets that the foot may crush them or the wild beast may trample them. She is hardened against her young ones, as if they were not hers. Though her labor is in vain, she is without fear. Because God has deprived her of wisdom, neither has He given her a portion of understanding. When the time comes, she raises her wings on high and scorns the horse and his rider.

Have you given the horse his strength? Have you clothed his neck with power? Have you made him spring like a locust? The glory of his snorting is terrible. He gallops in the valley and rejoices in his strength. He goes out to meet the clash off arms. He mocks at fear and is not afraid. He does not turn back from the sword. The quiver rattles on him, the glittering spear and the javelin. He swallows the ground with storm and rage and does not believe that it is the voice of the horn. Whenever he hears the horn he says "Ha! Ha!" and he smells the battle far off, the thunder of the captains and the shouting.

Does the hawk soar by your wisdom and stretch her wings towards the south? Does the vulture mount up at your command and make her nest on high? She dwells and stays on the rock, on the crag of the rock and the stronghold. From there she spies out the prey. Her eyes see it from far off. Her young ones also suck up the blood, and where the slain are, there she is....

Job chapters 38-39

In the end Job answered HaVaYaH and said:

I know that You can do everything, and no purpose can be withheld from You. Who is this that hides counsel without knowledge? Therefore, I spoke that which I did not understand, things too wonderful for me, which I did not know.... I had heard of You by the hearing of the ear, but now my eye sees You.

Therefore, I abhor my words and repent, seeing as I am dust and ashes.

ibid. 42, 1-6

Introspection and Contemplation

*C*oming to recognize the unfathomable mystery of creation can be a humbling experience. Man takes great pride in his knowledge and understanding: it makes him feel he is in control of things, at least temporarily. The realization that we are puny, fleeting mortals who know and understand very little about anything should induce in us a deep humility.

Humility is indeed necessary in order to attain true wisdom. Wisdom in Hebrew is called *ChoKhMaH*. Reversing the order of the first two Hebrew letters of the word *ChoKhMaH* gives us the words *Ko-aCh MaH*, "the Power (*Ko-aCh*) of What (*MaH*)". For true wisdom, *ChoKhMaH*, is an holistic vision of the Power-Source (*Ko-aCh*) that underlies and animates all that exists (*MaH*).

Such wisdom and perception can dwell only in one who is humble enough to be able to see beyond the boundaries of his own limited perspectives and self-interest. When a person effaces self and attains a state of genuine humility and "nothingness", the blinkers that usually narrow human perception fall away and he becomes open to the visionary consciousness of *Chokhmah*. Since humility is the prerequisite of true wisdom, the Bible teaches us that "Wisdom comes out of nothingness" (Job 26:20).

Adam's sin of "eating the fruit of the tree of knowledge" was essentially a selfish act. Wisdom and knowledge are divine faculties. God may share them with man as gifts of grace. But Adam wanted to steal them for himself. Instead of pursuing the kind of knowledge that connects man with the true Source of all creation, Adam wanted to snatch knowledge and understanding for his own aggrandizement so as to be able to gain control of things and manipulate them for his own selfish purposes. But any system of knowledge and understanding that fails to trace back the objects of that knowledge to their Divine Source can only be a warped, counterfeit wisdom.

Abraham's essential mission was to rectify Adam's stealing of the fruit of the tree of knowledge and the intellectual arrogance that has afflicted mankind ever since. Since Abraham sought true wisdom, *ChoKhMaH*, he was obliged to climb the most challenging "mountain" of all: the mountain of genuine humility, which is the quality that is the very foundation of wisdom.

Humility is called a "mountain" because paradoxically, meekness and lowliness are the "highest" of all spiritual qualities. The summit of spiritual achievement can be attained only through years of steady work chipping away at all one's selfish, negative traits one by one, until finally all traces of self-centeredness are erased. Abraham had this humility. Even as he stood arguing with God in prayer, Abraham knew what man is: "I am dust and ashes" (Genesis 18:27).

Abraham's Attributes as Seen in the Kabbalah

In the Kabbalah, Abraham is seen as the living embodiment of the divine attribute of *Gedulah* ("greatness"), which is also often called *Chessed*, expansive loving kindness. In all the various things that Abraham did during his life, he manifested character traits or soul-powers that teach us especially about these particular divine attributes. For example, the hospitality and charity Abraham showed when he entertained wayfarers, dug wells, planted trees and the like help us gain insight into the kindness, hospitality and charity of God Himself. In relation to God, all of us are "guests" whose needs He provides without receiving anything in return.

"The universe is built on kindness (*Chessed*)" (Psalms 89:3). The Godly attribute of *Chessed*, personified in Abraham, is the foundation of the whole creation. For the entire creation is a loving gift from God in order to enable us to find Him and forge a relationship with Him through the things of this finite world despite our puny status in relation to God's infinite greatness. God's kindness in allowing us to enter into a relationship with Him is itself a manifestation of His true greatness (*Gedulah*). For only the very greatest is great enough to be connected even with the very smallest.

In Kabbalah, the attribute of *Chessed* is associated with the Water Element (*Mayim*). [The four fundamental "elements" of all creation, spiritual and physical, are "Water", "Fire", "Air" and "Earth". The first three -- "Water", "Fire" and "Air" -- manifest themselves in and through the "Earth" element.] Water humbly flows ever downwards from the greatest heights to the lowest depths. Water is the indispensable basis of all life from the tiniest organisms to the most complex and sophisticated. Pure, vitalizing, cleansing, rejuvenating water symbolizes the expansive love and kindness that flow through the entire creation.

The opposite of water is fire (*Esh*). When left to itself, fire burns up and destroys creation, returning everything to nothing. Yet fire is equally indispensable to the creation, as long as its raw energy is harnessed and directed in a focused way. Fire is associated with the polar opposite of outflowing, unstinting *Chessed*: namely *Gevurah*, strength, discipline, limitation, restriction and severity. The attribute of *Gevurah* is embodied in Isaac (as will be discussed in Part II.) These two opposing poles of *Chessed* (thesis) and *Gevurah* (antithesis) are held in balance by a third, mediating quality: *Tiferet*, synthesis, harmony and beauty, embodied in Jacob and associated with air (or wind or spirit – *Ru'ach*. See Part III.)

Chessed and *Gevurah* are the "right" and "left" poles of the "tree" of the Kabbalah. This "tree" is the conceptual structure that expresses the interrelationship between the various divine qualities and attributes through which we are able to begin to understand and forge a connection with God. The structure of the kabbalistic "tree" corresponds directly to that of the human body, since "God created man in His own image" (Genesis 1:27). Each attribute is associated with one of the main parts of the human body.

Chessed and *Gevurah* correspond respectively to the right and left arms/hands of the body, while *Tiferet* -- in the center -- corresponds to the heart. The two "arms" of *Chessed* and *Gevurah* are the two fundamental poles of the creative process: expansive, active "giving" (*Chessed*, Water), and retractive, passive "taking/receiving" (*Gevurah*, Fire). The mediating quality of *Tiferet* is reflected in the ever-repeated cycles of successive expansion and contraction of the heart, which are governed by *Ru'ach*, Vital Spirit, Air.

The qualities of *Chessed*, *Gevurah* and *Tiferet* are visible and manifest in innumerable specific phenomena throughout the creation. But just as the visible activity of the arms and all other parts of the human body is governed by invisible intentions and ideas within the brain, so too the energy manifested within the creation via the "arms" is in fact governed by a higher-level master-system inside the "head". Here in the "brain" the creation is conceived and planned, and from here divine power is channeled "down" into the creation itself -- the "body" -- in such a way as to bring about God's ultimate purpose, which is that we should all become connected with Him.

Thus, the triad of *Chessed*, *Gevurah* and *Tiferet* -- the qualities that govern process within creation -- is itself under the control of the higher master-triad of *Chokhmah* ("Wisdom"), *Binah* ("Understanding") and *Daat* ("Knowledge") in the "brain", namely the spiritual level above and beyond creation. *Chokhmah*, Wisdom, is the holistic vision of what creation is to be. *Binah*,

Understanding, is the analytic intelligence that explores and maps out in detail the various specific concepts involved in bringing this conception of creation into being. *Daat* is the knowledge, consciousness and connection that comes from combining *Chokhmah* and *Binah* so as to see the whole vision in relation to all its parts and each of the parts in relation to the whole. This ensures that everything in creation works together harmoniously to bring about the ultimate goal, which is that all creation should know and be connected with God.

Each of the individual attributes in the *Chessed-Gevurah-Tiferet* triad is particularly rooted in the corresponding attribute in the higher *Chokhmah-Binah-Daat* triad. *Chessed*, the expansive, flowing kindness manifest within the creation, is especially rooted in *Chokhmah*, the profound Wisdom of the overall divine plan of creation. Thus, the Divine Name *EL* associated with the quality of *Chessed* has the numerical value of 31 (*Aleph* = 1 plus *Lamed* = 30). This is because *Chessed* is especially rooted in *Chokhmah*, which according to the Kabbalah consists of "thirty-two pathways of wisdom". Thirty-one of these pathways can be revealed within the creation through the attribute of *Chessed/EL*. However, the first and highest "pathway", the transcendent unity of the Infinite God, cannot be openly revealed within the finite, created world because this is the realm of limitation and plurality.

Hitbonenut: Contemplation

The finite human mind is well adapted to deal with the created world we live in, with its hosts of different phenomena, many of them seemingly disconnected from or even at war with one another. Particularly suitable for examining this world is *Binah*-thinking, which analyzes the individual phenomena making up a larger whole, investigating them in themselves and in relation to one another. [*Binah*-thinking traces the distinctions *between* one thing and another. "Between" in Hebrew is *BeiN*, which is obviously related to the root of *BiNah*, understanding. Moreover, by tracing the interrelationships between things as well, *Binah*-thinking connects and joins the individual entities together, as it were, building them into a larger structure. The Hebrew word for a "structure" or "building" is *BiNYaN*, the root of which is also related to that of *BINaH*.]

The discipline of actually using and applying *Binah*-thinking is in Hebrew called *HiTBoNeNuT*. This word is a noun made from the reflexive verb-form *HiTBoNeN* ("contemplates"), the root of which is *BiN*, to "understand". By thinking and thinking about something, examining it this way and that, one "makes oneself understand".

The created world, though founded on God's *Chessed* -- His loving will to "reach out" and reveal Himself -- could nevertheless only come into being through successive acts of self-limitation (*Tzimtzum*, "contraction") through which the Infinite Creator brings into being a finite realm suitable for the finite creatures destined to receive this revelation. Thus, the finite world of plurality came about through the divine attribute of *Gevurah*, the disciplined, focused application of the exact power necessary at each stage in each place in order to bring about God's purpose. The attribute of *Gevurah* is associated with the Divine Name *ELoHIM*, which literally means "the Powers". God -- *ELoHIM* -- is the unified Source of the plurality of specific, limited powers that are revealed in this world.

Just as the attribute of *Chessed* is especially rooted in *Chokhmah*, so too that of *Gevurah* is especially rooted in *Binah*, which traces out the specific details and limits of each of the various different powers involved in the creation. For this reason, *Binah*-thinking -- *Hitbonenut*, careful study and contemplation -- is particularly appropriate when starting to examine the phenomena of this world of plurality. As we seek to make sense of our surroundings we have no option but to begin with rational-analytic thought in order to investigate and try to understand the various different phenomena we find all around us.

But just as God's creation of the world is essentially driven by His expansive *Chessed*, His loving will to reveal Himself to all His creatures, so too the yearning of those creatures -- namely *US* -- to understand and make sense of this creation (in order to discover who we are and where we are going) is also fueled by a quality of *Chessed* within *US*. We are made in the image of God, and we therefore have this force of *Chessed* rooted deep within our souls. This is the inner urge that drives us to use our own creative spiritual powers in such a way as to transcend our limitations and penetrate to the unity that underlies the whole creation.

Abraham, who is the very embodiment of this *Chessed*, had no option but to begin his search for the Source from within the created world in which he found himself. Abraham was alone. He was the first. There was no tradition of religious revelation to guide him in his quest. Abraham had no alternative but to begin his search with *Hitbonenut*, contemplative examination of the phenomena of the world that he could see with his own eyes: the stars and planets and all the other hosts of creation. But the driving *Chessed* within him spurred him always to direct his *Binah*-contemplation towards *Chokhmah* perception, so as to see how all the individual entities in the world are in fact part of the single overarching, unifying Whole.

Abraham as a Student of Nature

Abraham was always journeying to the Mountain -- the humility and self-transcendence that bring one to true wisdom, *Chokhmah*. In his quest for God Abraham must have spent many years of his life in solitary contemplation, meditation and prayer on the blessed mountains of Israel, the Holy Land. It is indeed from the peaks of physical mountains that one can best survey the entire span of the heavens above and look down over all the territories stretching away below!

In his search for the unified Source of all the hosts of heaven and earth, Abraham had to direct his inner eye beyond the visible world. But it was from the visible, natural, physical world that he began. Indeed, Abraham was one of the most outstanding students of nature that ever lived, and especially of the planets and stars.

"And God took Abraham outside and He said, 'Look up to the heavens and count the stars...'" (Genesis 15:5). According to tradition, when God took Abraham "outside", He was raising him to a level of perception that lay beyond the astronomy/astrology of which he was already a master (see *Rashi* ad loc.). The sages and priests of the Babylon culture in which Abraham had grown up were expert sky-gazers and star-worshippers. For them it was a given that the planets and stars rule over all that takes place on the Earth to which they shine.

Abraham knew the skies as well as anyone. He had no doubt that radiations from the stars and planets influence everything on earth. But Abraham had a driving urge to find *EL*, the Power, the Source of all things. This urge caused the inner eye of his contemplative soul to rise above and beyond the disparate parts of the system in order to perceive the Whole. For Abraham, everything we can see in this world derives from and is a teaching to us about the unified Source of the world. Through intense *Hitbonenut*, the proper application of *Binah*-thought to the phenomena of this world, we have the power to rise to *Chokhmah*-perception and see that all these phenomena are part of the flow of God's *Chessed*.

Sefer Yetzira

HaVaYaH our Ruler, How glorious is Your Name throughout the earth, while Your majesty is expressed above the heavens. You have put strength into the mouths of little babies and children [i.e. the power of speech given to man] in order to still your enemies and adversaries. When I look at Your heavens, the work of Your fingers, the moon and the stars that You have established: What is man that You remember him and the son of man that You take account of him? Yet You made him only a little lower than the angels; You have crowned him with glory and honor. You have given him power over the works of Your hands. You have put all things under his feet. Sheep and oxen, all of them, and also the beasts of the field. The fowl of the air and the fish of the sea; whatever passes through the paths of the seas. *HaVaYaH* our Master, How glorious is Your Name throughout the earth!

Psalm 8

*A*braham gave expression to his perceptions in his *Sefer Yetzira*, the "Book of Creation (or Formation)", the most ancient of all known kabbalistic texts. (For a full English translation and commentary, see *Sefer Yetzira*: The Book of

Creation, In Theory and Practice, by Rabbi Aryeh Kaplan, Samuel Weiser Inc. 1990.)

The *Sefer Yetzira* is a short work of six chapters, each consisting of an average of about ten paragraphs in the style of *mishnah* -- concisely-expressed oral traditions handed down from generation to generation (presumably with some editing on the way.) The original Hebrew is terse, intense, vivid and pregnant with allusions and overtones.

While the *Sefer Yetzira* can be studied as a teaching about how to look at nature, it is many, many other things besides. It is one of the most important of all kabbalistic works, providing the keys to the entire kabbalah system both as a way to view the world and as a practical pathway of meditation, prayer and devotion leading to supreme levels of divine connection, prophecy and spiritual power.

Underlying the scheme of the *Sefer Yetzira* is the idea that "from my flesh I see God" (Job 19:26): namely, the structure and functioning of the human form gives us insight into God's relationship with creation as a whole. For man is "made in the image of God", and therefore features of our very bodily make-up -- such as the bipolarity of right and left, the design and arrangement of the brain, heart, lungs, stomach, liver, kidneys and other organs, etc. -- reflect in microcosm key aspects of the macrocosmic universe.

Man is distinguished from all other creatures by the complexity and subtlety of his vocal apparatus. Man's ability to build a limited number of basic sounds into innumerable different meaningful words and thought-structures has enabled him to develop the most amazing array of social, cultural, economic, technological, scientific, intellectual, artistic and other products of human inventiveness and creativity throughout the ages. Not only is speech the basis for our interactions with each other. It is also the basis for our ability to communicate with our very selves and with God.

Abraham's insight was that speech is actually the foundation of the entire creation. In the words of the Psalms: "By the *word* of *HaVaYaH* the heavens were made and through the air (wind, spirit) of His *mouth* all their hosts..." (Psalms 33:6).

When a human being performs a willful action, underlying the visible outward behavior is an inner intention or idea in his mind that gives this action meaning. The person may express his intention to others in words, or it may remain concealed within his mind. Even within our minds, our thoughts are expressed on some subtle level in words. The words of thought are built out of "letters" just as are the words of human speech.

Abraham grasped that just as all this applies on the level of the microcosm -- individual human thought and action -- so it must apply on the level of the macrocosm as well. The physical "actions" manifest in the creation all around us are outward expressions of meaningful Divine intentions. Just as human thoughts and intentions are expressed in letters, the building blocks of words, so too are the thoughts and intentions of God. The fundamental building blocks of the creation are the twenty-two letters of the Hebrew alphabet.

The entire creation is a *communication* from God to man. The universe is thus a *SePheR* ("book"): the "book" is the medium through which the communication is made. The book has its *SoPheR*, the Writer. He is both source of the actual "book" and Author of the message of the book, which is the *SiPPuR*, the "story."

The entire *SiPPuR* or "story" comes about because underlying forces emanating from God begin to interact with one another to bring about the Creation. These fundamental forces are the *SePhiRot*, the root spiritual forces underlying all creation, spiritual and physical. The power of the *Sephirot* radiates to the creation through the twenty-two letters of the Hebrew alphabet. These are the building blocks of creation. Innumerable different combinations of letters govern the structure and functioning of all of the different aspects of creation.

The underlying spiritual structure or essence of anything is in Hebrew called its *TzuRa*, "form" -- as opposed to its *ChoMeR*, "substance". Thus, the potter takes primal, formless matter -- clay -- and shapes it into a vessel having form, purpose and utility. The potter who creates the form and inscribes it in the clay is in Hebrew called the *YoTzeR*. The act of formation or creation is called *YeTziRa*.

Abraham's *SePher YeTziRa* is a quest for the inner wisdom underlying the *TzuRa*, the form of creation as a whole, as designed by the Master Artist, God, Creator of all the worlds. For when man discovers the secrets of the letters that power the spiritual and physical creation, man himself gains the power both to influence the existing creation and to bring new creations of his own into being.

God struck His Covenant with Abraham and commanded him to cut the sign of the Covenant into his very flesh by removing the foreskin of the membrum (Genesis 17, 1-27). Circumcision is a sign of our willingness to control our innate materialism and selfishness in order to elevate ourselves so as to become co-creators with God. On the physical level this includes curbing the sexual urge and elevating it in order to bring pure, holy children into the world so as to bring humanity to its destiny.

But Abraham grasped that God's Covenant applies not only to man's sexual creativity but even more to his mental and spiritual creativity through the organ that distinguishes him from all other creatures: his mouth. When man is willing to train and discipline his mouth and dedicate it to the work of holy speech, prayer and devotion, He becomes God's partner in creation as a whole.

From the Sefer Yetzira

Chapter 1:

Invocation of God; Basic concepts of the "Book", the "Writer", the "Story" and the Ten Sefirot corresponding to the ten fingers/ten toes.

> With thirty-two mystical paths of Wisdom engraved Yah the Lord of Hosts, the God of Israel, the Living God, King of the Universe, El Shaddai, Merciful

and Gracious, High and Exalted, Dwelling in eternity, Whose name is Holy -- He is lofty and holy -- and He created His universe with three books: with A Book, A Writer and A Story.

Ten Sefirot of Nothingness and twenty-two foundation letters: three Mothers, Seven Doubles and twelve Elementals.

Ten Sefirot of Nothingness, in the number of ten fingers, five opposite five, with a singular covenant precisely in the middle, in the circumcision of the tongue and in the circumcision of the membrum.

Ten Sefirot of Nothingness, ten and not nine, ten and not eleven. Understand with Wisdom, Be wise with Understanding, Examine with them and probe from them. Make each thing stand on its essence, and make the Creator sit on His base.

Ten Sefirot of Nothingness. Their measure is ten which have no end. A depth of beginning, a depth of end; a depth of good, a depth of evil; a depth of above, a depth of below; a depth of east, a depth of west, a depth of north, a depth of south. The singular Master, God, faithful King dominates over them all from His holy dwelling until eternity of eternities.

Ten Sefirot of Nothingness, their vision is like the "appearance of lightning", their limit has no end,

And His Word in them is "running and returning". They rush to His saying like a whirlwind and before His throne they prostrate themselves.

Ten Sefirot of Nothingness. Their end is imbedded in their beginning and their beginning in their end, like a flame in a burning coal. For the Master is singular, He has no second, and before One, what do you count?

Ten Sefirot of Nothingness. Bridle your mouth from speaking and your heart from thinking. And if your heart runs, return to the place. It is therefore written, "The Chayot running and returning" (Ezekiel 1:24). Regarding this a covenant was made.

Chapter 2:

The twenty-two letters of the Hebrew alphabet, elemental powers of Creation. These consist of three "mother" letters (see Chapter 3), seven "doubles" (these are the seven letters of the Hebrew alphabet that are sometimes hard, sometimes soft, such as Beit/Veit or Pe/Phe, (see Chapter 4), and the remaining twelve "simple" letters (see Chapter 5). Combination and permutation of letters.

Twenty-two foundation letters: three mothers, seven doubles and twelve elementals. The Three Mothers are Aleph Mem Shin. Their foundation is a [scales with a] pan of merit, a pan of liability, and the tongue of decree deciding between them. Three mothers: Aleph, Mem, Shin. Mem hums. Shin hisses and Aleph is the Breath of Air deciding between them.

Twenty-two foundation letters: He engraved them, He carved them, He permuted them, He weighed them, He transformed them, and with them He depicted (*TzaR*) all that was formed (*yeTzuR*) and all that would be formed.

Twenty-two foundation letters. He engraved them with voice, He carved them with breath, He set them in the mouth in five places: Aleph, Chet, Heh, Ayin, in the throat; Gimel, Yud, Kaf, Kuf in the palate; Dalet, Tet, Lamed, Nun, Tav in the tongue; Zayin, Samekh, Shin, Reish Tzadi in the teeth; Beit, Vav, Mem, Peh in the lips....

He permuted them, weighed them, and transformed them, Aleph with them all and all of them with Aleph, Beit with them all and all of them with Beit. They repeat in a cycle and exist in 231 Gates. It comes out that all that is formed and all that is spoken emanates from one Name.

He formed substance out of chaos and made nonexistence from existence.

Chapter 3:

The three mother letters, corresponding to the underlying Chessed (Right) vs. Gevurah (Left) polarity of the sefirotic tree, with Tiferet (Center) mediating between the two. The roots of the Chessed-Gevurah-Tiferet triad lie in the first three sefirot, Chokhmah, Binah and Daat/Keter. This root triad corresponds to the three main elements of creation, Water, Fire and Air, which are expressed through the medium of the Earth element.

Three Mothers: Aleph, Mem, Shin. Their foundation is a pan of merit a pan of liability and the tongue of decree deciding between them.

Three Mothers: Aleph, Mem, Shin. A great mystical secret covered and sealed with six rings, and from them emanated Air, Water and Fire and from them are born Fathers and from the Fathers, descendants.

Three Mothers: Aleph, Mem, Shin. He engraved them, He carved them, He permuted them, He weighed them, He transformed them, and with them He depicted three mothers AMSh in the Universe, Three Mothers AMSh in the Year, Three Mothers AMSh in the Soul. ["Universe" and "Year" are respectively the Time and Space coordinates of Creation, while "Soul" is the inner vitality of the living creatures within that creation.]

Three Mothers AMSh in the Universe are Air, Water, Fire: Heaven was created from Fire, Earth was created from Water, and Air from Breath decides between them.

Three Mothers AMSh in the Year are the hot, the cold and the temperate. The hot is created from fire, the cold is created from water, and the temperate from Breath decides between them.

Three Mothers AMSh in the Soul, male and female, are the head, belly and chest. The head is created from fire, the belly is created from water, and the chest, from breath, decides between them....

Chapter 4:

The seven "double" letters correspond to the seven "lower" sefirot (Chessed, Gevurah, Tiferet, Netzach, Hod, Yesod and Malkhut). These sometimes express themselves in a mode of Chessed (soft), at other times in a mode of Gevurah (hard).

Seven Doubles: Beit, Gimel, Dalet, Kaf, Peh, Resh, Tav: they direct themselves with two tongues, Beit-Bheit, Gimel-Ghimel, Dalet-Dhalet,

Kaf-Khaf, Peh-Pheh, Reish-Rheish, Tav-Thav, a structure of soft and hard, strong and weak.

Seven Doubles: BGD KPRT, their foundation is Wisdom, Wealth, Seed, Life, Dominance, Peace and Grace.

Seven Doubles: BGD KPRT in speech and in transposition. The transpose of Wisdom is Folly. The transpose of Wealth is Poverty. The transpose of Seed is Desolation. The transpose of Life is Death. The transpose of Dominance is Subjugation. The transpose of Peace is War. The transpose of Grace is Ugliness.

Seven Doubles: BGD KPRT, Up and Down, East and West, North and South, and the Holy Palace precisely in the center and it supports them all....

Seven Doubles, BGD KPRT, Seven and not six, Seven and not eight. Examine with them and probe with them. Make each thing stand on its essence and make the Creator sit on His base.

Seven Doubles: He engraved them, He carved them, He permuted them, He weighed them, He transformed them, and with them He formed Seven Planets in the Universe, Seven days in the Year, Seven gates in the Soul, male and female.

Seven planets in the Universe: Saturn, Jupiter, Mars, Sun, Venus, Mercury, Moon; Seven days in the Year [i.e. time]: the Seven days of the week.

The seven gates in the Soul, male and female, two eyes, two ears, two nostrils and the mouth....

[The *Sefer Yetzira* goes on to detail the individual "double" letters and their corresponding planet, day of the week and human attributes. See original text.]

Seven Doubles BGD KPRT: with them were engraved seven universes, seven firmaments, seven lands, seven seas, seven rivers, seven deserts, seven days, seven weeks, seven years, seven sabbaticals, seven jubilees and the Holy Palace. Therefore, He made sevens beloved under all the heavens.

Chapter Five:

The twelve simple letters corresponding to the twelve constellations of the Zodiac, the twelve months of the year, and twelve basic human functions.

Twelve Elementals: Heh, Vav, Zayin, Chet, Tet, Yud, Lamed, Nun, Samekh, Ayin, Tzadi, Kuf. Their foundation is speech, thought, motion, sight, hearing, action, coition, smell, sleep, anger, taste, laughter.

Twelve Elementals: H V Z Ch T Y L N S O Tz Q: Their foundation is that He engraved them, carved them, permuted them, weighed them and transformed them, and with them He formed twelve constellations in the Universe, twelve months in the

Year and twelve directions in the Soul, male and female.

Twelve constellations in the Universe: *T'leh* (the Ram, Aries), *Shor* (the Bull, Taurus), *Te'umim* (the Twins, Gemini), *Sartan* (the Crab, Cancer) *Arieh* (the Lion, Leo) *Betulah* (the Virgin, Virgo), *Moznayim* (Scales, Libra), *Akrav* (the Scorpion, Scorpio), *Keshet* (the Bow, Sagittarius) *Gedi* (the Kid, Capricorn), *D'li* (the Water Drawer, Aquarius), *Dagim* (the Fish, Pisces).

Twelve months in the year: Nissan, Iyar, Sivan, Tamuz, Av, Elul, Tishrei, Cheshvan, Kislev, Tevet, Shevat, Adar.

Twelve directions in the soul, male and female: the two hands, the two feet, the two kidneys, the gall bladder, the intestines, the liver, the esophagus, the stomach, the spleen.

[The *Sefer Yetzira* continues detailing each of the twelve simple letters in relation to its corresponding constellation, month of the year and "direction" of the soul. See original text.]

Houses of Prayer

Dedicated study and contemplation of the profound teachings in the *Sefer Yetzira* will open many horizons in understanding the view of Creation brought into the world by Abraham. The schema of the Water, Fire and Air elements as expressed through the Earth element is found throughout later biblical, talmudic, midrashic, kabbalistic, chassidic, philosophical and other Judaic writings. Abraham's astrological system is implicit in many important Jewish religious practices throughout the year [see the classic 18th century text, B'ney Yissaschar.]

Yet the *Sefer Yetzira* is far more than a book of "spiritual science", unveiling the mysteries of the Universe. First and foremost, it is a book with a practical purpose. It sets forth the basis of the Jewish system of prayer, which uses letter-combinations in the form of words and sentences to actually influence and change the creative process.

When we pray to God -- as Abraham did many times -- we become co-creators with God, building the world with letters and words. Thus. the *Sefer Yetzira* states:

> Two stones build 2 houses. Three stones build 6 houses. Four stones build 24 houses. Five stones build 120 houses. Six stones build 720 Houses. Seven stones build 5040 houses. From here on go out and calculate that which the mouth cannot speak and the ear cannot hear (4:16).

The "stones" are the letters of speech: the building blocks that make up our words, especially those of our prayers. Two letters can be permuted in two ways: for example, Aleph-Beit (*AV*, father) or Beit-Aleph (*BO*, Come). Three letters can produce six permutations, four can produce one twenty-four, and so on... When we combine letters into words and express ourselves in multiple different ways in prayer, we are able to bring immeasurable blessing into the world.

Being alone, Abraham never had a teacher: he lived before the Torah -- the "teaching" -- came in the world. Since he was the first, Abraham's only way to find God was through the yearnings of his heart, which he poured out in prayer. Abraham is the archetypal *Cohen* (Priest), who serves God through prayer, service of the heart. Abraham laid the foundation of this pathway for all time -- for his descendants and for all humanity.

Abraham was the pioneer. The end goal and purpose was to build the House, the place where mankind will unite in the service of God through prayer. But before it would be possible to build the House, it was first necessary to prepare the building blocks and stones. These are the letters that build the words, the "Houses of Prayer".

Abraham was the first. He was the one to hew the stones out of the mountain-rock in order to build the House.

Judaic View of Nature

*T*he view of creation that emerges from the *Sefer Yetzira* is implicit throughout biblical and rabbinical literature. Concepts like those of the Four Elements and the creative power of the Hebrew letters appear in various places throughout the Talmud, Midrash and other later writings.

The Judaic view of nature is expressed with the utmost clarity -- albeit in somewhat different terms from those of the *Sefer Yetzira*, and without its mystical dimension -- at the very beginning of the *Mishneh Torah*, the classic fourteen volume compendium of Jewish law by the great Rabbi Moshe ben Maimon, known as Rambam (or Maimonides, 1135-1204).

As well as being one of the towering Torah scholars of all time, Rambam was well-versed in Greek and Arabic philosophical literature. Yet in the section presented here below, where Maimonides systematically presents the fundamentals of the Torah view of the natural world, all the ideas are rooted in earlier biblical or rabbinical sources.

There has been much discussion about whether Rambam was privy to the kabbalistic tradition, which in his time was still not known outside of various secret circles of scholars and mystics. Whether Rambam was familiar with the details of the kabbalistic system as expressed in the *Zohar* and other *Zohar*-related literature is open to question. On the other hand, it is quite likely that he knew of the *Sefer Yetzira* and its contents. The *Sefer Yetzira* is explicitly mentioned in some manuscripts of the Jerusalem Talmud (*Sanhedrin* 7:13 (41a)). The first commentaries on the *Sefer Yetzira* had been circulating for at least a hundred and fifty years before Rambam's birth, including that of the outstanding sage and philosopher, the revered Rabbi Saadia Gaon.

The Judaic View of Nature

From Rambam's *Mishneh Torah, Hilkhot Yesodei HaTorah* (Laws Relating to the Fundamentals of Torah) Chapters 2-4

Contemplation of God's works

It is a positive duty to love and fear the glorious, awesome God, as written in the Torah: "And you shall love *HaVaYaH* your God" (Deuteronomy 6:5) and "Fear *HaVaYaH* your God" (Deuteronomy 6:13).

The way to come to love and fear God is by contemplating God's amazing works and creations and seeing the infinite wisdom expressed in them. This will immediately bring one to love God and want to praise and glorify Him. One will experience tremendous longing and yearning to know God's great Name. In the words of David: "My soul thirsts for *ELoKiM*, the living Power" (Psalms 42:3). As one contemplates further on these very things, one will immediately recoil in fear and awe, realizing that one is a tiny, lowly, dark creature standing with his flimsy, limited wisdom before the One Who has perfect knowledge....

Form and Matter

Everything which the Holy One, blessed-be-He, created in His universe comes into one of three categories:

- Creations made up of a combination of form (*TzuRA*) and matter (*ChoMeR*). These are constantly coming into being and ceasing to exist: for example, the bodies of man and animals, plants and metals.

- Creations made up of a combination of form and matter that do not change from body to body or from form to form in the same way as those in the first category. The form of the creations falling into this second category is permanently fixed in their matter, and they do not change as the others do. Examples are the spheres and the stars and planets that revolve in them. The matter of which they are constituted differs from other kinds of matter and their forms from other forms.

- Creations that consist of form but no matter, for example the *MaLaChiM*, angels. ["Angels" is the usual English translation of *MaLaCh*, but the Hebrew root, which is related to the word *MeLaChaH*, meaning "work" or the application of energy, indicates the spiritual "force" that is responsible for some process or other phenomenon in the world.] The creations in this category do not possess bodies or corporeal being, but rather are forms that are separate from one another...

What is meant by the prophet's statements that they saw an angel of fire, or with wings? All these are prophetic visions and parables....

Since the angels do not have bodies, what separates the form of the various angels from one another is that each one is below the level of the other and exists by virtue of its influence.

Everything exists through the power of the Holy One, blessed-be-He, and His goodness. By saying one angelic force is *below* another, we are not talking about physical space and height the way we do when we say one person is sitting higher up than another. Rather, we are talking about their relative spiritual level, just as one might say of two sages, one of whom is greater than the other, "One is on a higher level than the other". Similarly, that which is the *cause* of something else is said to be "above" it....

All of these spiritual forms (*TzuRoT*, the "angels") are alive. They know the Creator and have the most enormous consciousness of God, each according to its level, though not in proportion to God's true greatness.

Knowing God

Even the highest angel is unable to form any conception of the true essence of God as He really is, since the angel's mind or consciousness is too limited to know or grasp Him. Yet this highest angel does know and experience more of God than the form below it.

All existence except for the Creator -- from the very first form down to the smallest mosquito in the depths of the earth -- came into being through God's truth. Since God knows Himself and knows His true greatness, beauty and truth, He knows everything. Nothing is hidden from Him. The Holy One, blessed-be-He, recognizes His truth and knows it as it is. He does not know with a knowledge that is external to Him the way that humans know. This is because we humans are not one and the same as the knowledge we possess, whereas in the case of the blessed God, He, His knowledge and His life are a complete and total unity.... He is the Knower, He is the Known, and He is the Knowledge itself. All is one. It is beyond the ability of our mouths to explain this or our ears to take it in, nor is man's heart able to grasp this in its entirety....

The Heavenly Spheres

The heavens are made up of spheres. There are nine spheres. The closest to us is that of the moon. Above it, the second sphere contains the planet *Kochav* (Mercury). Above this, the third sphere contains the planet *Nogah* (Venus). The fourth sphere contains the Sun. The fifth contains the planet *Ma'adim* (Mars). The sixth sphere contains the planet *Tzedek* (Jupiter). The seventh contains the planet *Shabbtai* (Saturn). The eighth sphere contains all the stars we see in the sky. The ninth sphere revolves from east to west every day. It surrounds and encompasses everything. The planets and stars all appear to be in a single sphere even though one is higher than another. This is because the spheres themselves are pure and refined like glass or sapphire.... This is why the stars in the eighth sphere may appear lower than the first sphere.

Each of the eight main spheres containing the planets and stars is itself divided into many individual spheres, one above the other like the layers of an onion. Some of these spheres revolve from west to the east, others from east to west..... There is no empty space between any of them.

None of the spheres are light or heavy. They are neither red, black nor any other color. Although we see them as blue, this is only our perception because of the height of the atmosphere. Similarly, they have neither taste nor smell, because those qualities are present only in lower forms of matter. All these nine spheres surrounding the world are spherical like a ball, and the Earth is suspended in the middle....

From knowing the daily movements of the stars and planets, their positions north or south in the sky and their distance from or closeness to Earth, it is possible to know the total number of spheres and the way they revolve. This is the science of astronomy. Many books about these subjects were written by the wise men of Greece.

The Zodiac

The ninth sphere, which encompasses all the others, was divided by the sages of the early generations into twelve sections. They gave each of these sections a name based on the shapes that appeared to be formed by the stars in the corresponding section of the eighth sphere just below it. These are the mazalot (lit. sources of influence): the Ram (Aries), the Ox (Taurus), the Twins (Gemini), the Crab (Cancer), the Lion (Leo), the Virgin (Virgo), the Scales (Libra), the Scorpion (Scorpio), the Bow (Sagittarius), the Goat (Capricorn), the Bucket (Aquarius) and the Fish (Pisces).

The ninth sphere itself has no divisions and does not possess any of these shapes or stars. Rather, the larger stars in the constellations of the eighth sphere are seen in the shape of these forms or in a form resembling them. These twelve forms corresponded to these divisions only at the time of the Flood, which is when they were given these names. However, at present they have already moved slightly, because all the stars in the eighth sphere move just like the sun and the moon. It is just that these stars move more slowly....

All the stars and spheres possess a soul, knowledge and intellect. They are alive and stand in recognition of the One who spoke and brought the world into being.

According to their size and level, they all praise and glorify their Creator, just like the angels. And just as they are aware of the Holy One, blessed-be-He, they are also conscious of themselves and of the angels above them. The level of consciousness of the stars and spheres is less than that of the angels but greater than of humans.

The Four Elements

Below the sphere of the moon, God created a type of matter which differs from the matter of the heavenly spheres. [This is matter as we know it here on Earth.] He created four forms (*TzuRoT*) for this lower kind of matter different from the forms of the matter of the upper spheres.

Each of these four forms was fixed in part of this lower kind of matter, and the four parts together make up the totality of matter as we know it on Earth. The first of these forms is that of Fire. When the form of Fire was joined to its portion of the totality of matter, the two produced the "body" of Fire. The second of these forms is that of Air. When this form was joined to its corresponding portion of matter, the two produced the "body" of Air. The third of these forms is that of Water. When the form was joined to its portion of matter, the two produced the "body" of Water. The fourth of these forms is that of Earth. When it was joined to its portion of matter, the two produced the "body" of Earth.

[In speaking of the "bodies" of Fire, Air, Water and Earth, Rambam does not appear to be talking of actual physical fire, air, water -- H_2O -- and solid rock and dust the way most people think of them today so much as of four fundamental kinds of energy states underlying all the different solid, liquid, gaseous and radiational phenomena in the physical world.]

Thus, below the heavens there are four different states of matter, one above the other, each encompassing the one below on all sides like a sphere. The first of these physical "bodies", which is closest to the sphere of the moon, is that of fire. Below it is the air. Below this is the water and below this the body of the Earth. There is no empty space devoid of all matter between them.

[Rambam's above statement may be more comprehensible if we think of a panoramic land- or seascape and consider how the earth is at the bottom, above it stand the waters of the seas and lakes, above this the air, and above the air the light, heat and other radiations ("fire") coming down from the sun, planets and stars.]

These four "bodies" do not possess a soul, nor are they conscious or self-aware. They are more like dead bodies. Each possesses its unique characteristics, but not consciously. They are unable to change their characteristics.

This does not contradict David's words (Psalms 148:7-8): "Praise God from the Earth, sea-monsters and all the depths, fire and hail, snow and vapor..." The verse means: Men, praise God for His might, which is visible in the fire, hail and other creations seen in the realms below the heavens, because their power is always visible to both the great and the small.

Fire, Air, Water and Earth

These four "bodies" -- fire, wind, water and earth -- are the fundamental elements or foundations of all the creations below the heavens. Anything that exists -- man, animal, bird, crawling insect, fish, plant, metal, precious stone, diamond, rock, mountain or lump of earth -- is a specific body composed of some combination of these four basic elements.

Thus, all the specific bodies found below the heavens (with the exception of these four underlying physical elements) are combinations of form and matter in which the matter consists of a combination of these four basic elements. The four basic elements themselves are a combination of matter and form. [The word "form" (*TzuRA*) here refers to the spiritual qualities and structure of an entity and not merely its physical shape.]

The tendency of Fire and Air is to rise upwards from the depths of the earth out towards the sky. The tendency of Water and Earth is to go downwards from the sky towards the midpoint of the earth. These inherent tendencies stem not from conscious volition on the part of the basic elements but are functions of their natural make-up.

The nature of Fire is warm and dry. It is the lightest of these basic elements. Air is warm and moist, Water cold and moist, while Earth is dry and cold. Earth is the heaviest of the four elements. Water is lighter than earth, which is why it is found above it. Air is lighter than water, which is why it hovers above it. Fire is even lighter than wind.

Combinations of the Elements

Since these are the fundamental elements, the matter constituting every single individual body -- man, animal, bird, fish, plant, metal or stone -- is a combination of fire, wind, water and earth. When any one of them combines with the others it undergoes a change. For this reason, the various visible combinations of elements are not like any of the elements as it would be if it were to stand alone. In any given combination, you will never find even the tiniest portion of pure Fire, pure Air, pure Water or pure Earth. In combining to form a single body they all change.

Any body made up of a combination of these four basic elements will have some combination of cold and warmth, moistness and dryness. Some bodies have a higher proportion of Fire -- for example, creatures with living souls. Accordingly, they have a higher temperature. Conversely, there are some bodies with a greater concentration of Earth -- for example, stones. Accordingly, they are very dry. Similarly, some bodies have a higher concentration of Water, and accordingly they are moist.

One body may be warmer than another that is itself warm, or one body may be drier than another body that is itself dry. Some bodies are markedly cold, others particularly moist. In some bodies, coldness and dryness are equally noticeable. The proportion of a given element in the combination making up a particular body will express itself in particular characteristics found in that body.

Decomposition of Matter

Every entity that is a combination of these four basic elements will ultimately decompose and separate back into them. Some will decompose after a mere few days, others only after many years. But it is not possible for something made out of some combination of them not to decompose in the end and separate back to them. Even gold and ruby have to decompose eventually and return to their basic elements, part of them becoming Fire, part of them Water, part of them Air and part of them Earth.

Since every entity must eventually decompose and separate into these four basic elements, why was Adam told: "You will return to *dust*," [implying that man will turn back into the Earth element alone]? The reason is that earth is the major component of man's physical body. Just because an entity decomposes, this does not mean it separates back into the four basic elements immediately. Rather it will decompose and change into another entity, which will then change into another entity, and so on, until eventually it turns back into the four basic elements. Thus, all entities are constantly returning to their elemental state in a cyclical manner.

The four basic elements are in a constant state of flux, with a certain portion of each one -- though never the element in its entirety -- changing into another element every day and every moment. For example, part of the Earth closest to Water dissolves and actually becomes Water. Similarly, part of the Water closest to the Air evaporates and becomes Air. Part of the Air closest to the Fire changes and turns into fire. Similarly, part of the Fire closest to the Air changes, contracts and turns into Air. The wind closest to the Water changes, contracts and becomes Water. And the Water closest to the earth changes, contracts and becomes Earth.

This cycle of change proceeds little by little over the course of time. It will never happen that one of the basic elements will change completely into another. For example, the Water will never all turn into Wind, nor will all the Air turn into Fire, because it is not possible for one of the four basic elements to entirely cease to exist. Rather, a portion of the Fire will change to Air, and a portion of the Air to Fire.

There is an unremitting cycle of interchange between each pair of the four. This cycle is caused by the revolution of the sphere, which causes the four basic elements to combine to bring into being the matter of which humans, animals, plants, stones and metals are constituted. God gives each individual body the form appropriate to it.

Mind and Matter

You will never actually see matter without form or form without matter. It is the human mind that thinks about bodies and understands that they are combinations of form and matter. The mind grasps that some bodies consist of matter that is made up of a combination of the four basic elements, that other bodies (the planets, stars and spheres) are constituted of matter that is simple and uniform, and that there also exist pure forms (*TzuRoT*) that have no matter and cannot be seen by the physical eye. These last can be discerned only by the eye of the heart. We can know that they exist just as we know that God exists even though we do not see Him with our eyes.

When we speak of the *soul* of any living creature [such as an animal] we are referring to the form (*TzuRaH*) this creature was given by God. The extra dimension found in the soul of man is *TzuRaT HaADaM*, the Form of Man. Concerning this form, God said: "Let us make man in Our image and in Our likeness" (Genesis 1:26). Man has been given a form that is capable of knowing and communing with forms and ideas that are not material, like the angels, which are form without body, until man himself can be like them. When we speak of "form" (*TzuRaH*), we are not referring to the physical form of a body as seen by the eye -- the mouth, nose, cheeks and other parts of the body. In Hebrew that is called the *To'ar* ("shape").

This *Tzurat HaAdam* or Soul in man is not to be identified with the animal soul that causes it to eat, drink, reproduce, feel and think. Rather it is experienced in the higher consciousness of the inner soul. It is this inner soul or form that is referred to in the verse "in Our image and in Our likeness". Frequently this form is referred to as Nefesh or Ru'ach [in Kabbalistic terminology, the *Nefesh Eloki*, Godly Soul, or *Neshamah*].

This Soul is not a combination of the basic elements such that it must ultimately decompose and separate back into them. Nor is it merely a derivative of the animal soul such that it would need the animal soul the way the animal soul needs the body. The Soul comes from God, from Heaven. For this reason, even after the body, composed as it is of the four basic elements, decomposes, and even after the animal soul ceases to exist (for the animal soul can only exist in conjunction with the body and needs the body for everything it does), even so, the Divine Soul will never cease to exist, for it does not need the animal soul in order to act.

Rather, the Divine Soul knows and comprehends realities that are above matter, it knows the Creator of all things, and it exists forever. Solomon said in his wisdom: "The dust will return to the Earth as it was and the Spirit will return to God who granted it" (Ecclesiastes 12:7).

Rambam concludes:

All the ideas we have explained in this connection are like a mere drop.... They are very deep and profound.....

When a person meditates on them and comes to recognizes the different orders of creation -- the angels, the spheres, man and so on -- and appreciates the wisdom of the Holy One, blessed-be-He, in all these creations, his love of God will grow, his soul will thirst for God, and his very flesh will crave with love of God.

Love and Kindness

... You must also understand that the Rabbis in many cases explained fundamental mystical concepts using examples from nature or science. When they explained things with reference to science, they used concepts that were meaningful in terms of the theories current among students of nature and science in their time. But the main point in such explanations is not the scientific example as expressed in terms of once-current theories, but rather the mystical concept they wanted thereby to elucidate. It has no bearing on the truth of the mystical idea whether the external "garb" in which they clothed it -- the scientific theory -- is actually true or not [according to later thinking]. Their only intention was to express the mystical secret in terms used by the learned in those times. The actual secret could equally well have been clothed in another garb drawn from ideas and theories of later times, and the Rabbi giving the explanation would himself have put it in those terms had he lived later on.

The Rabbis view all physical phenomena as being governed and controlled by spiritual forces of various kinds, whether holy angels or demons and destroyers. Everything in this lowly material world is under the power of a higher, spiritual realm. Conversely, physical actions have an influence on that spiritual realm. Someone who does not understand this view will never be able to understand rabbinical thought...

Rabbi Moshe Chaim Luzzatto ("RaMChaL"), *Maamar al Agadot*, printed as an introduction to *Midrash Rabbah*

The wise men of Athens asked Rabbi Yehoshua ben Chananiya: "Where is the center of the Universe?" He raised his finger and said: "Here!" They said to him, "How do you know?" He replied: "Bring ropes and measure it!" (*Bekhorot* 8b)

*I*t may be grating to the modern mind to discover that the Judaic view of nature is unapologetically geocentric. It is clear from the *Sefer Yetzira*, Rambam's *Mishneh Torah* and other classic sources that the Earth is the center of the universe, while the sun, the moon and the other planets and stars are in orbit around it, each following its own unique path through the skies.

Many moderns will look with disdain at such pre-Copernican ideas. Even though large numbers of people evidently do regard themselves as being at the center of the universe, they would still consider it "subjective" and "unscientific" to view the sun and other celestial bodies as essentially dancing around *us* and shining especially for *us* -- even though that is the way it seems when you watch the sun and other heavenly bodies on their magnificent east-west circuits day after day.

But after a few hundred years of post-Galilean astronomy and several decades of space travel, many today would probably consider it more "objective" to take a "scientific" view and look back down at the solar system from some imaginary standpoint way above, in which case Earth would seem to be "just" another planet -- i.e. a "mere" appendage of the sun, which in any case is apparently "merely" another star.

Contemplating the numberless galaxies stretching away from us endlessly in all directions, one might easily conclude that the universe has no order and no center. Once Earth is dethroned from being the center of everything, the more democratic view would seem to be that all the stars, young and old, are equal -- and all equally meaningless, chance explosions of some gas that came out of nowhere for no reason.

Where is the Center?

Post-Copernican theories may well provide better explanations of the observable movements of the members of the solar system *than the geocentric rotating-sphere theory found in the Rambam.* But it is a mistake to conclude that just because science has displaced Earth from being the *physical* center around which all the stars and planets are orbiting, this means we are not at the *actual* center of the Universe.

Saying that we are at the center of the Universe is not a statement about our physical position in some closed system. The Universe appears to be endless, and therefore cannot meaningfully be said to have a physical center. There are in fact many physical "centers". The sun is clearly a "center", since it evidently holds major bodies, such as the Earth and planets trapped in its gravitational field. Earth is also a center, keeping you and me and all the rest of its inhabitants very close to the ground most of the time through the power of its gravitational pull.

When we speak about the Center of the entire Universe, we are not talking about a physical center but rather the *Absolute Center*. This is not a physical concept. For the Absolute Center of all centers is the One Creator, who in Himself is not like any of His creations. God is beyond the physical parameters of space and time that He created for this finite universe. The concept of physical center is simply inapplicable to God. Being one single unity in every respect, God is simultaneously at the center of all things, large or small, at all times. Or to put it another way, the Center is everywhere.

What this means is that wherever you are at any time, you are always right by the very center!

This is what Rabbi Yehoshua ben Chananiya said to the wise men of Athens when they asked him where is the center of the Universe. "Right here!" he said, raising his finger and pointing. When they asked him how he knew, he said, "Go and measure it!" Obviously, it is impossible to measure the Universe since it goes on for ever, being the work of the Infinite One, who is beyond all measure and limit. And because of His very infinity, God -- Creator of all things and Center of all centers -- is at all times simultaneously present in all places, including "Right here!" Wherever you are, you are always right next to the very Center!

Does the Universe Have Meaning?

It is easy to look up at the endless stars and galaxies and sneeringly dismiss the entire Universe as a massive fluke. This is the reaction of an arrogant ignoramus who will not admit that there could be any meaning in something he himself does not understand.

Insisting on only looking "down" at the sun, earth, planets and stars from some imaginary standpoint "up there" (the supposedly "objective," "scientific" viewpoint) as opposed to gazing up at the heavenly bodies in awe and wonder from "down here" on Earth, which is how the heavenly light-show was *meant* to be seen -- is like going to a wonderful movie and spending the entire time trying to figure out the projection system. This may be a most fascinating exercise, but you will miss the whole show!

The heavenly-light show -- the incessant spinning of the sun, the moon, the stars and planets around and around our skies -- is part of the overall live "movie" or *Sippur*, the "story" God is causing to unfold in front of our eyes here on Earth through the medium of the Universe, the Creation, which is the *Sefer*, the "book" (or "screen").

From our viewpoint here on Earth, the story is being enacted amidst the fabulous setting of the circuiting sun, the moon, the planets and stars. It is certainly a wonderful privilege to live in an age when men have traveled in space and looked back down on Earth from "up there", and have even walked on a tiny portion of one of the main projectors, the moon. But why be overly worried about the mechanics that are making the heavenly light-show work the way it does, while totally ignoring the actual radiations of light and other influences these celestial beings are sending down to us right here where we are on Earth?

Without doubt, if we were living on a different planet in a different galaxy the radiations would be different and so would the "story" they tell. It would be a completely different world, and we would be different beings. But the fact is that we are living here on this Earth, exactly where God has put us, and He is shining the lights of the sun, the moon and the stars in just the way He wants in order to tell us the part of the "story" that relates to us.

Above the Stars

Abraham, outstanding astrologer that he was, knew full well that the sun, the moon, the planets and stars are all shining directly to US with all kinds of radiations and influences. The *Sefer Yetzira* provides the foundations for a complete astrological system tracing influences present in the spiritual physical worlds to the stars and planets.

Yet Abraham understood that the Source of these influences is above the stars. Abraham did not merely project himself up to some imaginary standpoint above the solar system and look down the way the scientifically-minded might wish to do.

Abraham took a far greater leap -- a leap of faith -- above and beyond the entire physical universe.

> "And God took him to the outside, and He said, Look over the heavens...." (Genesis 15:5).

> "He took him out from the space (*ChaLaL*) of the universe and lifted him up *above* the stars. This is why the word 'look over' is used in the verse, having the connotation of looking from above down below." (*Rashi* ad loc.)

The humble Abraham was able to rise above the limitations of normal, everyday, materialistic, ego-bound thinking. Through the power of faith and holistic Chokhmah-vision, Abraham took a leap beyond physical space altogether -- to the ultimate, absolute Unity underlying the entire universe. This was how Abraham rose "above the stars". For he made connection with *HaVaYaH*, the Supreme Power that makes them shine.

The Hebrew word for star is *KOKhaV*. The word is made up of two pairs of letters, *Kaph Vav* and *Khaph Beit*. The numerical value of the letters of the two pairs is respectively twenty-six and twenty-two. (*Kaph*, 20 and *Vav*, 6 = 26. *Khaph*, 20 and *Veit*, 2 = 22.)

Twenty-six is the numerical value of the holy name of *HaVaYaH*, Creator of the Universe. At the very core and "center" of each *KO-KhaV* -- this star, itself a center, an individual sun radiating with light -- is the Absolute Center, the Source and Cause of all things: *HaVaYaH*. God. The specific power of this particular star derives from its inner *Tzura*, the God-created spiritual "form" that is the "soul" of the physical star. The power radiated by the *Tzura* is defined by the "name" of the star, which is made up of a particular combination of the elemental "letters" of creation. Altogether there are twenty-two elemental letters: the twenty-two letters of the Aleph-Bet. The Hebrew word for star, *KO-ChaV*, indicates that the power of the unified Creator, *HaVaYaH* (= 26 = *KO*) radiates via the physical star by means of the *Tzura*, the "form" or "angel" of the star, whose power is channeled via *KhaV* (= 22), the twenty-two letters of the Hebrew alphabet. *Ko-ChaV!*

It is these elemental letters that are writing the story being beamed down to Earth by the sun, the moon, the planets and stars with their many different kinds of light and different influences.

Love and Kindness

Abraham grasped that all this light shining down into the world -- giving life to the plants and to all other life-forms on Earth -- is a gift of pure kindness and charity. In the words of Rebbe Nachman:

> All the heavenly spheres and cycles are governed by *Tzedakah*, charity and kindness. This is the idea of "the way of the eagle in the skies" (Proverbs 30): the

eagle is a symbol of kindness and charity (*Zohar Yitro* 80b)"

Likutey Moharan I, 31:1

Seeing all this kindness and charity flowing down into the world, Abraham knew that it was directed to him. For He knew that God is so great, He is intimately involved in every single detail of creation. That is why "Each person must say, The entire world was created only for me" (*Sanhedrin* 37a).

And the humble Abraham asked: "Who am I to be the receiver of all this? How can I show my gratitude for this gift? What can I do to play *my* part in this amazing system?" What can *I* offer?

His answer was: "Just as the sun and the stars and planets are all giving, I too must give. Just as they are all shining pure love, charity and kindness to me, so too I must shine the light on to others...."

For Abraham, it was not enough to study and contemplate nature as an idle spectator. Spiritual maturity is when a person realizes he must play his part not just as a taker but also as a giver in a system which is all about giving.

Having leapt beyond the stars to the Absolute Center and Source, Abraham knew that the Center is everywhere. Every tiny detail of creation is important. Each individual is important. Every single one makes a difference.

That means that I also make a difference. What I do is important.

It is the acts of practical goodness and kindness we show to those around us that build a sweeter, happier world. Kindness means helping people satisfy their material needs. And it means more. The truest kindness is to help people satisfy their deep inner craving for spiritual light and joy and for the fulfillment that can only come from knowing God.

This was why Abraham was always reaching out to others. He would go from place to place trying to awaken people to the truth about the world and heighten their awareness of God.

Thanks for the Food

One of the ways Abraham did this was by teaching people to appreciate the many blessings flowing to us every day, especially in our very food and drink.

> "...Abraham planted the *ESheL* in Be'er Sheva and he called there on the name of *HaVaYaH, El Olam*, Power of the World" (Genesis 21:33).

> The Rabbis taught: "The *ESheL* was a grove of trees, a place where travelers could rest. Our father Abraham made every passer-by call on God's Name. How did he do it? After his guests finished eating and drinking, they would get up to thank him. Abraham would say to them, "Why thank me? Was the food that you ate mine? The food you ate is the

gift of *El Olam*, the Power of the World! Give thanks and praise and bless the One who spoke and brought the world into being" (*Sotah* 10b).

When a person eats, it is an offering to oneself. After performing the very physical and necessarily self-centered act of eating, Abraham taught that we must take some moments to focus our minds on the goodness, grace and kindness with which God lovingly sends food and sustenance into the entire universe.

"Blessed are You, *HaVaYaH*, our God, Power of the Universe, Who nourishes the whole Universe in His goodness, with grace, love and kindness..." (from *Birkhat HaMazon*, the Blessing after Bread).

By reminding ourselves of the kindness and charity that pervades the universe, we will remember our obligation to give something back in return.

It is necessary to offer such prayers of gratitude and praise regularly, in order to draw our awareness of God's love and our obligation to Him deep into our being. For, in the words of the beloved moralist, R. Bachya Ibn Paquda (who lived in the 10th century):

> Human beings are like foolish animals when they come into this world. As the wise man said, "When a man is born, he is like a wild ass's colt" (Job 11:12). People grow up surrounded by a superabundance of divine favors which they

experience continuously, and to which they become so used that they come to regard these as essential parts of their being, not to be removed for their whole life. Even when their minds and intelligence develop, they foolishly ignore the benefits God has given them, feeling no obligation to be thankful. For they are unaware of the true value of these gifts and the infinite greatness of the Benefactor.

They are like a baby found in the desert by a kind-hearted individual. He took pity on the child, carried it home, brought it up, fed it, clothed it, and provided for it most generously until it was old enough to understand the many benefits it had received. The same kind individual heard about someone who had fallen into the hands of his enemies and had been starved and kept naked and treated with extreme cruelty for a long time. The kind man was able to arrange for the prisoner to be freed, and he then took him home and showed him kindness, though to a lesser extent than he showed to the abandoned child. Yet the freed prisoner was more grateful to the kind man than the child who had been surrounded with kindness from infancy....

Since this is so, men of wisdom have deemed it their duty to awaken those who are unaware of God's beneficence and to teach them to recognize the benefits. There are many good things that people never enjoy simply because they are unaware of how good they really are. As soon as they are made aware of the true benefits they are receiving, they will offer greater praise and thanks to God, gaining pleasure and happiness in their life in this world as well as their heavenly reward in the next.

from Duties of the Heart (*Chovot Halevavot*) Second Treatise, by R. Bachya Ibn Paquda

Speech

To thank and bless God is to take the human faculty of speech, which people mostly use to communicate with other humans, and direct it *inwards* to self and soul and *upwards* to God.

Not only are our words of thanks and blessing a way to inculcate ourselves with greater awareness of God as we concentrate on the meaning of these words. These selfsame words are also the most precious offering to God we could make. For speech is man's highest faculty. Out of all creation, man alone was made "in the image of God". God "speaks". With letters and words, He brought into being all the *Tzurot*, the various "forms" of created beings from the highest to the lowest. The greatness of man is that his speech is also vested with creative power.

Since "every physical action has an influence on the spiritual realm", the very air of the breath with which we express the words of the blessings causes vibrations in the whole Universe. Just as the Word of God brought into being many forms and angels radiating love and light, so the words of our prayers and blessings send "kindness and charity" into all creation.

Having eaten and benefited from the fruits, vegetables and other foods that could only grow with the loving light of the sun, the moon and the stars, we take the time to bless God. We reflect on the flow of love manifest in the vast cosmic process of sustenance. And we open our mouths in praise and thanksgiving in order that the words and vibrations flowing from our lips should send blessings into the whole universe.

Adam sinned by stealing the fruit of the tree of knowledge for himself. Abraham taught people not to steal, but to eat what is rightfully theirs with thanks and gratitude to the One who gave it.

And God's love for us is such that when we -- tiny creatures in this vast, endless cosmic system -- bless God, our words are precious to Him. He takes these humble human words and letters and makes them vibrate through the entire universe, opening up the wellsprings of blessing and spreading goodness and peace throughout the world.

The Binding of Isaac

For years Abraham had no children. But at last his beloved wife Sarah bore him a son.

> "And *HaVaYaH* remembered Sarah as He said, and *HaVaYaH* did to Sarah as He spoke. Sarah conceived and bore a son for Abraham in his old age. Abraham called the name of the son that Sarah bore Isaac. Abraham was *a hundred years old* when his son Isaac was born" (Genesis 21:1-5).

The birth of Isaac to Abraham and Sarah at such an advanced age was a miracle that flew in the face of natural law and the ordinances of the stars.

It was twenty-five years since this couple had set off on their journey to the Land. At that time, they were still called by their original names, Avram and Sarai. They were already old then, and to all appearances they were congenitally incapable of ever having children.

Abraham knew this: as if the physical message of their old age and his wife's menopause was not clear enough, Abraham, the master astrologer, saw the facts written indelibly in the stars: "Avram cannot have children."

How many tears and prayers must he and Sarah have poured out to God to give them a child. Otherwise all their efforts to bring the knowledge of God to the world would die with them. How they must have longed and yearned for a successor that they could raise and train in perfect purity in order to establish the pathway of obedience and devotion to *HaVaYaH* for all time.

They were not interested in setting up a dynasty. They craved for a son because they wanted to do more than merely salvage tarnished souls from the prevailing degeneracy. They wanted to raise a whole new breed of human beings who would be pure from the very time of conception onwards, holy people fit to be priests and ministers of *HaVaYaH*. Only this way would the entire world be cleansed of its corruption and creation brought to its destiny.

Abraham and Sarah continued praying despite everything. They paid no attention to biological "facts" or the passing of year after year without their seeing an answer. People thought they were crazy. When the aged Abraham walked about the Land calling on God's name and preparing for the perfect society his descendants were to build, the Canaanite inhabitants jeered and taunted him. What senile madness was this for a barren old man to dream that his seed -- his descendants -- would inherit the land for ever?

Still Abraham and Sarah did not give up. They carried on yearning and pouring out their prayers. They knew that the teaching they were bringing to the world was so vital that it *had* to survive them and endure for ever. Again and again, they poured out torrents of words and prayers from the depths of their hearts.

And the words won. Their prayers prevailed. Abraham and Sarah's words became the Word of God.

"And He took him outside and said, Look over the heavens and count the stars, if you can count them. And He said, So will be your seed." (Genesis 15:5).

In taking Abraham "outside," God was saying: "Go out from your astrology. You've seen in the stars that you are not going to have a son. *Avram* has no son. But *Abraham* will have a son. *Sarai* will not give birth. But *Sarah* will have a child. I will call you by a different name, and this will change the *mazal*." (*Rashi* ad loc.)

The decree of the stars was that *Avram* and *Sarai* were indeed permanently barren. This was a physical fact -- a reality caused by the radiations from the *mazalot*, the constellations, into the material world and inscribed in their actual bodies, which were biologically incapable of procreation.

But the nature of things in the physical world is governed by their *tzurot*, the spiritual forms or "angels" that make them what they are. These *tzurot* are the letters and formulae that govern the structure and functioning of the *chomer*, the material substance to which they give form. However, one who has the power to change the *tzurah* can change the very physical nature of the *chomer* to which it is bound. The right change of words and letters can bring about a total change of *tzurah* that generates a corresponding change in the *chomer*. This can lead to a complete miracle -- a phenomenon that simply and blatantly flies in the face of natural probability and the "ordinances of the stars".

Words have the power to alter *mazal*, the flow of influence from the angels and stars into the actual physical world. *Avram* and *Sarai* could not have a child. But *Abraham* and *Sarah* could have a child.

The wisdom of *tzurot* -- letters and words -- was the very wisdom Abraham had mastered and taught in his *Sefer Yetzira*. The mystical foundations of this wisdom are the deepest of the deep. Yet the wisdom can be applied in the simplest way by practically anyone. Abraham's pathway is the path of prayer: speaking out the innermost yearnings of our hearts sincerely and honestly in the simplest of words and offering them to *HaVaYaH* as the "charity of our lips", a service performed for the simple reason that this is what He wants of us: to turn to Him and ask Him for everything we need and desire. For this is the way to come to know and understand that everything in the world is from *HaVaYaH*.

Just as *HaVaYaH* created everything through His Word, so He has the power to change everything at will through words and bring entirely new creations into the world. When we recognize this, and offer Him *our* words, our will becomes His will and our very words themselves become the Word of God that determines what will be.

The amazing rejuvenation of the aged Abraham and Sarah followed by the miraculous birth of their beautiful new baby Isaac was a most awesome manifestation of the supreme power of God to bring about anything He wants. Isaac was living proof of the power of prayer -- Abraham's way of using words to bend reality.

A whole new era was beginning. Abraham had searched so long to discover the trail. He had struggled so hard to break his way through. From now on, under the leadership of Isaac -- who would follow the discipline of prayer and prophecy from the very outset -- this tough, inaccessible mountain track would turn into a readily accessible field that others too would be able to learn to work in order to bring the world to perfection.

To the Mountain

There was Isaac eagerly binding himself to the yoke and throwing himself with all the strength of youth into the work of ploughing the field, practicing the ways of justice, charity, prophecy and prayer.

As Abraham watched his beloved son -- living proof of the power of words -- could he have any doubts about the truth of the chilling prophecy that suddenly came to him through those same trusted methods?

> "And He said to him: Take your son -- your only son whom you love -- Isaac, and go to the land of Moriah and offer him up there as a whole offering

on one of the mountains that I will tell you." (Genesis 22:1-2).

This was the ultimate mountain, Abraham's supreme test. The familiar prophetic voice was telling him to sacrifice his son to God.

From his earliest years Abraham had been destined for priesthood. The woman who wanted him to bring a sacrifice to Terach's idols felt instinctively that Abraham understood about divine ministry. The question was not whether to bring offerings but to whom. Abraham saw the absurdity of bringing offerings to powerless idols, but he knew a great deal about offerings and self-sacrifice to *HaVaYaH*.

Did the path of prayer and devotion really lead to literal human sacrifice?

This is not the place for a discussion of the profound mysteries of the Binding of Isaac, which has been discussed at length by philosophers and moralists throughout the ages. The fact is that in the end it turned out that it was *not* the will of God to shed human blood -- not even for the sake of a holy sacrifice, let alone in murder and warfare.

After three days of anguish following the prophecy, Abraham finally reached Mount Moriah. This was the place from whose Earth Adam's body was formed. This was where Noah offered sacrifices after the Flood. This was the place which was -- and will be -- the site of the Holy Temple of God.

They came to the place that God told him, and Abraham built the altar there and arranged the wood and bound Isaac his son and put him on the altar on top of the wood. And Abraham stretched out his hand and took the knife to slaughter his son.

And the angel of *HaVaYaH* called to him from the heavens and said: "Abraham! Abraham!" And he said, "I am ready!" And He said, "Do not put your hand to the boy and do not do anything to him. For now, I know that you revere God and you did not hold back your only son from Me". *(ibid.* 9-12)

It was not Isaac's blood that God wanted. Isaac's very *life* was to be the sacrifice. He was to be the exemplar of total submission to God and obedience to His law.

Yet Abraham was not satisfied. Had he climbed all the way to the top of the mountain in total surrender, only to leave without surrendering anything?

Abraham raised his eyes and saw that there was a ram caught by its horns in the thicket. Abraham went and took the ram and offered it up as an offering in place of his son. And Abraham called the name of that place "*HaVaYaH* sees, as it is said this day, On the Mountain *HaVaYaH* is seen." *(ibid.* 13-14).

Here was the mountain, the place where mankind can attain the peak of connection with God -- seeing and being seen -- by climbing to the very summit of lowliness, humility, submission and self-sacrifice.

When Adam ate the forbidden fruit, the sin was that of arrogant selfishness. Now, through Abraham's willingness to make the supreme sacrifice, it would be possible to rectify the sin. The very earth from which Adam's body was formed would be the place of the atonement altar of his descendants for all time. Through the Temple sacrifices humanity would learn what it is to slaughter one's own willfulness and selfishness, placing what God commands over and above what man desires.

What God most wants of man is that he should know God. Mount Moriah, the place of sacrifice and prayer, would be the place for all mankind to come to know God. For "My House will be called the House of Prayer for all the nations" (Isaiah 56:7).

Abraham had conquered the Mountain.

Spiritual Retreat
in the Mountains

Spiritual retreat to the mountains has been a Jewish practice from biblical times until the present day.

Just prior to the redemption from Egypt, Moses, preparing himself for his role of leadership, went back to the ancestral practice of Abraham and took himself to the mountain:

> And Moses was tending the flock of Jethro, his father-in-law, Priest of Midian. He led the flock to the farthest end of the wilderness and came to the Mountain of God to Horeb (Exodus 3:1).

Egypt was the all-time paradigm of degenerate city civilization -- center of every kind of vice and idolatry. The Israelite slaves were forced to build store-cities for Pharaoh (Exodus 1:11) -- buildings, buildings and more buildings. The super-sophisticated Egyptian urban environment was so cluttered with idolatrous images and so shut off from all awareness of *HaVaYaH*, it was impossible even to pray there! When Pharaoh begged Moses to pray for an end to the plague of hail, Moses said, "When I *go out of the city* I will spread out my hands to *HaVaYaH*" (ibid. 9:29).

Getting free of Pharaoh meant leaving the slick man-made world of the city for the awesome natural grandeur of the wilderness. The whole Jewish People picked up, abandoned their houses in Egypt and went out to camp in the desert. It was out in nature, standing at the foot of a Mountain -- the humble, lowly Mount Sinai -- that the 600,000 souls of the Children of Israel had the peak spiritual experience in all of human history as they collectively witnessed God's Self-revelation to the world.

It was at this Mountain of Sinai that they received the Torah code that was to be their guiding light in building a new life in the Land of Israel on totally different foundations from those of Egypt-style civilization. Forty years later, when they first entered the Land under the leadership of Joshua, the entire nation went through a solemn ceremony of rededication to the Torah under the shadow of two mountains, the twin peaks of Ebal and Gerizim (Deuteronomy 27; Joshua 8:30-39).

From the time of Joshua onwards the mountains and deserts of the Land of Israel were places of retreat for spiritual seekers. Jephthah's daughter (who was supposed to be offered up as a sacrifice because of her father's thoughtless vow prior to his defeat of the Ammonites) went to the mountains to "bewail her virginity" (Judges 11:38). It was in the mountains and wildernesses that the young David -- in flight from King Saul -- found refuge (1 Samuel 19-26). Out of David's intense devotions in these dramatic natural surroundings were born many of the sublime prayers in the book of Psalms. The

Psalms include many passages of praise to God for the wonders of nature.

Mountains and wildernesses were the choice of those seeking to escape the corruption that developed in the days of the later kings of Israel. In flight from persecution at the hands of the idolatrous King Ahab and his wife Jezebel, Elijah the Prophet wandered far into the wilderness until he came back to Sinai. There God spoke to him:

> "And He said, Go out and stand on the *mountain* before *HaVaYaH*. And behold, *HaVaYaH* passed by, and a great, strong wind broke the mountains and smashed the rocks in pieces in the presence of *HaVaYaH*. But *HaVaYaH* was not in the wind. And after the wind, there was an earthquake. But *HaVaYaH* was not in the earthquake. And after the earthquake, a fire. But *HaVaYaH* was not in the fire. And after the fire, there was a still small voice...." (1 Kings 19:11-12)

It was his prophetic vision at Sinai that powered Elijah in the crowning achievement of his career when he successfully challenged the Prophets of Baal and brought about the mass repentance of the Israelites -- again, at a mountain: Mount Carmel (1 Kings 18).

Mountains were the setting for one of the most famous acts of repentance recounted in the Talmud:

They said of Eliezer ben Durdaya that there was not a prostitute in the world that he did not visit. Once he heard of a prostitute in a distant town who took a purse of gold coins as her fee. He took a purse of coins and passed through seven rivers to reach her. While they were together, she let out gas. She said, "Just as this gas will never go back where it came from, so Eliezer ben Durdaya will never be accepted back as a penitent."

[This remark shook him to the very core.] He went to the mountains and hills. He said: "Mountains and hills, ask for mercy for me." They said, "Before we ask mercy for you, we better ask mercy for ourselves, because it says (Isaiah 54:10): 'The mountains may depart and the hills may be removed.'" He said, "Heaven and Earth, ask for mercy for me." They said, "Before we ask mercy for you, we better ask mercy for ourselves, because it says (ibid. 51:6): 'For the Heavens will vanish away like smoke and the Earth will grow old like a garment.'" He said, "Sun and Moon, ask for mercy for me." They said to him, "Before we ask for you, we better ask for ourselves, because it says (ibid.24:23): 'Then the moon will be confounded and the sun ashamed.'" He said, "Planets and stars, ask for mercy for me." They said to him, "Before we ask for you, we better ask for ourselves, because it says (ibid. 34:4): 'And all the host of heaven will molder away.'"

He said, "I see that it's all up to me!" He put his head between his knees and wept and groaned until his soul went out of him. Then a heavenly voice came forth and said, "Rabbi Eliezer ben Durdaya is invited to the life of the World to Come!"

Avodah Zarah 17a

During the Second Temple period and the subsequent Roman occupation of Israel, spiritual seekers continued going to the mountains and wildernesses. Well-known examples are the Essenes, who formed spiritual communities in the mountainous desert regions around Yam HaMelach (the "Dead" Sea).

Retreat to such surroundings in order to escape city corruption is advocated in classic Jewish sources of later eras. In the words of Rambam (Maimonides):

People's attitudes and behavior are naturally influenced by their friends and associates and by the prevailing practice in the cities where they live. A person should therefore always associate with the righteous and sit with the wise in order to learn from their behavior. He should keep away from evil people so as not to be influenced by them....

Thus, if a person finds himself in a city where evil is the norm, he should move to a place where the people are walking the path of righteousness. And if all the cities he knows of and hears about are following the not-good path, *as is the case in our times*, or if this person is unable to move elsewhere because of war or illness, he should sit alone in solitude, as it says, "He will sit alone and keep silent" (Lamentations 3:28). And if the people where he lives are so evil and sinful that they will not leave him in peace unless he joins them in their evil ways, he should go out and dwell in caves and amidst desert thickets and wildernesses rather than follow the ways of the wicked, as it says, "If only I were in the wilderness in a wayfarer's hut" (Jeremiah 9:1).

Mishneh Torah, Hilkhot Deot (Personal Conduct and Attitudes) 6:1

In his classic devotional guide, *Mesilat Yesharim*: Path of the Just, Rabbi Moshe Chaim Luzzatto ("*Ramchal*", 1707-46) discusses ways of achieving a state of detachment from the mundane material world in order to lead a life of greater spirituality:

Most precious of all is the practice of *hitbodedut*, solitude. For when a person removes worldly affairs from before his eyes, he removes their attraction from his heart. King David spoke in praise of *hitbodedut* when he said, "If only I had wings like a dove! Then I would fly away and be at rest. I would wander far off, I would lodge in the wilderness, I would hurry to a shelter from the raging wind and storm" (Psalms 95:7-8). We find that the prophets Elijah and Elisha had their own special place in the mountains for secluded prayer and meditation. The early sages and saints followed the same pathway, finding *hitbodedut* the best way to attain a state of complete detachment from the mundane world in order that vanities of their contemporaries should not cause them to waste their lives away...

Mesilat Yesharim Chapter 15

Rabbi Israel Baal Shem Tov, founder of the Chassidic movement (and a contemporary of Ramchal) spent extended periods in solitude and devotion in the Carpathian mountains. Solitary prayer and devotion was one of the fundamental practices advocated by the Baal Shem Tov, and it was emphasized especially by his great grandson, Rebbe Nachman of Breslov.

One of Rebbe Nachman's followers related:

One summer day in Zlatipolia (in about 1801) the Rebbe worshipped very early. He suggested that we take a stroll together. We soon left the city and found ourselves walking in a grassy meadow. The Rebbe said: "If only you could hear the song of this grass. Each blade sings out to God without any ulterior motive, not expecting any reward. It is a wonderful thing to hear their song and serve God among them."

We walked a little further and came to a small mountain not far from the city. I asked why we were going there, and the Rebbe told me the secret of that mountain. He asked me to come with him. The mountain was hollow like a cave. Once you were inside you could not be seen from the outside. As soon as we entered the hollow, the Rebbe took a copy of *Shaarey Tzion* (a devotional work) from his pocket and began reading. He read it page by page, weeping bitterly all the time. I stood there holding the Rebbe's coat. I was amazed at how much he cried. We stayed there for a very long time. When the Rebbe finished he asked me to go out and see what time it was. The day was almost over and the sun was beginning to set. The Rebbe had spent an entire long summer day weeping in prayer without a break.

Rabbi Nachman's Wisdom #163

Until today, followers of Rebbe Nachman regularly go out to the hills and mountains of Israel and elsewhere in order to be alone with God. Those searching for the truth about the world and about God will continue to take themselves away from the vanity and falsehood of the big city in order to seclude themselves amidst the purity of natural surroundings until the day will come when we will be able to exclaim:

"How beautiful upon the mountains are the feet of the bringer of good news who announces 'Peace,' the bringer of good news who announces 'Salvation,' saying to Zion, Your God reigns..." (Isaiah 52:7)

"And Isaac went out to meditate in the field towards evening"

(Genesis 24:63).

PART II

The Field

ISAAC

MOTIFS: The Field / Sunset, Afternoon / Life cycles, Old age, Death / Element: Fire / Color: Red, Gold / Mother Letter: *Shin* / Divine Name: *ELOHIM* / Attributes: The Left Column -- Understanding (*Binah*), Power, Discipline (*Gevurah*) Splendor (*Hod*) / Torah Study / Prayer of the Day: Afternoon (*Minchah*) / Festival: Giving of the Torah (*Shavuot*) / Overcoming sexual lust / Submission, Discipline

The divine command to Abraham to offer up Isaac was as much a test for the son as it was for the father. Despite Isaac's youth and strength, he allowed the aged Abraham to bind him on the altar. Isaac, embodiment of power and

strength, thus became the prime exemplar of disciplined submission to the divine will.

Being bound on the altar was such a formative experience that Isaac revisited the site again and again, making it his place of meditation and prayer. For Abraham, it had been a "mountain", but Isaac turned it into a field, a place of regular labor: cultivation of the soul. For the only way to attain the exalted spiritual peaks to which we aspire is through regular, disciplined work.

Isaac's mission was to turn Abraham's revolutionary spiritual teachings into an accessible pathway that people would pursue in a steady, disciplined way in order to bring the entire world to perfection. Isaac taught that justice and charity have to be applied in the most practical details of our lives, including the way we cultivate the land or make a living by other means. Through giving tithes and applying the other "laws of the land", the land itself is blessed, bringing forth its produce in abundance.

Just as Abraham's distinctive quality of expansive flowing kindness, is in Kabbalah associated with right-brain holistic visionary thinking, so Isaac's distinctive quality of restraint, control and discipline is associated with rational analytic thinking. Careful observation of the details of the natural world, combined with acute inferential reasoning is characteristic of the Judaic way of viewing the surrounding world of nature, from the stars and planets in the heavens to the endless diversity of inanimate, vegetable, animal and human forms on Earth.

The purpose of such observation and study is to bring us to a deeper understanding of our role in the system, which is to offer up the letters and words of our prayers in order to draw divine blessings to ourselves and into the whole creation. This was Isaac's labor in the field. The spiritual pathway taught by Isaac leads man to his supreme destiny as the master of prayer, the words of whose blessings bring the entire holistic system of ecological and other cycles into balance and harmony.

Whereas Sarah bore Abraham only one son, Rebecca presented Isaac with twins -- Jacob and Esau, two very different types. While Jacob's preference was for "dwelling in tents", Esau followed after his father as the "man of the field". However, in the case of Esau -- the archetypal hunter -- Isaac's qualities of holy power and control expressed themselves in the form of brute force, cruelty and selfishness. These latter are indeed an integral feature of what might be seen as the darker side of nature, where the continued existence of so many creatures, including ourselves, is bound up with the systematic killing and consumption of other creatures. It is by cultivating Isaac's qualities of holy power and discipline that we are able to rectify this darker side of nature as it manifests itself in human selfishness and cruelty.

The spiritual work of "cultivating the field" through prayer and meditation has from Biblical times onwards been conducted in actual fields, meadows and other natural surroundings.

Power and Strength

Mountains are very beautiful and inspiring, but few are able to remain permanently on a mountain-top living the life of prayer and prophecy. For most people, the idyllic existence of Rebbe Nachman's Prayer Leader and his followers out in nature, surviving off wild fruits and spring-water, is not a practical option.

Visiting the mountains for spiritual retreats, hitbodedut, hiking, climbing and the like can be conducive to physical health and spiritual wellbeing. But these cannot be more than leisure-time pursuits for most people. Afterwards they must backtrack down the mountain and return to their normal lives in the civilized world. Mankind is still afflicted with the curse of Adam, and the majority can survive only through some kind of toil, whether literally out in the agricultural field, cultivating the land to provide food, or through some other metaphorical "field" of activity in a different sector of the economy.

The mountain is the place of vision -- the holistic vision of Abraham, who was the first, the breakaway, the revolutionary, the initiator. But after the drama and excitement of the vision comes the hard follow-up work of trying to actualize the vision in practice. Having set your sights on the peaks, you now have to break through the actual terrain. You have to keep going even when you can no longer see the grand view and get direction. You have to keep going even when the path gets extremely tough and you don't seem to be getting anywhere. This is the work of cultivating the field, the work of Isaac.

"Running" and "Returning"

In Ezekiel's vision of the Divine Chariot (*Merkavah*), the *Chayot* -- the vital (*Chai*) forces of creation ("angels") -- are described as "running and returning" (Ezekiel 1:14). They rise up in yearning to transcend their limitations as created beings in order to merge in unity with their Creator: they "run out" of themselves. But afterwards they "return" to themselves and their separate existence. For it is God's will that they should continue to be independent creatures.

This cyclical "running and returning" is one of the underlying dynamics of all creation from the highest spiritual levels down to actual physical matter. All human life consists of up and down cycles, such as waking and sleeping, satisfaction and hunger, and many others. This is particularly true in the pursuit of spirituality. We may have moments of self-transcendence and intimate closeness with God -- "running". But as long as we remain in this world, such moments must be followed by a "return" to ourselves, to normality and everyday activities. Our purpose in this world is to transcend ourselves and attain closeness to God of our own free will. But it would undermine this purpose if God did all the work for us, constantly taking us beyond ourselves with no effort on our part. We have to "return" in order to start working again in order to "run".

The phase of "running" is personified in Abraham, exemplar of *Chessed*, expansive outreach and kindness. Abraham broke away from the repressive tyranny of Nimrod's civilization-gone-mad in quest of freedom, vision, the Land, the Mountain, the stars, the Heavens, and the summits of true humility and divine connection.

However, "running" has to be complemented by "returning": coming back to the normal world in order to actualize the vision in and through practical everyday situations amidst all the constraints and pressures of reality. The phase of "returning" is personified in Isaac, man of the Field, the exemplar of *Gevurah*, the disciplined, controlled application of power.

"Running" is represented by the dawning day and the rising sun -- morning -- which is associated with Abraham, who typically "rose early in the morning" (Genesis 19:27; 22:3). According to tradition, Abraham established Shacharit, the Morning Prayer. "Returning" is represented by the declining, setting sun -- afternoon -- which is associated with Isaac, who "went out to meditate in the field towards evening" (*ibid.* 24:63). According to tradition, Isaac established Minchah, the Afternoon Prayer.

The morning begins with a fresh burst of energy and enthusiasm: the light breaks through on the horizon and the sun appears in all its glory, climbing higher and higher in the skies, radiating ever more light and heat. But then the sun reaches its ultimate noon peak, and then a constraining force -- the great wheel of the universe -- forces it to start its downward descent and decline, until at last it sinks beneath the horizon, leaving the world to darkness.

The expansive upward climb of the sun, radiating life to all the world, is a glorious manifestation of Godly power. Thus in Kabbalah, the associated divine attribute of *Chessed* (loving kindness) is connected with the divine name *EL*, which literally denotes "power". However, the counter-balancing attribute of *Gevurah* (strength, restriction, constraining force) leads to an even greater manifestation of power. For it is through the harnessing of raw power and energy and their controlled, disciplined application that their full potential becomes actualized in reality.

For example, the formidable power of electricity is manifested not so much in massive surges of current through a major power line, though this can instantly burn up any puny thing it touches, but rather in the way specific, limited amounts of electrical power are distributed to all kinds of different equipment and appliances in order to serve an endless variety of different purposes. Similarly, torrents of water can sweep away and destroy humans, animals, plants and even rocks. But it is the minute quantities of water that falls in individual rain-drops and finds its way into individual living cells that makes all life possible.

The attribute of *Gevurah*, power, strength and constraint, is associated with the divine name *ELOHIM*, which literally means "the Powers" -- alluding to the multiplicity of specific, defined and delimited powers manifested in different parts of the creation, all through the power of the single, unified God.

Just as Abraham expressed the divine attribute of *Chessed*, expansive kindness, in various different ways and on different levels throughout his career, so did Isaac express the divine attribute of *Gevurah*, power, discipline and strength, in his.

Torah

Abraham was the first. Without guides or teachers, he discovered the path of *HaVaYaH* for himself through the power of the yearnings of his heart and the outpourings of his lips in the letters and words of his prayers.

But Abraham did not merely want to find God for himself. He wanted to rectify the whole world and bring everyone to know God. He therefore had to teach his pathway to others. This was why he craved so much for a son that he could raise and train in the service of *HaVaYaH* from the very start.

Therefore Abraham "commanded his sons and his household afterwards to keep the way of *HaVaYaH* to practice charity and justice" (Genesis 18:19). Thus, what for Abraham was a new path discovered through the voluntary yearnings of his heart became for Isaac a revered tradition, a teaching, a Torah that carried with it a set of strict obligations. Thus, when God blessed Isaac, it was in the merit of Abraham's code of obedience, "Because Abraham listened to My voice and guarded My ordinances, My commandments, My statutes and My teachings" (*ibid.* 26:5).

A founder needs a follower; a teacher needs a student. A giver needs a receiver. Isaac was the follower, the student, the receiver. Abraham typifies the active principle of *Chessed*, "giving", while Isaac typifies the passive principle of *Gevurah*, "receiving". To receive means to submit to the power and will of the giver. It is as the exemplar of submission and obedience that Isaac himself became the teacher and giver of spirituality to others. Isaac's teaching is that the only way to come closer to God is through obedience to God's will as expressed in God's law.

Just as the binding of Isaac on the altar was a test for Abraham, it was equally a test for Isaac. Would he be unflinching in his willingness to submit even to the bitter end? The figure of Isaac bound on the altar is symbolic of perfect submission and obedience to the will of God.

Not that mindless obedience was all that was required of Isaac throughout his life. He faced many tests of his own. He had to take his own initiatives in order to hack out a way for himself on Abraham's path. For example, "the Philistines stopped up all the wells that his father's servants dug in the days of Abraham, and they filled them with earth... And Isaac dug the wells of water that they had dug in the days of Abraham his father which the Philistines had stopped up after the death of Abraham, and he called them names like the names his father had called them" (Genesis 26:15-18).

Besides their environmental significance as water supplies for the general welfare, Abraham's wells also signify the wellsprings of spiritual inspiration that he made available for all humanity. Because of human crassness, these water-sources became "stopped up and filled with earth", i.e. earthliness and materialism caused the dampening of spiritual enthusiasm. Isaac had to dig all over again in order to rediscover and reopen the wellsprings of spiritual inspiration. A major task for any second- or later-generation religious seeker is to rediscover the original freshness within time-encrusted traditions.

But it was to his tradition that Isaac had to bind himself. Indeed, through his very submission and obedience he attained his greatest spiritual heights. Tradition attributes Isaac's blindness to the fact that at the moment when he was bound on the altar with Abraham about to slaughter him, the heavens opened up and the ministering angels saw and wept, and their tears fell upon Isaac's eyes (*Rashi* on Genesis 27:1). The opening of the heavens and the falling of the tears from the "eyes" of the angels into those of Isaac indicate a transcendental vision attained by Isaac only through his perfect surrender.

Abraham is particularly associated with the festival of *Pesach* (Passover), which celebrates freedom from oppression. Abraham's escape from Nirmod's furnace was the paradigm for his descendants' liberation from slavery in Egypt. But the purpose of releasing the Jewish People from subjection to the man-made tyranny of Pharaoh was to bring them to submit to the higher service of *HaVaYaH* and His Torah that would lead to the rectification of the world. Thus, the journey out of Egypt into the wilderness necessarily led to Sinai, where the Torah was given.

The giving of the Torah at Sinai is celebrated on *Shavuot* ("the Festival of Weeks"), fifty days after the first day of

Pesach. Shavuot is particularly associated with Isaac. Just as Isaac was bound on the altar, so there was an element of compulsion in the Giving of the Torah. In a certain sense, the Jews had no real alternative but to accept it, as expressed in the rabbinical teaching that "God uprooted the mountain from its place and arched it over them like a huge tank, saying: If you accept it, good; if not, this will be your grave" (*Avodah Zarah* 2b). In a way, Mount Sinai actually turned into a field, for according to tradition, when the Torah was given this lowly desert mountain was verdant with plants and trees.

It is customary on Pesach to read the Song of Songs, which is a lyrical love-song between God and the Soul, replete with images of nature, flowers, fragrant herbs and fruits, groves of trees, springs of water, meadows and hillsides and "mountains of spices" (Songs 6:14). On Shavuot, it is customary to read the Book of Ruth, in which a major theme is harvesting the crops in the field and the associated laws of gifts of produce to the poor.

The Field

"And Isaac went out to meditate in the field towards evening" (Genesis 24:63)

*B*eing bound on the altar was such a formative experience for Isaac that he went back to the site again and again. It was here that his wife-to-be Rebecca first caught sight of him as she neared the end of her camelback journey from her native Padan Aram to the Land of Israel in order to marry Isaac.

Isaac had come out in the cool of the late afternoon to meditate and pray. The grammatical form of the Hebrew verb *Vayeitzei*, "he went out", indicates that he used to do this regularly. He had chosen this "field" as his place of meditation and prayer.

For Abraham, it had been a Mountain, the site of the supreme test of his life. But Isaac turned it into a Field, a place of regular labor: cultivation of the soul. For the only way to attain the high spiritual peaks to which we aspire is through regular, disciplined work.

The mountain symbolizes the summit or end-goal of human spiritual achievement, which is to attain such perfect humility and self-effacement that one becomes totally merged with God. This level is the crown of all levels (*Keter*). It is even higher than that of *knowing* God (*Daat*). For the concept of "knowing God" implies a separation between the knower -- the human being -- and God, the "object" of the knowledge. But God is not an "object". God is in truth the ultimate "subject". Ultimately there is *only* God: only God can truly say "I". It is the human sense of selfhood, separation and independence that is the illusion. To attain the ultimate connection with God, the seeker must surrender all sense of selfhood, self-interest and separate identity to the point that he is lifted beyond all limits to a state of total mystical union with the One God.

It is not possible for human beings in their bodily existence on earth to remain permanently in such states of mystic union with God. Normally these are attained fleetingly, perhaps at the climax of intense meditation, prayer and devotion, or sometimes quite unexpectedly and serendipitously. Even then they usually come only after considerable spiritual work and effort.

The question is how to attain the goal?

You cannot leap to the top of a mountain in one jump. You have to climb up step by step, starting from wherever you are now. This may often seem like the long way to go, but those who try to take short-cuts usually end up having to go the long way anyway. Taking things step by step one at a time is actually the simplest and easiest way.

Rebbe Nachman illustrated the point with a parable:

> A king once sent his son away to study. Finally, the son returned home fully versed in all the arts and sciences. One day the king ordered his son to bring an enormous stone up to the top floor of the palace.

The stone was so big and heavy, the prince couldn't shift it at all. It made him very depressed.

At last the king said to his son: "Did you really imagine I would tell you to do the impossible? Would I tell you to try to carry this stone up just as it is? Even with all your learning, how would you be able to do that? What you should do is take a hammer and break the stone into little pieces! This way you'll be able to carry them up one by one until you get the whole stone up to the top floor."

Tzaddik #441

Sometimes our personalities are like a heavy stone weighing us down and keeping us from God. We are asked to lift up our hearts and bring Godly awareness into every aspect of our being: "Know today and take to your heart that *HaVaYaH* is the only God in heaven above and on the earth below" (Deuteronomy 4:39). But the heart is a "heart of stone" (Ezekiel 36:26). The only way to lift up the heart is by taking a hammer, as it were, and breaking our major goals, ambitions and projects into small, practicable tasks.

It is the same principle that applies in cultivating a field. The end goal is to have produce to eat, but this is achieved only after a whole series of preliminary steps: removing the stones from the soil, plowing the field, planting the seeds, watering, weeding, pruning, etc. Even after harvesting the produce, it is necessary to separate the edible portions from the unwanted stalks and other refuse, and then peel, grind, mix, knead, bake, cook or otherwise process the food until it is ready for eating.

It is through the application of *Gevurah*, the discipline and control exemplified in Isaac, Man of the Field, that ambitious goals of any kind are attained. Major end-goals as we initially conceive them with *Chokhmah*-vision in our mind's eye can rarely be accomplished through a single leap. It is necessary to apply *Binah*-intelligence in order to break down the goal down into its component parts and develop a strategy with which to tackle each part of the overall project step by step in a disciplined way. *Binah*-intelligence is an aspect of *Gevurah*, as are the determination, strength and courage needed to carry the project through.

When a person wants to purify himself so as to open himself to spirituality and God-awareness, it is necessary to seek understanding of the various different aspects of his personality and how they function together (or conflict with one another) whether to bring him nearer to his goal or to hold him back. As he comes to understand the various ways in which his negative traits are holding him back, he must work on them steadily one by one. Spiritual work rarely proceeds in a strictly orderly way. Even so, without developing a general strategy and making an effort to follow it, the work will not proceed at all.

The Solitary Path

There are many avenues of spiritual growth that can be followed by people working together in pairs or larger groups, as long as those seeking together love each other dearly and feel able to be very honest and open with one another.

However, *hitbodedut* -- the secluded meditation and prayer that lead to self-transcendence and communion with God -- is by definition a solitary practice.

Rebbe Nachman defined the goal and method of hitbodedut in the following teaching:

> The only way to return to the roots of one's being and merge in the unity of God is through nullifying the self. One has to efface the self completely until one becomes wholly merged in God's unity. The only way to achieve this state of self-transcendence is through hitbodedut. By secluding oneself and giving voice to one's inner thoughts in the form of personal prayers to God, one is able to remove all negative traits and cravings to the point that one nullifies all materialism in oneself. Then one is able to become merged in the Source.
>
> True hitbodedut is practiced in the depths of night, at an hour when everyone is free from their toil in the material world. During the day people are so busy chasing after the material world that it distracts the spiritual seeker from attaching himself to God. Even if he personally is quite detached from the material world, the mere fact that everyone else is then busy chasing after the vanity of the world

makes it very difficult to attain self-transcendence at such a time.

Hitbodedut must also be practiced in a special place outside the city on a "solitary path" (*Avot* 3:5) in a place where no-one goes. For in a place where in the daytime hours people are busy chasing after the vanity of the world, even though they may not be there at this hour, it is still a distraction from hitbodedut, making it impossible for the spiritual seeker to attain the state of total communion with God.

For this reason, it is necessary to go alone at night on a solitary path to a place where no one goes even by day. There one should seclude oneself and empty one's heart and mind of all worldly involvements until one attains the state of true self-transcendence and communion.

This is a step-by-step process. First the person should devote this solitary night-time hitbodedut to talking and praying to God at length until he succeeds in nullifying one negative trait or desire. Next, he should devote his hitbodedut to working on nullifying a second trait or desire. He should go on like this night after night in this solitary spot until he nullifies everything.

Even then, something is still left of him, namely some residue of human pride and arrogance. He still considers himself to be something. He must persist with hitbodedut and carry on working hard until he nullifies this too, until nothing whatever is left of him and he is in a state of true self-transcendence. Then, when he attains true nothingness, his soul becomes merged in its root, namely in God.

Likutey Moharan I, 52

Go Out to a Grassy Field....

For many people, it may not be easy or practicable to rise regularly in the small hours of the night and go to a deserted spot for hitbodedut. Nevertheless, Rebbe Nachman's explanation of this practice brings out the extreme privacy and seclusion from the distractions of the world that are desirable in order to succeed in this most intimate and transformative of all spiritual practices.

In its simplest form -- meditation and direct talking to God -- Rebbe Nachman advocated hitbodedut for everyone. There is no need to feel that it may only be practiced at night in some remote spot. Hitbodedut can be practiced by anyone anywhere. Rebbe Nachman especially advocated meadows and fields as the place for hitbodedut.

> The best place to go to seclude yourself and meditate is in the meadows outside the city. Go to a grassy field, for the grass will awaken your heart.

Rabbi Nachman's Wisdom #227

Fields and meadows were Rebbe Nachman's preferred place for his own hitbodedut. His closest student, Rabbi Natan Sternhertz of Breslov, writes:

> He would often walk in the woods and fields and seclude himself in prayer. I once walked with the Rebbe through Medvedevka, where he lived earlier. We strolled all through the fields and hills. The Rebbe gestured toward the hills and meadows and said, "See all these fields and hills around the city. See all the other places near the town. I've been in all of those places. I've been to each one of them many times and secluded myself in prayer."

> *ibid.* #162

Simple Talk

The method of hitbodedut is simply to talk out all the issues in one's life with God one by one, using one's own words in one's own unique personal way.

Rebbe Nachman himself practiced this:

> The main way the Rebbe attained what he did was simply through prayer and supplication before God. He was very consistent in this. He would beg and plead in every way possible, asking God to be kind to him and bring him to genuine closeness and devotion. What helped him most were his prayers in his own native language, which was Yiddish. He

would find a secluded place and spend time expressing all his thoughts to God. Speaking in his own language, he would beg and plead with God. He would use every kind of argument, pleading with God to draw him closer and help him in his devotions. He kept this up constantly, spending days and years engaged in such prayer.... All his prayers had one goal: that he should
come closer to God.

Praises of Rabbi Nachman #10-11

Rebbe Nachman advised everyone to practice hitbodedut.

The Rebbe once spoke to a young man encouraging him to seclude himself and talk to God in his own words. The Rebbe told him that this was how prayer began. Originally prayer was each person's individual expression to God of his own inner thoughts and feelings in his own words. Rambam (Maimonides) discusses this in his code of Jewish law at the beginning of the section on Prayer. He states that this was originally the main form of prayer prior to the formalization of the liturgy by the Men of the Great Assembly (3rd century B.C.E. -- Rambam, *Mishneh Torah, Hilkhot Tefilah* 1:2-4) It was only then that a formal order of prayer was introduced. Even today, according to the Law, the original form of prayer is still foremost. Even though we follow the order of prayer instituted by the Great Assembly, the original form is still most beneficial.

Make a habit of praying to God from the depths of your heart. Use whatever language you know best. Ask God to make you worthy of truly serving Him. This is the essence of prayer. This is how all the Tzaddikim attained their levels.

Rabbi Nachman's Wisdom #229

Rabbi Nachman taught:

You must pray for everything. If your garment is torn and has to be replaced, pray to God for a new one. Do this for everything. Make it a habit to pray for everything you need, large or small. Your main prayers should be for fundamentals: that God should help you in your devotion and that you should be worthy of coming close to Him. Still, you should also pray even for trivial things. God may give you food, clothing and everything else you need even though you do not ask for them. But then you are like an animal. God gives every living thing its bread without being asked. He can also give it to you this way. But if you do not draw your life through prayer, then your life is like that of a beast. For a *man* must draw all the necessities of life from God only through prayer.

Rabbi Nachman's Wisdom #233

Courage

The path of prayer is often difficult. Worst of all is the sense of discouragement that comes from praying repeatedly without seeing results.

Rebbe Nachman went through all this as well.

> Even so, it always seemed to the Rebbe that all his prayers were being disregarded. He was sure that he was not wanted at all, and that he was being pushed further and further from any true devotion. For he saw the days and years passing, and still he felt far from God. After all his prayers, he felt he had not succeeded in coming close to God at all. It was as if his words were never heard and he had been totally ignored all this time. It seemed as if everything was being done to push him away from God.

> But the Rebbe's resolve remained firm and he did not abandon his ground. It was not easy, for there were many things to discourage him. He prayed and pleaded before God, begging to be worthy of true devotion, and still he saw no results. He felt as if he was being totally ignored.

> There were times when he became discouraged and let his conversations with God lapse for several days. But then he would remind himself that he should be ashamed for criticizing God's ways. He said to himself, "God is truly merciful and

compassionate... He certainly wants to draw me near to Him." This was how the Rebbe was able to again strengthen his resolve. He would begin anew, speaking and pleading with God. This happened very many times.

Praises of Rabbi Nachman #12

The courage and determination with which Rebbe Nachman coped with the inevitable disappointments and difficulties along the path of prayer are a vital aspect of the *Gevurah* -- power and strength -- of the Man of the Field.

In Hebrew, such courage and determination are called *HitGaBRut* -- "self-strengthening". The would-be strongman (*GiBoR*) must be *MitGaBeR*: he must apply his strength to himself in the sense of bringing his own instinctive tendency towards impatience under control. For "Who is strong? He who controls his bad impulses, as it says (Proverbs 16:32): Better is the person who is patient than the mighty warrior and better is the person who controls his own spirit than the conqueror of a city" (*Avot* 4:1).

The tiller of the field must wait patiently until the effects of his own labors combined with the power of the earth, the sun, the rains, the winds and God's other blessing cause his fruits to ripen and mature. So too one who follows the path of prayer must wait with consummate patience, until his eyes will be opened and he will see that his field is all abloom with flowers and rich in abundant fruits.

Cultivating the Land

"And Isaac sowed in that land, and he found in that year one hundredfold, and God blessed him" (Genesis 26:12).

"This comes to teach you that they made an estimate of how much the field was likely to produce, and it produced a hundred times the amount they expected. Why did they measure it in view of the principle that 'blessing is not found in that which has already been weighed, measured or counted' [i.e. once measured, the amount will not miraculously increase]? They measured it in order to make an exact calculation of the tithe due on the produce so as not to err because of a rough assessment"

(Midrash Rabbah Bereishit 64:6).

*N*ot only was Isaac the Man of the Field of Prayer; he was also a most successful agriculturist.

The Bible relates that when famine struck the Land, Isaac had to move temporarily to the Philistine kingdom of Gerar. There he encountered moral decadence of the kind his father Abraham had encountered both in Egypt and in Gerar, in both of which Sarah was actually kidnapped to the royal court. Now Isaac's wife Rebecca came near to being seized by the Philistine king (Genesis 26).

Isaac's mission was that of Abraham: to bring the knowledge of God to mankind and to teach humanity God's law. If the Philistine king had taken Rebecca, it would have been a violation of the prohibition against adultery and incest, which is one of the Seven Universal Laws of Mankind.

The others are: not to worship idols; not to curse God; to establish courts of justice; not to murder; not to steal; not to eat flesh from a living animal (*Sanhedrin* 56b). The near-kidnapping of Rebecca became the occasion for Isaac to teach people about these Universal Laws of Mankind. No civilization that does not honestly observe all these laws deserves to be called a civilization. Such culture as it may boast is no more than a veneer for barbarity, as in much of the world today, where corruption in government, sexual immorality, killing, stealing and other violations of these laws are so rampant.

Isaac, exemplar of *Gevurah*, is closely associated with *law*. *Gevurah* sets limits and boundaries. This is what a system of law does. It regulates what is within the bounds of the acceptable and permissible and what is not.

Man-made legal systems often serve to protect the strong at the expense of the weak, leading those who feel unjustly treated to hate and despise the law. Religious law can also become oppressive when people twist it for their own purposes. But the only purpose of God's authentic Torah is to bring about the conditions in which genuine love, kindness and blessing can be enjoyed by all the world in peace and harmony. For this reason, one of the main talmudic terms for the Torah (and its Author, for the two are one) is *Rachmana*, "The Loving One".

God's law is a teaching to each and every one of us as to how to bring balance into every area and every detail of our lives -- in order to elevate ourselves spiritually in this world without coming to grief because of its various pitfalls, including the powerful drives with which we are endowed. When humans willingly submit to God's perfectly-devised system of law to govern all their affairs, it brings balance and harmony into the world as a whole, enabling people to live peaceably without anyone hurting anyone else.

The Law of the Land: Charity

During his sojourn among the Philistines, Isaac taught a lesson about the underlying principle of God's law: charity. Abraham had grasped that charity is the fundamental dynamic of the entire universe and that man's task is to play his role, overcoming his instinctive selfishness and turning himself into a *giver*. Abraham thus instructed "his sons and his household afterwards that they should guard the way of *HaVaYaH* to practice charity and justice" (Genesis 18:19).

It is a basic, natural human instinct to think first and foremost about one's own needs and interests. This is indeed necessary for self-preservation and survival, for "If I am not for myself, who is for me?" (*Avot* 1:14). However, there is a widespread tendency for people to forget the corollary, "If I am *only* for myself, *what* am I?" (*ibid.*)

It is impossible to live without taking and consuming: from birth until death we have to eat and satisfy our other needs. But we must be aware that everything we eat and consume is a gift of God's goodness. The sun and the stars shine down to earth with perfect altruism.... Nature provides us with our food and other resources. If we take and take and consume without understanding what it is to *give*, we are worse than animals, pathetically unaware of the true nature of the system of love and kindness of which we are a part.

In order to grasp this underlying dynamic of altruism and charity, man has to incorporate it within himself by actually participating in the dynamic. Man must also give. The natural tendency is for people to hold on to what they feel to be theirs and guard it for themselves. To give charity is to do the opposite. One takes something of one's own that one values -- food, clothing, money or whatever else -- and gives it away to another person who is in need. Instead of thinking only about oneself, one thinks about the other person's needs and how things look from their point of view. Voluntarily curtailing our own consumption for the sake of others lifts us above our native selfish perspective on the world, making us become partners in the universal flow of divine goodness and kindness.

When a person eats and consumes only after first giving a share to others needier than himself, the remaining portion that he keeps for himself is indeed blessed. For he has turned himself into a giver. It is as a giver that he is now eating and consuming, in order to be able to gain the strength to be able to give more and more.

It is fitting that it is Isaac who teaches this lesson, for Isaac is the exemplar of *Gevurah*, the passive principle of taking, receiving, holding, as opposed to *Chessed*, the active principle of giving and kindness. Isaac showed that we have to apply our *Gevurah* -- our strength and control -- to our very selves. We have to curtail and put limits on our own native selfishness in order to *give* to others. Isaac taught this in the way he raised his crops even at a time of famine. From the very outset, he was thinking about how his first act before eating his harvest would be to give away tithes for the benefit of others.

"And Isaac sowed in that land, and he found in that year one hundredfold, and God blessed him" (Genesis 26:12).

The Midrash comments: "This comes to teach you that they made an estimate of how much the field was likely to produce, and it produced a hundred times the amount they expected. But why did Isaac measure the crops at all in view of the principle that 'blessing is not found in that which has already been weighed, measured or counted' (*Ta'anit* 8b). [This means that once measured, the amount will not miraculously increase.] The answer is that Isaac did not want to give his tithe on the basis of a rough assessment. He wanted to be exact" (*Midrash Rabbah Bereishit* 64:6).

The phenomenal blessing of abundance enjoyed by Isaac came because he was already thinking about giving even before he had received anything. According to the Midrash, even before he sowed, Isaac was already estimating how much the field would produce because he was already thinking about giving away tithes.

It is typical of Isaac to be making measurements: precision and strictness are aspects of *Gevurah*. Indeed, firm principles and accurate calculations are the only sound basis for a system of true charity. There has to be a precise calculation of how much it is proper for each individual to give in relation to his or her specific means. If charity is simply left to people's voluntary generosity and "rough assessments", although at times some will give more than their due, more often the majority are likely to give less than their due, much less. Then the needy will simply not be receive enough.

The system of Torah Law of the Land governs all the various aspects of agriculture, defining precisely how much of his produce the farmer should give away and to whom. Having sweated and toiled to raise his crops, the farmer is certainly entitled to eat the fruits of his labors himself. But only after he first makes himself deeply aware that all his produce is God's gift and blessing. This he does by first setting aside tithes and other gifts to others and only then sitting down to eat.

Synopsis of Torah Laws Relating to the Land

Gifts to the Poor: The farmer should leave a corner (*Pe-ah*) of his field or tree unharvested for the poor. One or two ears of corn or individual fruits etc. that drop to the ground during harvesting (*Leket*) are the property of the poor, as are sheaves forgotten in the field (*Shikhchah*).

The First Fruits: In Israel in Temple times the farmer presents his first ripe grapes, figs, pomegranates, olives, dates, wheat and barley (*Bikurim*) at the Temple, after which they are eaten by the Priests. Having put so much work into raising the crops, it would be tempting for the farmer to eat the first ones himself. Instead, he holds back and first gives thanks to God by presenting the choicest first-fruits in a joyous, colorful ceremony. A similar law for animal farmers is to present first-born calves, sheep and goats to the Priest.

Tithes and other gifts separated from produce:

Gift to the Priest: Before separating any other gift from his harvested produce, the farmer in Israel first puts aside around 2% as a gift (*Terumah*) for the priest (*Cohen*). This may be eaten only by priests and their households in strict ritual purity. Besides produce, priests are also entitled to various other gifts, such as bread (*Challah*) wool shearings

(*Reishit HaGez*) and portions of animal meat (*Matanot*) and certain sacrifices. Aside from their role in Temple rituals, the role of the priests is to teach Torah to the people. This they are best able to do when freed of the burden of earning a living through receiving their needs from the people. By regularly giving produce and other gifts to the priests, the farmer maintains an on-going relationship with these teachers, which enables him to bring greater spirituality into his life in and through his material activities.

First Tithe: Gift to the Levite: In Israel, after separating the priestly gift, the farmer next separates 10% (*Ma'aser*) of the remaining produce as a gift for the Levites. The role of the Levites (as opposed to the priests, *Cohanim*) is to be singers and ceremonial guards in the Temple, as well as to teach Torah in the wider community. Again, they are helped to do this through being supported with tithes. The Levite, who is thus a *receiver*, also has to *give* a gift of *Terumat Ma'aser* from his tithe to the Priest. For those in the contemporary money economy who do not have home-grown produce to give away, the gift that corresponds to the levitical tithe is the Money Tithe, *Ma'aser Kesafim*, ten per cent of one's net income that should be given to truly worthy charitable causes, such as the support of genuine students of Torah. This general tithe on people's income applies equally in Israel and throughout the world.

Second Tithe: In Israel, having separated the first tithe for the Levite, the farmer now separates 10% of the remaining produce as a Second Tithe, *Ma'aser Sheni*. In the first, second, fourth and fifth year in every 7-year Sabbatical cycle, the owner himself brings this Second Tithe produce or its monetary value to Jerusalem, where he and his family eat it in ritual purity, holiness and joy. Eating the fruits of one's own labors in this way brings Godliness into the whole process of production and consumption. In the third and sixth years of the Sabbatical cycle, the Second Tithe is given to the poor and needy.

Some other land laws:

The Sabbatical Year: The land of Israel is worked for six years and then left without being cultivated for the Sabbatical Year. By "abandoning" his fields in this way the farmer learns that the land really belongs to God, Who has granted him ownership, and that agricultural success depends not only upon human labor and effort but also on God's blessing.

Forbidden Mixtures: It is forbidden to plant various different kinds of crops in excessively close proximity to one another or to cross-graft different species (*Kilayim*). Similarly, it is forbidden to cross-breed animals or plow etc. with two species at once (e.g. an ox and a donkey).

Immature fruit trees: The fruit that grows on trees within their first three years (*Orlah*) should not be eaten or used in other ways. The fruit of the fourth year should be taken by the owner to eat in Jerusalem.

Jewish law includes many other detailed land-related laws such as the rules of good neighborliness, laws of damages, land use in and around cities, prohibition of cruelty to animals and general environmental responsibility.

* * *

All the problems in the world today ultimately stem from the sin of Adam eating the fruit of the tree of knowledge of good and evil. Adam took and consumed the fruit even though it was not his. He was therefore cursed with having to earn his bread with the sweat of his brow.

The sin was one of selfish, arrogant consumption. Ironically, the same problem is threatening to destroy the world today. It is selfish, excess consumption that is depleting resources and destroying the global environment. This is obviously a problem that can be rectified only by rectifying the selfishness and thoughtlessness with which people consume.

To do just this is the purpose of the Law of the Land and other Torah laws regulating the way people earn a living and consume. It behooves all who care about the future of the Earth to practice these fundamental principles of charity, kindness and justice and to teach them to others, just as Isaac did when he dwelled with the Philistines in Gerar.

Nature Study

The Place of Nature Study in Judaism * Binah-Thinking * On the examination of created things * How the Tzaddik looks at nature * The varieties of fruits * The language of animals, birds & trees

*H*umanity's constantly expanding stock of knowledge about the workings of the natural world gives us awesome power to exploit and manipulate nature through all kinds of agricultural, industrial and other technologies in order better to satisfy our material needs and desires.

In the Torah tradition, such knowledge is respected as being both necessary and desirable for the welfare of humanity as long as it is pursued and applied in full accordance with Torah law. This does not mean that science or nature study are the same as Torah. The purpose of true science (as opposed to pseudo-scientific speculation) is to establish facts about visible, observable natural phenomena and processes and to seek deeper understanding of their mechanics. Torah on the other hand gives us knowledge about the *meaning* and *purpose* of the various different aspects of this world and how God wants us to *relate* to them. Such knowledge could not be inferred merely through observation of the visible world around us; it had to be revealed by the Prophets.

Knowledge and understanding of certain aspects of the natural world can be important adjuncts to Torah knowledge. Among the areas of Torah law that involve knowledge and understanding of natural phenomena of various kinds are:

- **The Calendar:** The timing of all the Jewish festivals (with the exception of the weekly Shabbat) depends upon the lunar cycle. The Jewish calendar is based upon highly sophisticated and accurate astronomical understanding of the movements of the moon in relation to the sun and a system of leap years that keeps the lunar months perfectly synchronized with the solar years.

- **Diet:** The Torah distinction between pure (edible) and impure (prohibited) species of animals, birds, fish and insects presupposes familiarity with the different species. To be fit for Jewish consumption, not only must pure animals or birds undergo valid ritual slaughter (*Shechitah*); they must also be free from any kind of life-threatening physical defects (*Treifot*). Understanding of the complex rules of such defects involves a detailed understanding of animal and bird anatomy.

- **Procreation and the Menstrual Cycle:** The Torah emphasis on procreation coupled with the strict prohibition against marital relations from the onset of menstruation until after ritual purification by the woman encouraged the accumulation of a vast treasury of knowledge about all aspects of these basic functions.

- **Agriculture:** The detailed Torah code relating to agriculture involves all kinds of knowledge about different species of plants and trees, methods of cultivation and so on. The Talmud and other rabbinical literature includes references to a vast array of different plants and other natural phenomena.

Binah-Thinking

The systematic, scientific approach to exploring and understanding the world around us is linked with Isaac's quality of *Gevurah* -- control, restraint, strictness -- associated in Kabbalah with the "left hand", in contrast to Abraham's quality of *Chessed* -- expansiveness, outreach, kindness -- which is associated with the "right hand".

In the human mind, the left-pole *Gevurah*-linked faculty is *Binah*, rational-analytic thought, "left brain thinking", as opposed to the right-pole *Chessed*-linked faculty of *Chokhmah*, holistic-visionary perception, "right brain thinking"... Where *Chokhmah*-thinking is wide-angle vision of whole systems, *Binah*-thinking narrows the focus in order to examine the individual constituent parts of the system one by one in all their details and to trace how they relate one to another.

Both *Chokhmah* and *Binah* are necessary to attain *Daat*, complete, balanced Knowledge. In the words of the *Sefer Yetzira*: "Understand (*Bin*) with wisdom (*Chokhmah*), be wise (*Chakem*) with understanding (*Binah*)... Examine and probe... Make each thing stand on its essence, and make the Creator sit on His base" (*Sefer Yetzira* 1:4). It is through oscillating between *Chokhmah* and *Binah* that we attain *Daat*, Knowledge of the whole together with its constituent parts.

Abraham's revolutionary mental leap was to grasp that all of the individual *details* of creation -- the stars, the planets and all the other different entities in the universe -- are parts of one unified overarching system created by *HaVaYaH*. This holistic perception is one of *Chokhmah*.

Isaac's work, on the other hand, was to come down from the mountain of holistic *Chokhmah*-vision and get to work out there in the actual field, applying *Binah*-thinking to look at the world in detail, seeking to understand all the individual parts in themselves and how they connect one to another to make up the unified system of God's kingdom. "And Isaac went out to meditate in the field" (Genesis 24:63).

Binah-thinking is characterized by careful, accurate observation of details followed by the application of acute inferential reasoning to the resulting data in order to generate new knowledge and deeper understanding of interrelationships, causes and effects and so on. Thus, *Binah* is defined in the Talmud as "understanding one thing from another thing" (*Chagigah* 14a, *Sanhedrin* 93b, *Rashi* on Exodus 31:3).

The divine name associated with the left pole of *Binah/Gevurah* is *Elohim* (pronounced *Elokim* except when used in prayer). Although as a name of God this name almost always appears in the Bible with a singular verb, the grammatical form of the name itself is actually a plural. Literally, *Elohim* means "Powers", referring to the multiplicity of different powers possessed by God as revealed in the creation.

The numerical value of the Hebrew letters of *ELoHIM* -- 86 -- is the same as that of the letters of *HaTeVA*, "nature". This teaches us that all of the various different facets of nature embody and reveal different powers of God.

God as God is totally above nature, above the world, and utterly beyond the grasp of the human mind. Yet with the application of *Binah*-thinking it is possible for us to gain some faint apprehension of God's attributes through inferences based on that which we can discern and know in this world. Through deep contemplation of the various phenomena of this world, it can be seen that they all *point beyond* the world to their invisible Source.

Out of the four basic elements of Water, Air, Fire and Earth, it is Fire that is associated with *Binah* and *Gevurah*. Just as fire rises upwards, so the striving of *Binah*-intelligence is to track and trace these various pointers, understanding one thing from another, and thereby lifting the mind "up" step by step from the multiplicity of separate, visible, revealed phenomena within the creation to their ultimate, unified, unrevealed Source.

On the examination of Created Things

Study and contemplation of nature for the purpose of attaining deeper connection with God is discussed at length in R. Bachya Ibn Paquda's classic moralistic work, Duties of the Heart (*Chovot Halevavot*) Second Treatise, On the Examination of Created Things.

By this examination, is meant meditating upon the marks of divine wisdom manifested in all created things and earnestly evaluating them to the utmost of one's mental capacity... Contemplate, therefore, God's creatures from the largest to the smallest and reflect on those aspects of them that are at present hidden from you... (Chapter 1)

Is it our duty to study created things or not? The obligation to do so and thereby find proof of the wisdom of the Creator can be established by reason, from the Bible and from the rabbinical tradition.

By reason: It is evident to the intelligent mind that a rational creature's superiority over an irrational one lies in the rational creature's superior ability to perceive, understand and know the mysteries of the Supernal Wisdom -- mysteries whose existence is confirmed throughout the universe, as it says: "Who teaches us more than the beasts of the field and makes us wiser than the birds of heaven" (Job 35:11). When a human being contemplates these foundations of wisdom and studies the signs of this wisdom in the universe, his superiority over the dumb beast rises in proportion to his intelligence. But if he fails to observe and reflect, not only is he not equal to the beast, he is inferior to it, as it says: "The ox knows its owner and the ass its master's crib, but Israel does not know, My people does not consider" (Isaiah 1:3)."

From the Bible: It says: "Lift up your eyes on high and see Who created these!" (Isaiah 40:26). Similarly: "When I look at Your heavens, the work of Your fingers, the moon and the stars that You have established..." (Psalms 8:4).

From rabbinical tradition: The Rabbis said, "When a person has the ability to make astronomical calculations but fails to do so, the Bible says of him (Isaiah 5:12): 'And the harp and the viol, the tabret and the pipe and wine are in their feasts; but they do not regard the work of *HaVaYaH* and they do not contemplate the work of His hands' (*Shabbat* 75a). The Rabbis also said: "From where do we learn that it is a duty to make astronomical calculations? Because it says (Deuteronomy 4:6): 'Observe therefore and do them, for this is your wisdom and understanding in the sight of the nations that, when they hear all these statutes, they will say, Surely, this great nation is a wise and understanding people'" (*ibid.*) The Rabbis also said (*Eruvin* 100b): "If the Torah had not been given to Israel, we could have learned decency from the cat, chastity from the dove, etiquette from the cock and honesty from the ant." (Chapter 2)

What to Study

Rabbenu Bachya continues:

Examination of created things means a close study of the original elements of which the Universe is composed; the products that result from the combination of these elements; the character of the constituents of each compound; its various uses; the marks of wisdom exhibited in its production, form and shape, and in the purpose for which it was created; the beautiful spirituality of this world; its causes and effects and the complete perfection for which it was created; to know its contents -- spiritual and physical, rational and irrational, the immobile and the mobile, minerals and plants; its higher and lower parts; and to realize that the Creator created the Universe in a perfect and orderly combination -- each of its parts distinctly recognizable, so that it indicates and points to the Creator as clearly as a piece of work points to the workman or a house indicates the builder (Chapter 3).

It is possible to discern seven different kinds of signs of divine wisdom in created things:

The first is the mark of divine wisdom apparent in the primary and fundamental elements of the universe. The earth, we see, is at the center. Next to it above is water. Next to the water is the air, and above everything is fire -- all in a just and unchanging balance and measure. Every one of these elements maintains the proper position appointed for it...

The second is the mark of wisdom apparent in the human species -- a universe on a small scale that completes the ordered series of creation and constitutes its crowning beauty, glory and perfection.

The third is the mark of wisdom apparent in the formation of the individual human being -- his physical structure, the faculties of his mind, and the light of reason with which the Creator has set him apart from and above other living creatures...

The fourth cornerstone is the mark of wisdom manifested in other species of living creatures, from the least to the greatest -- those that fly or swim or creep or move on four legs with their various qualities, pleasures and uses.

The fifth is the mark of wisdom displayed in plants and other natural products such as minerals that have been provided for the benefit of the human race because of their usefulness to man in various ways in accordance with their natures, constitutions and virtues... Thus, it is said: "And he (Solomon) spoke of trees from the cedar in Lebanon down to the hyssop that grows in the wall; he spoke also of

beasts and birds, of creeping things and fishes"
(I Kings 5:13).

The sixth is the mark of wisdom discernible in the sciences, arts and crafts which the Creator, blessed be He, provided for man to benefit him, to enable him to obtain a livelihood and gain other benefits of a general and particular character...

The seventh is the mark of wisdom exhibited in the appointment of the Torah and its statutes, to teach us how to serve the Creator and secure for one who consistently lives according to their dictates immediate happiness here and recompense in the life to come hereafter. To this should be added the customs by which the government of other nations is regulated together with their useful features... (Chapter 4).

According to R. Bachya, our primary duty is to study that which is closest to us: the human being.

It is our duty to study the origins and birth of the human, the form and structure of his physical frame, how the various body parts are connected and function together, the purpose of each individual part and the need for it to take its present form. Next, we should study man's advantages, his various temperaments, the faculties of his soul, the light of his intellect, his qualities -- those that are essential and those that are accidental; his desires, and the ultimate purpose of his being. When we have arrived at an understanding of the matters noted in regard to man, much of the mystery of this universe will become clear to us, since the one resembles the other... as Job said (Job 19:26): "From my flesh I see God." (Chapter 5)

R. Bachya continues with a remarkable passage discussing at length and in great detail the human body from birth to death, human development and growth both physical and psychological, the various basic human functions, traits, skills and technological abilities. After this, R. Bachya adds:

> The study of other species of animals, their habits and their sustenance will not be ignored by one who observes them and reflects upon the marks of divine wisdom to be discerned in them.... The foods assigned to different living creatures are too numerous to specify... And so too when one studies the course of the heavenly spheres distinguished by their various movements and the individual luminaries, all contributing to the order of the universe, he will see in them evidence of power and wisdom such as the human mind cannot grasp and would become weary in attempting to describe... Reflect on that most perfect of God's gifts to living beings and to plants -- the rain, which besides falling in its due season, descends in showers when needed.... How astonishing too is the growth of foods from seeds. A single grain produces a

thousand grains and more... We also come across gigantic trees whose roots have sprung out of a single seed or short. Praise be the All-Wise and Gracious One, Who brings into existence such vast effects from causes so small and weak... (Chapter 5)

How the Tzaddik Looks at Nature

Rabbi Nachman of Breslov sums up the fundamental orientation of the spiritual seeker in examining the details of the natural world:

> The Tzaddik is constantly searching to discover and reveal what God wants. At the root of everything lies the will of God. This applies to the universe as a whole: there is a reason why God wanted to create the universe as a whole. So too in every individual item and detail of creation there lies the will of God. Namely God wanted this item to be exactly the way it is with its own unique form, power and nature, while something else has a different form, power and nature.

> The Tzaddik constantly hunts and searches to discover and reveal the will of God in each thing. For example, why was it God's will that a lion should have this form, structure and nature and possess this degree of strength and power while a tiny mosquito has a totally different form, structure and nature and is extremely weak? The same question applies to specific details. For example, in

the lion itself: why does one limb have one form and power while another limb has a quite different form and power? The same applies to everything else in the world, inanimate, vegetable, animal and human... On every level, there are innumerable different kinds and species and countless varieties within each species. Every single individual item has its own unique idiosyncrasies down to the smallest details of every single limb. This applies to plants, trees and all the other details of the creation. There are countless different creatures, all with their own unique forms, powers and qualities. Everything is the way it is because the Creator, blessed be He, willed that this should be like this and that one should be like that. And the Tzaddik constantly searches to discover and reveal the will of God in each particular.

Likutey Moharan I:17

The Varieties of Fruits

An example of the Kabbalah way of viewing natural phenomena is found in the following passage about the different kinds of fruits based on teachings by R. Chaim Vital (1542-1620), principal disciple of the outstanding kabbalistic master, Rabbi Isaac Luria, the "*ARI*":

Even though God has established His rule over the earth through the individual angels that are appointed over each species, even so every individual item in creation has its roots in the supernal attributes, the sefirot...

Every single plant is unique and has its own unique roots in the supernal world. There are thirty species of fruits of trees. Ten of them correspond to the ten sefirot as revealed in the world of *Beriyah*. They are far from impurity and close to the supreme "world" of *Atzilut*. For that reason, the corresponding fruits have no husk or peel either inside or outside. They are eaten just as they are. Examples are grapes, figs, apples and pears.... There are ten other kinds of fruits that are intermediaries between the world of *Beriyah* and that of *Asiyah*. They correspond to the ten sefirot as revealed in the world of *Yetzira*, which is not as close to impurity as the world of *Asiyah* yet not as far removed from it as the World of *Beriah*. Accordingly, the pits of these fruits are found inside the fruit. They are not edible because they are not soft like the seeds in the fruits that correspond to the sefirot of the world of *Beriyah*. Examples of this latter type are olives and dates... Then there are ten other kinds of fruits corresponding to the ten sefirot of the world of *Asiyah*, which is closest to the realm of impurity. In the case of these fruits the edible portion is inside, surrounded by an inedible peel which has to be removed and discarded. Examples are pomegranates, nuts and almonds, etc.

(*Pri Etz Hadar*)

The language of animals, birds and trees

According to tradition, certain outstanding saints and sages attained such exalted levels of perception that they could understand not only the meaning of the outward form and structure of natural phenomena such as plants and animals but their very languages.

Foremost among those credited with such knowledge was King Solomon, as alluded to in the verse: "And he spoke of trees from the cedar in Lebanon down to the hyssop that grows in the wall; he spoke also of beasts and birds, of creeping things and fishes" (I Kings 5:13).

Of Rabban Yochanan ben Zakkai (1st Century C.E.), the Talmud relates: "Hillel the Elder had eighty disciples. The greatest of all of them was R. Yonatan ben Uziel, the smallest of all of them was Rabban Yochanan ben Zakkai. They said of him that he had comprehensive knowledge of Mishnah, Talmud, law, exposition, logical inference, astronomy, mathematics, incantations of angels, the language of the demons, the *language of trees* and the proverbs of launderers and foxes..." (*Succah* 28a).

Rabbi Chaim Vital writes in a similar vein of his master, the *ARI*, stating that among his many other areas of expertise were the language of trees, the language of birds and the speech of angels (Introduction to *Etz Chaim*).

Similar knowledge was attributed to the Baal Shem Tov. The following story is told of one of his foremost disciples, R. Leib ("the Preacher") of Polonnoye:

R. Leib of Polonnoye had a powerful yearning to understand the language of the animals, birds and trees. He decided to travel to the Baal Shem Tov to ask him to teach him this wisdom. When he arrived, there were many people in the Baal Shem Tov's house and the latter paid no attention to him. It was a long time before he even greeted him, and when he finally did, it was with great casualness. R. Leib was quite surprised as the Baal Shem Tov usually showed him great affection since he was one of his closest students. However, R. Leib did not pay too much attention because of his great desire to learn this wisdom. He waited for the right time to broach the subject.

One day the Baal Shem Tov had to go on a journey and he asked R. Leib to come with him. R. Leib was delighted. He was sure that on the way the Baal Shem Tov would accede to his request... As they traveled in the carriage the Baal Shem Tov said to R. Leib: "I know that the main reason you came to me was to learn the conversation of animals and birds. And now I will teach you...

"From the face of the Man in the Supernal Chariot (the *Merkavah*) vitality is drawn down to man in this lowly world. From the face of the Ox vitality comes down by a downward chain of causes and effects from level to level with contraction after contraction to all the animals (*Behemot*) in the lower world. From the face of the Lion vitality is drawn to all the wild animals (*Chayot*). And from the face of the Eagle vitality is drawn to all the birds in the lower world. This is the secret of the *Perek Shirah* (literally, Chapter of Song, a collection of Biblical verses put into the mouths of various different species of trees, plants, animals, birds and other natural phenomena). The formulae of words expressed by the various forms in the Supreme Chariot determines the vitality that comes down into the lower world to the various species of animals and birds and so on... This is the general principle, but there are awesome and wondrous secrets in all the details...."

The Baal Shem Tov explained the entire subject until R. Leib had a thorough understanding. The Baal Shem Tov explained many relevant passages in the *Zohar* and *Tikkuney Zohar*. With one ear R. Leib listened to the words of the Baal Shem Tov while with the other he listened to what the birds and animals were saying. The Baal Shem Tov carried on teaching him until they approached the town. Then he said to R. Leib, "Have you understood everything?" "Yes" replied R. Leib.

The Baal Shem Tov passed his hand over R. Leib's face, and R. Leib promptly forgot all the secrets which the Baal Shem Tov had revealed to him. All R. Leib could remember was the Baal Shem Tov's opening words about the Supernal Chariot.

The Baal Shem Tov smiled and said, "If you had a need for this wisdom in order to serve God, I myself would have been in a hurry to teach you. I only told you what I did in order to satisfy your thirst. And you forgot it all because you have no need for it! Serve God with simplicity!"

Sipurey Baal Shem Tov

Prayer

*I*f all the birds and animals and even the very trees and plants are constantly uttering the deepest secrets, why did the Baal Shem Tov not teach his students how to hear and understand them?

His answer was: "If you needed this wisdom in order to serve God, I would have hurried to teach you.... But you have no need for it! Just serve God with simplicity!"

The simplest way of serving God is through prayer, which the sages called *avodah*, "work", "labor" or "service".

This was Isaac's act of service when he "went out to meditate in the field" (Genesis 24:63). Isaac, diligent disciple of his father Abraham, set himself to the task the way an ox submits to the yoke and patiently plows the field.

Isaac was following the path of Abraham's *Sefer Yetzira*, which teaches that by manipulating the "letters of creation" in prayer and meditation, man has the ability to influence creation according to his will. That man should play this exalted role was indeed the very purpose of his creation. God "placed Adam in the Garden of Eden to *work* it and *guard* it" (Genesis 2:15). Creation was intended to be a magnificent garden of wisdom and harmony, with man in the role of the gardener and orchestrator, tending and developing it to perfection. Order, meaning and blessing come into the world through following all aspects of the divine code -- the Torah -- and especially through prayer, which aligns the entire creation with its Creator:

Praise *HaVaYaH* from the heavens; praise Him on high. Praise Him all His angels, praise Him all His hosts. Praise Him, sun and moon, praise Him, all bright stars. Praise Him, highest heavens and you waters that are above the heavens...

Praise *HaVaYaH*, O you who are on earth, all sea monsters and ocean depths, fire and hail, snow and smoke, storm wind that executes His command, all mountains and hills, all fruit trees and cedars, all wild and tamed beasts, creeping things and winged birds, all kings and peoples of the earth, all princes of the earth and its judges, youths and maidens alike, old and young together.

Let them praise the name of *HaVaYaH*, for His name, His alone, is sublime; His splendor covers heaven and earth!

Psalms 148 1-4, 7-13

Fixing the Creation

Adam failed to rise to his destiny of bringing the world to God. Instead, pride and greed made him to seek to manipulate the world for his own selfish purposes, treating it as a separate realm from which God had somehow become detached, a pleasure-ground for him to exploit in any way he wished without thinking about the consequences. Adam ate from the forbidden fruit. And today, thousands of years later, we are witness to the terrible despoliation and destruction of the world we live in due to the same pride and greed.

The mission of Abraham, Isaac and Jacob was to forge the pathway that would enable mankind to rectify Adam's failure. Isaac's going out to "labor in the field" exemplifies the Torah of prayer taught by his father Abraham in order to bring man and the world back to God.

The essential labor of prayer is to affirm that God governs the entire universe and to bring this knowledge into the innermost recesses of our hearts in order to overcome the egotistical human tendency to suppose that we are in control of things. By steadily working in the "field" of hitbodedut day after day, prayerfully laboring to refine and elevate the raw elements of our personalities, we turn ourselves into true servants of *HaVaYaH*, manifesting His total unity and power. We are then ready for the highest level of prayer, which is to pray selflessly for the welfare of the whole world.

In the words of Rebbe Nachman: "According to the rabbis, every person must say, The whole world was created only for me! (*Sanhedrin* 37a). If the world was created for me, it follows that I must constantly examine how I can rectify the world and fulfill its needs and *pray for the world...*" (*Likutey Moharan* I, 5:1).

The classic Jewish prayer book, the Siddur, composed by the Men of the Great Assembly (2nd century B.C.E.) -- outstanding sages, saints and prophets -- consists of elaborate structures of Hebrew letters, words and holy names all of which are aligned to the underlying *TzuRoT* (forms or codes) through which God made and runs the creation. These sages' profound knowledge of the secrets of *Sefer Yetzira* enabled them to compose prayers that would accomplish the necessary rectification.

"Every Blade of Grass Has an Angel That Strikes It..."

To understand how prayer has the power to rectify and benefit the entire world, it is necessary to understand the underlying cosmology of the Kabbalah as taught by Abraham, Isaac and all subsequent masters and teachers of the Torah tradition.

The patriarchs lived in a world where people were very aware of the influence of the sun, the moon and other planets and stars upon Earth. Whether these are seen as gods, angels or lumps of lifeless matter formed by exploding gases, it is obvious that these celestial bodies are vital sources of light and all kinds of other influences upon Earth. All life on Earth, plant, animal and human, depends upon the interplay of light and other radiations from these celestial bodies with the various gases, liquids and solids that make up Earthly matter.

Awareness of the heavenly influences upon life on Earth down to the very plants of the field is implicit in the well-known rabbinic dictum: "There is not a blade of grass that does not have a star in the skies that strikes it and says: Grow!" Examining the original context of this saying will help elucidate its meaning.

Rabbi Simon said: You will not find a single blade of grass that does not have its *mazal* -- constellation of stars and/or angel -- in the heavens that strikes it and says to it "Grow!" as it says: "Do you know the ordinances of Heaven? Can you establish its rule (*Mishtaro*) over the earth?" (Job 38:33). The word for rule, *miShTaRo*, is from the root *ShoTeR*, signifying a "police officer" who gives blows to enforce the law [alluding to the "striking" of the plant by the *mazal*.) The same passage continues: "Can you bind the chains of the stars of the Pleiades or loosen the bands of Orion?" (*ibid.* v.31). The Pleiades ripen the fruits and give them flavor, while Orion lengthens the stalks of the plants to let the fruits grow. "Can you lead forth the Mazarot in their season? Or can you guide the Bear with her sons?" (*ibid.* v.32). This is a constellation that sends winds to blow over the plants and cleanse them of their wastes...

Midrash Rabbah Bereishit 10:6

According to the above-quoted Midrash, each plant has its own *mazal* that strikes it and says "Grow!" The word *mazal* means both a "constellation of stars" and "an angel", for the two are interrelated. The physical energy -- the light that "strikes" the plant and makes it grow -- comes from the physical star, the sun, etc. But this physical energy derives from and is channeled by a spiritual power-source, an "angel" or "form" (*Tzura*) that governs the physical process through a formula of *words* ("and *says*: Grow!").

The interface between the physical and spiritual worlds is explained by Rabbi Moshe Chaim Luzzatto ("*RaMChaL*") in his classic exposition of the Judaic worldview, "The Way of God".

Creation in general consists of two basic parts: the physical and the spiritual. The physical is that which we experience with our senses and is in turn divided into the terrestrial and the astronomical. The terrestrial includes everything in the lowest sphere: the earth, water and atmosphere, and every detectable thing they contain.

The spiritual consists of all entities which are not physical and which cannot be detected by physical means. These in turn are also divided into two categories: souls and transcendental beings. Souls comprise a class of spiritual entities destined to enter physical bodies. Transcendental beings comprise a class of spiritual entities that are not meant to be associated with physical bodies. Transcendental beings are also divided into two categories: Forces ("*Kochot*") and Angels....

Everything in the physical world has a counterpart among these transcendental Forces. Every entity and process in the physical world is linked to these Forces following a system decreed by God's wisdom. These Forces are therefore the roots of all physical things, and everything in the physical world is a branch and result of these Forces. The two are thus bound together like links in a chain. Every physical entity and process is under the charge of some type of angel. These angels have the responsibility of maintaining each of them, as well as bringing about changes within them according to God's decree.

The main existence and true state of the physical universe thus emanate from these highest Forces. Whatever exists in the physical world is a result of something that takes place among these Forces. This is true of both what existed in the beginning and what transpires with the passage of time. These forces were the first things created, and they were arranged in various systems and placed in different domains. Everything that came about later was a result of this, following rules willed by God, linking these Forces to the physical world. Everything that happens in the past or present thus has its origin in processes taking place between these Forces. The existence, state, pattern and every other quality that exists among these Forces are a result of what is relevant to them by virtue of their essential nature. The existence, state, arrangement and other phenomena involving physical things in turn depend on what is transmitted and reflected to them by these Forces, following the essential nature of these physical entities.

The Way of God Part I, Chapter 5

The central figure in the entire creation is man. Thus, Rabbi Moshe Chaim Luzzatto continues:

There is one exception to the rule that every physical phenomenon originates among the highest Forces. This exception includes all things that depend on man's free will. God willed that man should be able to choose freely between good and evil, and therefore made man absolutely independent in this respect. Man was thus given the power to influence the world and its creatures in any manner his free will desires.

The world therefore contains two opposite general influences. The first is that of natural determinism, while the second is indeterministic. The deterministic influence is directed downward from on high, while the indeterministic is directed upward from below. This is because the deterministic is the influence that stems from the highest Forces, and therefore, when it is directed toward the physical world, it is directed downward. The indeterministic influence, on the other hand, is the result of man's free will here in the physical world.

Since both man and his actions are physical, the only direct influence that he can have is on physical things. However, because of the linkage between the physical world and the highest Forces, every time a physical thing is influenced, it also has an effect on its counterpart among these Forces. Since man's deeds in the world are what influence these Forces on high, man's influence is said to be directed upward. It is thus the exact opposite of the natural deterministic influences....

God arranged things so that every matter falling within the realm of man's free will should be able to affect the transcendental forces through this indeterministic influence according to the measure and degree set forth by God. This is true not only of man's deeds *but even his speech and thoughts.*

Every indeterministic influence also results in deterministic influences. When the highest Forces are influenced by man's free will, they in turn influence the physical things that are inherently linked to them.

ibid.

The crucial point that emerges from Rabbi Moshe Chaim Luzzatto's explanation of the interface between physical and spiritual is that every single human being has the power to influence the root Forces of creation through our actions in this world and through our very words and thoughts.

The highest way of influencing these root Forces for good is through Prayer, which is simultaneously a spiritual and physical process. When we pray, our inner thoughts and feelings on the level of spirit and consciousness are bound to the physical words that we form with the movements of our mouths. These cause vibrations of actual physical air together with rippling chains of spiritual influence that fan out to the highest Angels and root Forces of creation.

The Word of God

Rabbi Nachman explains that the power of prayer derives from the fact that through expressing Divine names and other supremely powerful formulae on his lips, man's word actually becomes the Word of God (*Dvar HaVaYaH*). And it is through the Word of God that the entire creation came into being and remains in being.

"Through the word of *HaVaYaH* the heavens were made and all their hosts by the breath of His mouth" (Psalms 33:6). These "hosts" include both the spiritual Angels and everything contained in the physical creation, including ourselves.

It is from the Word of God that the Angels and other spiritual forces receive their power, as explained by Rebbe Nachman in the following passage:

Know that from every single word that came from the mouth of the Holy One, blessed be He, an angel was created (*Chagigah* 14a). And every single word was divided into many sparks "as a hammer smashes a rock" (Jeremiah 23:29, and see *Shabbat* 88b), and many, many angels were created corresponding to the multitude of sparks. A word consisting of many sparks created a ruling angel who is chief over all the angels created from the sparks, and these secondary angels make up his camp. Each individual angel is in charge of something. Even the trees and herbs all have captains over them, as our Sages said: "There isn't a single blade of grass down below that does not have an angel in the world above overseeing it." Each angel receives vitality from the Word of God that brought it into being, and in turn sends vitality into the thing it is in charge of, be it a blade of grass or something else.

Likutey Moharan I, 57

The Angel, then, receives power from the creative Word of God that brought it into being, and it then hands on this power to the physical entity over which it rules.

But man has a power that goes above that of the Angels. For when man uses his God-given faculty of speech in prayer, he manipulates the Letters of Creation themselves. Then man's own words themselves become the Word of God, bringing blessing and influence into all creation.

In the words of Rebbe Nachman:

Every single plant receives its powers from its own particular planet or star. Every planet and star receives its power from the stars above it, and the highest stars from the higher powers, until they receive power from the supreme angels, as we are taught (*Tikkuney Zohar* #44, #79b) "All the stars borrow one from another: the moon borrows from the sun, etc. "for one higher than the high guards, and over them are those who are even higher" (Ecclesiastes 5:7). All of the stars borrow one from the next, until they receive and borrow from the supreme angels, and the angels receive from the powers beyond them, one higher than the other, until they all receive from the root of all things, which is the Word of God, as it is written, "Through the word of God the heavens were made and all their hosts by the breath of His mouth" (Psalms 33:6).

Likutey Moharan II, 1

According to Rebbe Nachman, when a man rises to pray, the very herbs and plants of the field put their power into his prayers. This is because prayer is the "Word of God" which is the root of all things. When a man rises to pray -- and the prayers coming from his mouth are the "Word of God" -- all the plants and herbs of the field are obliged to give back their power and put it into his prayers, which as the "Word of God" are their supreme Source.

The reason is that when a person attains true prayer, the "Word of God" -- which is the supreme Source from which the highest angels and hosts of heaven receive their power -- then all the angels and hosts of heaven become his debtors. For "all the stars borrow one from another" and thus all of them are debtors, right up to the supreme Source, which is the Word of God, which the Master of Prayer has attained. He is thus the Great Lender, to whom all the hosts of heaven and all the powers in the world are in debt.

Thus, it is written: "And the hosts of heaven bow to You" (Nehemiah 9:6). This means that all the hosts of heaven bow down to and humble themselves before their root, which is the Word of God, which the Master of Prayer has attained.

Because of the exaltedness of the letters and words of the prayers coming from his mouth -- the "Word of God" -- the Master of Prayer becomes the Creditor from whom the entire creation is receiving a flow of power and blessing. Since he is their creditor, all the Angels and all the plants and trees have to pay him back, as it were, pouring back their power into his words, which are now bringing blessing into all creation. This is the idea in the verse: "And Isaac went out to pray (la-SuaCH) in the field" (Genesis 24:63). Isaac's prayer was *with* the herbs (SiaCH) of the field, because all the herbs of the field returned their power and put it into his prayer, which was their root.

Praying in Fields and Meadows

The natural surroundings of the fields and meadows are most conducive to prayer and meditation. In the words of Rebbe Nachman: "Go to a grassy field, for the grass will awaken your heart" (Rabbi Nachman's Wisdom #227).

Grassy fields, meadows, woods and other natural surroundings can be most enchanting. Yet the idea is more than that they should serve simply as a pleasant backdrop for spiritual work. The grasses and other plants and trees actually contribute to our prayers. The plants and trees have their own song. As Rebbe Nachman told one of his students as they walked through a grassy meadow early one summer morning: "If only you could hear the song of this grass! Each blade is singing out to God for no ulterior motive, not expecting any reward. It is most amazing to hear their song and serve God among them" (Rabbi Nachman's Wisdom #163).

Especially in the spring and early summer, as the plants return to life after the winter, they themselves yearn to enter into the prayers of the person who has gone out to meditate and pray among them. The very yearning of the plants comes into this person's prayers, filling him with yearning and longing for God.

In the words of Rebbe Nachman:

In the winter, all plants and grasses die. Their strength is dissipated and they are like the dead. But when the summer comes, they awaken and return to life. It says: "And Isaac went out to meditate in the field" (Genesis 24:63). The Talmud teaches us that this meditation was prayer. When summer begins to approach it is very good to meditate in the fields. This is a time when you can pray to God with longing and yearning. The Hebrew word for meditation and prayer is *SIChah*. The Hebrew word for a bush of the field is *SIaCh*. When every bush (*SIaCh*) of the field begins to return to life and grow, they all yearn to be included in prayer and meditation (*SIChah*).

Rabbi Nachman's Wisdom #98

In the last years of Rebbe Nachman's life, when he was seriously ill with the tuberculosis that was to take his life, he would often ride to the outskirts of the city and take walks in the fields. In the words of his leading student, Rabbi Natan:

During these strolls, we heard many wonderful teachings and discussions by the Rebbe. It was on one such occasion that we heard a lesson on the verse, "And Isaac went to meditate in the field" [see below]. We had taken the coach out of the city, and we stopped in a field to walk. We had got down from the coach and were standing around the Rebbe, who was still sitting there. It was time for the afternoon (Minchah) prayer. We were about to begin the service in the field. The Rebbe said that when one prays in the field, every blade of grass enters into his prayers (*ibid.* #144).

The lesson Rebbe Nachman gave on that occasion is printed in his collected teachings, *Likutey Moharan* II, 11:

The Produce of the Land

Know that when a person prays in a field, all the grass and herbs come into his prayers and help him and put strength into his prayers. This is why prayer is called *SiChaH*: the Hebrew word is related to the word *SIaCh*, herb, as in "the herb of the field" (Genesis 2:5). For all the herbs of the field put strength into the person's prayers and help him.

This is the underlying idea in the verse: "Isaac went out to pray (*la-SUaCh*) in the field" (*ibid.* 24:63). His prayer was with the help and strength that came from the field. For all the grass and herbs -- *SIaCh* -- of the field put their strength into his prayer and helped the prayer. This is why prayer is called *SIChaH*.

Conversely, among the curses is that "the land will not give its produce (*YeVUL*)" (Deuteronomy 11:17). For all the produce of the earth is supposed to put power and strength into our prayers to help them. When this power and strength fail to enter our prayers for some reason, this is the negative situation expressed in the curse: the land does not give its produce. Even when a person is not actually praying in a field, the produce of the land still puts power into his prayers and helps them. For all the food and drink and other things a person consumes -- all of which are "the produce of the land" -- also put power into his prayer.

The difference is that when the person is actually in the field, he is very close indeed to the plants, and then all the grasses, herbs and other "produce of the land" put power and strength directly into his prayer. The Hebrew letters of the word *YeVUL* ("produce") are the initial letters of the Hebrew words making up the verse "And Isaac went out to meditate in the field" (*Vayeitzei Yitzchak Lasu-ach Basadeh*). This indicates that all the plants and produce of the field prayed with him.

Likutey Moharan II:11

The field in which Isaac prayed was the site of the Holy Temple destined to be built by his descendants. Isaac's labor of prayer in the field laid the foundation of the Temple as the "House of Prayer for all the nations" (Isaiah 56, 7) -- the place where the prayers of mankind will bring the world back to the Creator and shine peace and blessing into all the world.

The Dark Side of Nature

A deer is in desperate flight from a lion. The deer's grace and beauty are of no avail when at last, exhausted, it falls prey to the powerful lion, which mercilessly savages the deer's tender neck to gratify its lust for meat and blood.

An eagle digs its claws into its terrified prey... A snake sinks its teeth into the flesh of its victim and injects its deadly venom.... A spider bites to death the helpless fly trapped in its web...

Similar scenes of predators and their prey are repeated constantly day after day on every level of the chain of life from the lowest, simplest and most primitive to the highest, most complex and sophisticated. Millions and millions of cows, sheep, chickens, fish and other creatures are slaughtered every day for human consumption.

Sooner or later, man's time also comes. Throughout his life he was the confident master. Now he becomes the frightened victim. One way or another the Angel of Death always gets his prey, and man's body goes back to the earth to decompose and be consumed by worms, molds and the like. These in turn provide food for other life-forms which in turn become the food of others. And so the food chain goes on and on.

Cycles

No sensitive person can fail to be troubled by the plight of the victims as they meet their bitter end in the mouths of their predators. At the same time, we cannot but accept that the vast, awesome process of life feeding off life is one of the most fundamental of all universal cycles. In water and on land the bodies of lower organisms are recycled through being consumed by and turning into the bodies of higher organisms. They in turn end up providing food and energy for other organisms.

The Hebrew word for a cycle is *galgal*, literally a "wheel". The spinning of the wheel is called *gilgul*, a term which in Jewish mysticism is particularly associated with the "recycling of souls", i.e. reincarnation. In other words, not only are physical materials constantly being recycled through the water, carbon, nitrogen, oxygen and other natural cycles. Souls and spirits also spin around on the wheel of cosmic destiny. Human souls may enter the bodies of animals, birds, fish or even plants, and vice versa. These great cycles are in turn governed by higher, more exalted spiritual cycles. These are the Sefirot. (The word *SeFiRaH* has the connotation of a rotating sphere.)

For the earthbound humans of pre-modern times, as indeed for any truly aware, thinking person today, one of the most profoundly moving and striking of all examples of cycles was and is the way the sun, the moon, the planets and the stars seem constantly to circle the earth in their various orbits.

Consider the orbiting of one heavenly body around another. The body in orbit is unable to travel off freely on a path of its own out into space because its forward movement is constrained by the gravitational pull of the larger body. Without entering into the complexities of the actual orbital paths of planets (which are elliptical) the orbiting body essentially travels an endless circular path around the greater body.

A circle is the shape described by any moving point whose forward motion is constrained in a specific way by some other point -- the "center" -- around which the former is moving. The moving point maps out a circle because it is unable to move any closer to or further from the center point. This far but no further!

The concept of circularity and cycles is thus bound up with that of force and constraint. A center point of some kind exerts a force upon all the points circling around it, keeping them all in their place. The size of the circle described by any given moving point is a function of the distance of that point from the center (i.e. the radius of the circle) and the mathematical ratio known to mathematicians as *Pi*, which is approximately 314:100. Significantly, 314 is the numerical value of the Hebrew letters of the Divine Name that expresses the constraining aspect of the creative process, *Shadai*, "the Eternal God" -- "Who said to His universe, *Dai*, enough! This far and no further!" (*Chagigah* 12a).

Isaac and the Afternoon Sun

The concept of power and constraint is particularly associated with Isaac, who embodies the quality of *Gevurah*, strength and strictness. This is associated with afternoon, time of the setting sun.

Abraham was the first, the initiator, the embodiment of *Chessed*, expansive, unrestricted love and kindness. Abraham is associated with the morning, time of the rising sun, which gets ever more brilliant and hotter as it climbs up and up, ascending to the heights of the heavens.

But then comes noon. The sun reaches the peak of its strength and glory, and its upward climb is now constrained. At first indiscernibly, then gradually more and more markedly, the sun descends, the day begins to cool and the brightness of the skies starts to fade, until at last the sun sinks magnificently down to the western horizon and finally disappears, leaving the world to dusk and the darkness of night.

In the early hours after sunrise the path of the sun may have seemed like a straight upward climb from the east. But as the day progresses the upward movement of the sun seems to be constrained by a force that pulls it in a circle across the skies and down to the west.

The sun's daily rising and setting symbolizes the constantly repeated expansive-*Chessed* and contracting-*Gevurah* phases that characterize all kinds of different oscillations and cycles on all levels of creation. Thus "Abraham [*Chessed*] rose *early in the morning* [sunrise]" (Genesis 19:27 & 22:3), while "Isaac [*Gevurah*] went out to meditate in the field *towards evening* [sunset]" (Genesis 24:63).

Cruelty

It can be very fascinating to contemplate vast cycles of creation such as reincarnation of souls and the food chain -- as long as you are not the one being eaten. For most people, it is sobering and indeed fearful to think about the quality of *Gevurah* as it actually manifests itself in human life in the form of limitations, obstacles, hardship, pain, illness, decline, old age and death. In contrast to Abraham's quality of unstinting mercy and kindness, Isaac's quality of power and control is characterized by a relentless strictness that may turn into veritable harshness. The emotion associated with *Gevurah* is fear. It was with fear and awe that Isaac experienced God, as it says: "the Fear of Isaac" (Genesis 31:53).

When we think of the terrible things that happen to people, the world can seem like a very cruel place. The cruel face of *Gevurah* is epitomized in the figure of Isaac's son Esau. Whereas Sarah bore Abraham only one son, Rebecca presented Isaac with twins, Esau and Jacob, two very different types. While Jacob's preference was for "dwelling in tents" (this will be the focus of Part III of this book), Esau followed after his father as a "man of the *Field*" (Genesis 25:27).

Isaac's activity in the field was the constructive work of physical cultivation of the land and cultivation of the soul through meditation, prayer and good deeds. On the other hand, Esau's love of the field was as a place to throw off the restrictions of civilized life in order to surrender himself to his primitive selfish lusts and passions even to the point of barbaric cruelty.

"And Esau came in from the field" (Genesis 25:29). According to tradition, the day on which Jacob cooked soup and fed it to Esau in exchange for his birthright was the day Abraham died. The soup was of lentils, which Jacob was preparing for the customary meal of consolation given to mourners, in this case his father Isaac. Jacob chose lentils "because they are round like a *wheel*, for mourning is a revolving wheel that recurs again and again in the world" (*Rashi ad loc.*).

In other words, when Abraham died and *Chessed* reached its end point, as it were, the quality of *Gevurah* came to the fore as expressed in the severity of death and mourning, which are inevitable aspects of the universal cycle. And on that same day the harsh extreme of *Gevurah* manifested itself in the person of Esau.

"Esau raped an engaged girl, as it is written (Deuteronomy 22:27) `for the rapist found her in the *field*'. And he committed murder, as it says `And Esau came from the *field* and he was *tired*' -- tired from killing (see Jeremiah 4:31)....

He also robbed, denied God and worshipped idols"

(Midrash Rabbah Bereishit 63:12; Baba Batra 16b).

Esau embodies the unholy extreme of *Gevurah* -- power used with merciless brutality for the gratification of self. This is the ultimate in taking and grabbing, as opposed to Abraham's selfless giving to others. Abraham himself had been the polar opposite of the selfish, power-loving Nimrod. Now the cycle swung around again, and Abraham's revelation of *Chessed* was followed by the terrifying manifestation of the opposite, wickedness and crime. According to tradition, the beautiful clothes that Esau possessed (Genesis 27:15) had actually been Nimrod's. One day, Esau saw Nimrod wearing them and desired them for himself, so he killed Nimrod and took them *(Midrash Rabbah Bereishit* 65:16).

Esau's exploitation and slaughter of others for his own self-gratification -- "My life before yours!" -- makes him a fitting symbol of the Angel of Death. Death is the ultimate constraint.

Sweetening the Severity

> "And God saw all that He had made and it was *very good*" (Genesis 1:31). "Very good" -- this refers to Angel the of Death"

(Midrash Rabbah Bereishit 9:12).

Cruel and heartless as it may at times seem, *Gevurah* is an indispensable part of creation (though this should never be used to justify outright cruelty by humans, who have the freedom to act otherwise).

The Infinite God is all good, and wants to share that goodness with all His creatures. However, it would simply be impossible for God's creatures to experience this goodness incessantly, for then they would no longer exist: they simply would be absorbed and merged in God's infinity. The only way for any created being to exist is within limitations of some kind. It is these very limitations that give it a specific identity of its own. As we have seen, even the Chayot, the vital forces ("angels") of creation, exist in a mode of "running and returning" (Ezekiel 1:14). They "run out" of themselves in yearning to rise up and merge with God, but then they "return" to themselves and their separate existence. This cyclical "running and returning", expansion and contraction, is one of the underlying dynamics of all creation.

Just as the world needs Abraham, the founder, the leader, the teacher, the giver, the man of *Chessed*, so it also needs Isaac, the follower, the student, the receiver, the man of *Gevurah*..

Isaac's holy mission is to teach how to rectify the harsh aspect of *Gevurah* -- selfish excess, as embodied in Esau -- by directing one's very power and strength back in upon oneself in the form of self-discipline, restraint and the focused application of power and strength for the sake of accomplishing true good. *Gevurah* has to be "tied up" and bound in the service of *Chessed*, as symbolized in the binding of Isaac on the altar by Abraham.

The labor of Isaac in the field thus includes the tough spiritual work of facing and resolving inner conflict, fear, pain, torment, depression, doubt and other forms of negativity and darkness. This is an integral part of the work of hitbodedut. The essence of the work is to search for the sparks of good within darkness and negativity.

The Blessings

> Isaac was old and his eyes were dim so that he could not see. He called Esau, his elder son, and said "I am old: I do not know the day of my death. Please take your weapons, your quiver and your bow, and go out to the field and catch me venison. Make me tasty food the way I love and bring it to me so that I may eat in order that my soul may bless you before I die." (Genesis 27:1-4).

According to tradition, "When Isaac was bound on the altar with Abraham about to slaughter him, the heavens opened up and the ministering angels saw and wept, and their tears dropped down and fell into Isaac's eyes, weakening them" (*Rashi* on Genesis 27:1).

Isaac's willingness to be bound on the altar symbolizes his perfect willingness to apply his quality of *Gevurah* to himself through total self-surrender and submission to the will of Abraham, *Chessed*. This in itself lifted Isaac to a most exalted level of spiritual perception way beyond people's normal level of perception in this world. This elevation is expressed in the idea of the ministering angels shedding tears into Isaac's eyes, which represents their superior angelic power of vision coming into Isaac (cf. *Likutey Moharan* 1, 250 end).

Isaac's higher vision of the ultimate cyclical forces (sefirot, angels) that underlie all worldly processes tends to make him "blind" in the sense of being apparently insensitive to the everyday ups and downs that upset most people. This is because Isaac keeps his eyes focused on their long-term meaning and purpose.

Adam and Eve's original mistake in selfishly stealing the fruit of the tree of knowledge was itself caused by a flaw of vision. They looked at the immediate, the superficial and the temporary -- "The woman *saw* that the tree was good to eat" (Genesis 3:6). Adam and Eve ate, "and the eyes of both of them were *opened*" (*ibid.* v.7). Isaac rectified this flaw by closing his eyes to the vanities of the transient world and keeping his inner vision focused on higher truths.

Whether Isaac really intended to hand on the blessings he received from his father Abraham to the wicked Esau and if so, why, has been the subject of extensive discussion by biblical commentators. This is not the place to enter into the mysteries of what the wise, dim-sighted, far-gazing Isaac intended in calling on Esau to bless him, or why the eminently shrewd, down-to-earth Rebecca saw fit to disguise her favorite Jacob as Esau and send him in to take the blessings for himself.

Here our focus is on a single facet of Isaac's conduct in this episode: how he ate. For it teaches us a lesson about the rectification and elevation of the quality of *Gevurah*.

Of the three patriarchs Abraham, Isaac and Jacob, Isaac is the only one in the biblical narrative whom we actually see eating. All three patriarchs are portrayed as preparing and giving food to others. Abraham gave hospitality to the angels (Genesis 18:4ff). Isaac made a feast for Avimelech and his men (Genesis 26:30). Jacob gave the lentil pottage to Esau (*ibid.* 25:28) and he called his sons and Laban to eat bread (*ibid.* 31:56).

But Isaac is the only one who is explicitly shown to us eating and drinking in the episode of the Blessings.

"Isaac was old and his eyes were dim so that he could not see. He called Esau, his elder son, and said `I am old: I do not know the day of my death. Please take your weapons, your quiver and your bow, and go out to the field and catch me venison. Make me tasty food the way I love and bring it to me so that *I may eat in order that my soul may bless you* before I die.'" (Genesis 27:1-4).

Whenever we eat, we take something that was alive -- animal or vegetable -- and we ingest it in order to give ourselves life. When someone says he "loves" meat, he does not love the poor animal at all. He loves his own taste buds and stomach much more, which is why he puts a quick end to the animal's life to gratify his own desires.

We have already discussed how the quality of *Gevurah* is bound up with taking for oneself as opposed to giving to others. It is a universal law of the food chain that the greater consumes the lesser. But to what end? Isaac wants to eat the venison not merely to gratify a lust for meat but "in order that my soul may bless you": Isaac eats so as to have the strength to pass on Abraham's blessings of kindness to the next generation. Isaac takes in order to give.

The food eaten by higher forms of life is actually elevated by the process. In the words of Rebbe Nachman:

Through eating, the food turns into the one who eats it. When an animal eats grass or plants, the very grass turns into the animal through being digested and becoming part of the animal's body. The same happens when a human eats an animal. The animal turns into the human. Wherever the nutrients from that food enter into the tissues of the person who ate it, they turn into that tissue. For example, the part of the food that goes up to the brain turns into brain; that which comes into the heart turns into the heart, and so on.

Likutey Moharan 1, 129

When a human uses the energy derived from his food to pursue animal activities, the food is degraded with the person. But when a person devotes his energy to the pursuit of justice, kindness, Torah study, prayer and other Godly purposes, the very plants and animals he consumed are elevated in the process. For their energy is being used to influence the cosmos in ways far more exalted than anything they could have accomplished it had they remained in their original form.

The Torah teaches that killing of an animal or bird for human consumption (*Shechitah*) is a most solemn moment. The slaughterer invokes his privilege under God's law to mankind (Genesis 9:2-5) to take the knife, symbol of *Gevurah*, and swiftly slit the animal's windpipe and gullet according to God's command (Deuteronomy 12:21).

Before the slaughterer may take the animal's life, he is obliged to invoke the name of God: "Blessed are You, God, Ruler of the World, Who has sanctified us with His commandments and commanded us concerning *Shechitah*).

The invocation of God's name on his lips is man's highest act. The quality that distinguishes man from the animals is the power of speech, manipulating the letters of creation. When the slaughterer offers the blessing just before taking the animal's life, the holy words of the blessing become the medium of ascent of the animal's spiritual soul to the higher worlds.

But if the slaughterer treats the blessing as a meaningless formula to which he pays no attention, or worse still, if he fails to make a blessing at all, the animal's soul has no medium through which to ascend to the higher spiritual realms and it remains caught in the rut of cosmic destiny until the wheel will eventually swing back again (see *Likutey Moharan* 37:6).

In the words of Rebbe Nachman, "Woe to this slaughterer! Woe to the soul that killed a soul and gave her over into the hands of her enemies!" (*ibid.*)

The same could be said to apply to all eating. The person who eats is the "slaughterer" who puts an end to the life of the food item he is about to eat in order to give himself life. If the person understands that the foods he is eating contain holy souls that are waiting to be elevated and if he uses these energies for Godly purposes, he then elevates these souls. This is accomplished especially through invoking God's name when eating the food through blessing Him before and afterwards. But when a person eats purely for selfish animal gratification and lust, he degrades these souls just as he degrades himself, for a human who behaves like an animal is lower than an animal.

"Make me tasty food the way I love and bring it to me so that I may eat in order that my soul may *bless*!" Isaac's act of eating had the purpose of elevating the energies in the food in order to spread blessing further and further.

Rebecca knew her two sons better than did Isaac. She knew that Esau was unfitted to receive Isaac's blessings as he would want to keep them selfishly for himself rather than spread them further and further to others like Jacob.

Rebecca herself prepared food for Isaac and, disguising Jacob as Esau, sent him in with the food to Isaac in order to receive the blessings.

"And Isaac said, `Bring the food near to me and I will eat of my son's venison in order that my soul may bless you. And he brought it near to him, and he ate. And he brought him wine, and he drank. And his father Isaac said to him, `Come near now and kiss me, my son'. And he came near and kissed him. And he smelled the smell of his clothes and blessed him and said:`See, the smell of my son is as the smell of a field which *HaVaYaH* has blessed. So, God will give you the dew of the heaven and the fat places of the earth and plenty of corn and wine. Let peoples serve you and nations bow down to you. Be master over your brothers and let your mother's sons bow down to you. Cursed be everyone that curses you and blessed be every one that blesses you.'" (Genesis 27:25-29).

Isaac smelled on Jacob the fragrance of "a field that God has blessed". Isaac, holy man of the field, knew that the son who brought him his food was the one who was worthy to receive the blessings, for he too had the smell of the field: the true field -- the field that God has blessed.

The Site of the Holy Temple

This "Field" is the same as Isaac's field -- the place where he went to meditate, the place where he had been bound on the altar on the Temple Mount in Jerusalem. This is where Isaac fulfilled his holy mission to rectify the quality of *Gevurah*, power and strength. And this is the place where the rectification of *Gevurah* is to take place as a continuous process through the service in the Temple, God's House of Prayer for all the nations.

In the following teaching, Rabbi Nachman explains how the various cycles of creation are bound up with the Temple.

The world is a rotating wheel. It is like a Dreidel (the spinning top customarily played with on the festival of Hanukkah), where everything goes in cycles. Man becomes angel, and angel becomes man. Head becomes foot and foot becomes head. Everything goes in cycles, revolving and alternating. All things interchange, one from another and one to another, elevating the low and lowering the high.

All things have one root. There are transcendental beings, such as angels, which have no connection with the material. There is the celestial world, whose essence is very tenuous. Finally, there is the world below, which is completely physical. All three come from different realms but all have the same root.

All creation is like a rotating wheel, revolving and oscillating. At one time, something can be on top like a head with another on the bottom like a foot. Then the situation is reversed. Head becomes foot and foot becomes head. Man becomes angel and angel becomes man. Thus, our sages teach us that certain angels were cast down from heaven. They entered physical bodies and were subject to all worldly lusts. Other angels were sent on missions to our world and had to clothe themselves in physical bodies. We also find cases where human beings literally became angels. (*Targum Yonatan* on Genesis 6:4, 18:2 and 5:24; Numbers 25:12, etc.)

For the world is like a rotating wheel. It spins like a Dreidel, with all things emanating from one root.

The feet of some are also higher than the heads of others. For in the transcendental worlds, the lowest level of an upper world is higher than the highest level of a lower one. And still, everything revolves in cycles.

The primary concept of the Temple is the revolving wheel. The Temple was in the category of "the superior below and the inferior above". God lowered His presence into the Temple and this is "the superior below". The Temple's pattern was engraved on high: "the inferior above".

The Temple is therefore like a rotating wheel, where everything revolves and is reversed. The Temple refutes philosophical logic. God is above every transcendental concept, and it is beyond all logic that He should constrict Himself into the vessels of the Temple. "Behold the heaven and the heaven of heaven cannot contain You, how much less this Temple!" (I Kings 8:27). But God brought His presence into the Temple and thereby refuted philosophical logic. Philosophy cannot explain how man can have any influence on high. It cannot say how a mere animal can be sacrificed and rise as a sweet savor giving pleasure to God. They explain that this pleasure is the fulfillment of His will, but how can we even apply the concept of desire to God?

But God placed His presence in the Temple and accepts the animal as a sweet savor. He made the fact contradict philosophical logic. Such logic is crushed by the Dreidel, the rotating wheel which brings the "superior below and the inferior above".

Rabbi Nachman's Wisdom #40

Out in the Meadows

*I*saac was 123 years old when he blessed Jacob, and directly afterwards he instructed him to leave home and go out of the Land of Israel to Padan Aram, home of his mother Rebecca's family, to find a wife. From this point on until the end of the Book of Genesis the tumultuous life of Jacob and his wives and children becomes the central focus of the biblical narrative, though in fact Isaac lived on for another 57 years until the age of 180 (*Rashi* on Genesis 27:2; *ibid.* 28:1ff and 35:28).

Having taught the true meaning of holy *Gevurah*, power and strength, how to use it and how to sweeten its harshness, Isaac's work was essentially complete. Through the personalities and careers of Abraham and Isaac, holy *Chessed* (love and kindness) and *Gevurah* (power and strength) -- the two main poles of creation, "right" and "left" columns of the sefirotic "tree" -- had been manifested in all their beauty. The stage was now set for the supremely wise Jacob to show how to join these two opposing poles together to make the perfect synthesis: *Tiferet*, Beauty. Jacob's life and some of its lessons for the contemporary age will be the subject of Part III of this book.

Isaac's task had been to continue and develop Abraham's pathway of charity and justice with the utmost self-discipline and devotion. Central to this task was the inner discipline of prayer and meditation: "And Isaac went out to meditate in the field towards evening" (Genesis 24:63).

The Field chosen by Isaac for this supreme labor -- on the Mountain where his father Abraham had bound him as a sacrifice -- would become the site of the Holy Temple, God's House of Prayer for all the nations. Our understanding of the meaning of the Temple and its significance for mankind today can be greatly deepened by contemplating the different ways in which each of the three patriarchs envisioned it, Abraham as a Mountain, Isaac as a Field and Jacob as a House.

A field yields its best fruits through systematic work combined with faith and trust in the Creator. Isaac's unswerving pursuit of justice combined with his devotion to prayer and meditation are reflected in the Temple later built on the site of Isaac's field.

By the side of the main Temple courtyard was the regular meeting place of the Sanhedrin, the Supreme Council of Torah Sages. Isaac had taught that all success, both in this world and the next, depends upon the pursuit of charity and justice. This lesson is to go out to all the world from the Sanhedrin in Jerusalem, whose mission is to teach the world God's law: the Seven Universal Laws that apply to all mankind and the six hundred and thirteen commandments specifically given to the Children of Israel. "From Zion will go forth the Torah..." (Isaiah 2:3).

The same verse continues: "... and the Word of *HaVaYaH* from Jerusalem" (*ibid.*). The whole purpose of God's law is to bring the entire universe back into harmonious unity with God. This can only be accomplished when people learn that in any and every field of human activity human endeavors can bear genuine fruits only when we conduct ourselves as partners with God in the work of creation. Man's uniqueness in the creation derives from the fact that he has been vested with the very keys of creation, the letters of speech, which he has the power to manipulate in prayer and meditation. It is through prayer that man draws divine blessing into all that he does. When man attains his destiny, his very words become *Dvar HaVaYaH*, the "Word of God". As a place of prayer and devotion, the Temple is a lesson to all mankind that our words of prayer, song and praise have the power to influence the highest realms. For "My House will be called the House of Prayer for all the nations" (Isaiah 56:7).

Fields and Meadows

Although the "field" in which Isaac pursued his work of prayer and devotion is especially associated with the Temple Mount in Jerusalem, actual fields and meadows have been favored by Jewish mystics and spiritual seekers throughout the ages for spiritual work of various kinds.

The theme of the field as a place for spiritual communion recurs in many biblical passages (e.g. Genesis 37:7 & 15, Judges 13:9, Samuel I, ch. 19, Ruth ch's 2-3, etc.).

In later times, many rabbis and teachers have discussed the benefits of spending time in fields and meadows, including the practical health benefits, as in the following passage from the classic collection of rabbinic wisdom on spiritual and physical healthcare, *Tav Yehoshua* ("Joshua's Note") by R. Yehoshua Briskin, who was a rabbi in Odessa in the mid-19th century:

> "One should always be careful to rise like a lion early in the morning in time for the sun-rise and to spend *three or four hours* in the open fields breathing the clear, pure air, walking about in the fields, the hills and mountains. One should do this every day for health, strength and complete healing...."
>
> Tav Yehoshua 3:3

It is sad that many people trapped in today's enormous, sprawling urban agglomerations are simply unaware of the benefits to health, bodily and spiritual, of spending time in the peace and quiet of open fields and meadows. All the more reason why we should remind ourselves of teachings about the value of this practice, as echoed in the words of Rebbe Nachman:

> "It is best to seclude yourself and meditate in the meadows outside the city. Go to a grassy field, for the grass will awaken your heart" (Rabbi Nachman's Wisdom #227).

"When summer begins to approach it is very good to meditate in the fields. This is a time when you can pray to God with longing and yearning. When every bush of the field begins to return to life and grow, they all yearn to be included in prayer and meditation." (*ibid.* #98).

Those who do not have access to open fields and meadows on a regular basis can greatly benefit from periodic retreats to some peaceful spot to reconnect with nature and with their inner selves. Many followers of Rebbe Nachman practice this regularly until today, whether for a few hours from time to time or even for periods of several days or more. The same applies to followers of other schools, such as Novardok, whose adherents try to take time out in the countryside each year, especially in the springtime in preparation for the Passover festival and in the late summer in preparation for Rosh Hashanah, the New Year.

Besides recommending going to the fields and meadows for prayer and meditation, chassidic masters such as the Baal Shem Tov and Rebbe Nachman would also sometimes give over their teachings to their students out in nature (see Rabbi Nachman's Wisdom #144).

In teaching Torah out in the fields and meadows, these chassidic masters were following a most ancient tradition. It is evident in numerous passages throughout the *Zohar*, where many of the teachings by Rabbi Shimon bar Yochai and his other companions were first taught while they were walking through the open countryside. Similarly, the outstanding 16th century kabbalistic master, Rabbi Yitzchak Luria (*ARI*), explained many of the details of the kabbalistic scheme to his outstanding student, Rabbi Chaim Vital while they walked around the hills and meadows of the Galilee in northern Israel (see *Shaar Hagilgulim*, etc.).

It is fitting that it was the *ARI* (who himself bore the name of Isaac, man of the Field) who made the Field a part of Jewish consciousness every week at the commencement of the Shabbat. The *ARI* did this through his "Kabbalat Shabbat" practice of going out into the fields with his students late Friday afternoons in order to welcome the Shabbat "Queen". Facing west towards the setting sun they would sing, dance and rejoice together. This practice is recalled in synagogues throughout the world when in the Kabbalat Shabbat service at the commencement of Shabbat the worshipers chant all or part of the "*Lecha Dodi*" ("Come, my beloved!") song of welcoming the Shabbat while facing west instead of the normal direction of prayer towards Jerusalem.

In the *Zohar* and other mystical works the true spiritual seekers are called the "reapers of the field" (*Chatzdei Chakla*). In the words of one of the *ARI*'s Shabbat songs, "Rejoice, reapers of the field!" (Shabbat Morning Zemirot). "Those who go about weeping bearing the burden of the seed will surely return in joy bearing sheaves!" (Psalm 126:6). May we speedily see the fruits of all our labors and witness the rebuilding of the Temple quickly in our days. Amen.

"Jacob dreamed: There was a ladder with angels ascending and descending.... And Jacob awoke from his sleep and he said, Indeed HaVaYaH is in this place and I did not know. And he was filled with awe, and he said: How awesome is this place, this is none other than the House of God and this is the gateway to Heaven" (Genesis 28 vv.11 & 16-17).

PART III

The House

JACOB

MOTIFS: The House / Night / Rebirth / Element: Air / Color: Yellow-Green / Mother Letter: *Aleph* / Divine Name: *YHVH* / Attributes: The Center Column -- Truth (*Emet*), Knowledge (*Daat*), Justice (*Mishpat*), Harmony & Beauty (*Tiferet*), Foundation & Procreation (*Yesod*) / The labor of Torah Study and

Adam's eating from the tree of knowledge ruptured man's primal harmony with God, throwing us out of alignment with nature. To complete Abraham and Isaac's work to rectify the sin, Jacob taught humanity about the House. Only if we learn to lead lives of harmony within our very homes and houses -- the most basic units of human organization -- will humanity be able to make peace with the environment and survive.

Jacob's entire life was devoted to house-building: the building of his own household of four wives, twelve sons and a daughter, and preparing for the building of the House of Prayer for All Mankind destined to stand in the Mountain-Field where Abraham and Isaac had worshipped.

In flight from his vengeful brother Esau, Jacob arrived at this place of destiny and lay down to sleep. He dreamed of a ladder with angels ascending and descending. Awakening, Jacob understood: "This is none other than the House of God and this is the Gate of Heaven" (Genesis 28:17). Laying the corner-stone, he took a solemn vow of dedication to God.

Jacob's work of construction began in earnest when he arrived in Charan at the house of his deceptive Uncle

Laban and embarked on twenty years of labor, first to earn the wives with whom he built his family and then to breed the livestock that were their means of support.

Jacob's supreme moment came as he returned with his family to the Land of Israel, only to find Esau advancing towards him with four hundred armed warriors. Jacob's main struggle was on the spiritual level against Esau's guardian angel. Overcoming the angel, Jacob was given the name Israel, "for you have striven with God and men and you have prevailed" (Genesis 32:29).

Esau went on his way, while Jacob "journeyed to Succot and built himself a house, and for his livestock he made huts" (Genesis 33:17). In an act of collective repentance, Jacob brought his entire household and all who were with him to Beit El, the House of God.

Jacob's heritage to his descendants is the priceless fabric of spiritual teaching and practice that keeps our awareness constantly focused upon the wonders of God's creation day to day, from week to week, from month to month, on the festivals, and from year to year. Cherishing these traditions will deepen people's spiritual awareness and reverence for God's creation, thereby greatly contributing to current efforts to protect the global environment.

The House

*W*hen Adam violated God's command and ate from the forbidden fruit, it ruptured the original innocent harmony that had existed between man and God. In consequence, man's alignment with nature was also upset. Before, in the Garden of Eden, all Adam's needs were immediately available. But from now on: "The land is cursed because of you: through toil you will eat all the days of your life. Thorns and thistles, it will sprout for you, and you will eat the grass of the field. By the sweat of your brow you will eat bread..." (Genesis 3:17-19).

Until today the great majority of humanity still struggles to eke out a bare living from an often hostile environment. Even those who have everything they need and more are often plagued by a deep-rooted insecurity about the future. It is this insecurity that drives people to the compulsive pursuit of wealth, fueling endless strife and wars over conflicting interests.

Today we watch helplessly as reckless greed, extravagance and waste cause irreversible damage to the global environment. More and more people recognize the serious threat to long-term human survival. Yet for all the talk about environmental responsibility, the practical protective measures being taken by governments, industry and others fall far short of what is necessary to halt the destruction.

This is not surprising since the secular materialistic culture dominant in most of the world is actually fueled by waste and extravagance. "Eat, drink and be merry for tomorrow we die!"

The mission of Abraham, Isaac and Jacob was to forge a path for all humanity in order to transcend the innate selfishness that caused Adam to sin and which today threatens his descendants' very survival. These Founding Fathers came to teach mankind that, for all our human intelligence and ability, we must recognize that God is above all of us. If we want it to go well for us, we have no alternative but to submit to God's superior wisdom and follow His law.

For Abraham, the service of God was a lofty Mountain. For Isaac, it was a Field of steady toil and effort. However, great mountains and even fields are beyond the range of many people's normal experience. The exalted spiritual service taught by Abraham and Isaac still had to be brought down to a level where it could be understood and applied practically by everyone, men, women and children, each on his or her own level. For only when all humanity can understand and pursue the service of God will it be possible to rectify Adam's sin and restore man's harmony with God.

Jacob's mission was to make serving God comprehensible and applicable to everyone. He did it by explaining the service of God in terms of the idea of a House.

In the words of Rebbe Nachman:

The nations of the world cannot know the greatness of the Holy One except through Jacob. Thus, in time to come all humanity will say, "House of *Jacob*, go, let us walk in the light of *HaVaYaH*" (Isaiah 2:5). For Jacob revealed God more than the other founding fathers. "Abraham called it a mountain and Isaac called it a field" (*Pesachim* 88a). A field is more understandable and more necessary to people than a mountain. But "Jacob called it a *House*" (*ibid.*) A house is more of a place of human habitation than a field. In other words, Jacob called the place of the Holy Temple, which is a place of prayer, a *House*. A house is a place that people live in all the time. Jacob elevated prayer -- the service of God -- from being a distant mountain or field to being a *House*. This is an idea that people grasp more readily than that of a mountain or a field. Everyone understands the idea of a house, as it says, "For My *House* will be called the House of Prayer for *all the nations*" (Isaiah 56:7).

Likutey Moharan I:10

Jacob's vision of the House is of crucial importance to humanity today as we face the challenge of surviving on Earth and creating a meaningful global culture.

A house is a building. Houses -- and factories, offices, shops, schools, colleges, places of entertainment, medical facilities and all kinds of other buildings -- are the basic spatial units around which civilized human life is organized. It is houses, houses and more houses that make up the vast urban agglomerations in which almost half the human race already live and which form the main centers of the materialistic culture that is destroying the global environment.

This culture encourages people to make their homes and houses a major focus of their materialistic aspirations, equipping them with lavish comforts, conveniences, entertainment technology, jacuzzis, exercise machines, etc. etc. all in a phantom quest to create a pseudo-paradise in which to relax and enjoy all the delights of the flesh, each according to his tastes.

Jacob came to teach mankind a different way. We must put *soul* into the spaces in which we live. We must devote our main efforts into *sanctifying* our homes and houses so as to make them dwelling-places of divine light, love, kindness, peace and harmony. Our homes and houses should be places where we not only sleep and eat but also pray, meditate, study, talk about God and discuss ways of serving Him, rejoice with one another, sing together, dance...

Jacob taught this especially through the idea of the Temple, the House of Prayer for all the Nations. The Temple is a kind of model house, a centerpoint for all mankind to direct themselves towards in order to gain inspiration about how we should live and conduct ourselves in our own homes and houses. It is precisely because everyone understands the idea of a house that it is such a powerful metaphor through which to teach mankind about God and how to serve Him.

We must learn to revere God in our homes and houses and indeed in the most intimate areas of our lives. We must learn to revere God as the *source* of our lives, the source of our very food and drink and everything else we consume. We must learn to moderate our consumption according to the rules and norms laid down in God's wisdom. Only then will humanity be able to make peace with the natural environment -- God's creation. Only then will we survive.

House-Building

"How goodly are your tents, Jacob, your dwelling places Israel"
(Numbers 24:5)

*F*rom the very outset, just as soon as the contrasting characters of Isaac's twin sons Jacob and Esau started to become apparent, it was clear that Jacob's preference was to be *inside*. "Esau was a man who understood hunting, a man of the field, but Jacob was a sincere man sitting in tents" (Genesis 25:27).

There were two tents in particular in which the young Jacob used to sit: those of his two august teachers, his grandfather Abraham (who lived until Jacob was aged 15), and his father Isaac. Abraham and Isaac were polar opposites. Abraham, the breakaway, the originator, founder of the tradition, was all *Chessed*, expansive outreach, love and kindness. Isaac, the assiduous student, the follower and receiver of the tradition, was the model of *Gevurah*, submission, strict discipline and judgment.

Chessed and *Gevurah* both absolutely need each other. By themselves, wild, untrammeled love and cold, compassionless justice can each be destructive in the extreme (as exemplified in Ishmael and Esau, who embodied the unholy aspects of their respective fathers' special traits). Jacob's task was to show how to bring the polar opposites of *Chessed* and

Gevurah into balance in order to make a perfect whole. This was an integral part of Jacob's work of building his House.

For this reason, Jacob sat in the tents of each of his masters learning from both. The Hebrew word for tent, *Ohel*, has the connotation of shining light (see Job 31:26). A tent or canopy "shines down" in the sense of giving definition to the space beneath it. The contrasting ways and teachings of the two founding fathers Abraham and Isaac were two canopies of light shining down upon the young Jacob. To put it in terms of dialectics, Jacob took Abraham's thesis and Isaac's antithesis and fused them into the unique synthesis that would be Jacob's heritage to all his descendants, the Children of Israel.

Whereas the twin lights of Abraham and Isaac shone *down* from above to below, Jacob's light was to be a pillar of ascent from below *upwards*. Jacob's synthesis enables the spiritual seeker to return to God's original unity, which could begin to be revealed initially only through first revealing plurality in the form of the two apparent opposites *Chessed* and *Gevurah*, the two fundamental poles of creation as embodied in Abraham and Isaac. Jacob completed the holy triad by revealing the unifying quality of *Tiferet*, synthesis, harmony and beauty, forging a dynamic unity out of the contrasting aspects revealed in *Chessed* and *Gevurah*.

Tiferet strives ever upwards transcending these two counterpoised poles to rise to their source in the unifying root quality of *Daat*, "Knowledge", and then rising yet higher, beyond the counterpoised aspects of *Chokhmah* (holistic

"Wisdom") and *Binah* (analytic "Understanding"), right up to *Keter*, the Crown, the Will of Wills, the Supreme Source: ultimate unity.

Outside and Inside

Abraham and Isaac's nomadic life in tents, on the mountain and in the field, suggests a certain lack of permanence. For the Godly revelations they each embodied, were stages in the unfolding of a greater whole that was still to be completed and perfected. It was Jacob who was to give the holy tradition the permanence of a House, a fixed and enduring structure.

Abraham, the man of the Mountain, and Isaac, man of the Field, are both associated with the outdoors. But if Jacob was the builder of the House, that is not to say that he only knew about life indoors. On the contrary, at the end of twenty years of exile from his parental home and land, Jacob, defending himself against the accusations of his father-in-law Laban, reminds him: "These twenty years that I've been with you [shepherding your sheep in the outdoors] ... scorching heat ravaged me by day and frost by night..." (Genesis 31:38-40). Jacob was just as much an outdoors person -- a profound student and lover of nature and a watcher of the heavens -- as his fathers and teachers, Abraham and Isaac.

In fact, Jacob was able to build his House only by first knowing the outside -- the Mountain and the Field -- "inside out". Jacob became a master of both. He began his journey to Laban with a visit to the very Mountain where Abraham had gone to sacrifice, namely Isaac's Field (Genesis 28:11; see next chapter). Twenty years later, confronted by Laban, Jacob himself "sacrificed on the *mountain*" (*ibid.* v.54), albeit a different mountain. Jacob was also a man of the field, as when he "sent and called Rachel and Leah to the *field*" (Genesis 31:4) and when he came to Isaac to receive the blessings and Isaac said: "See the smell of my son is like the smell of a *field* that *HaVaYaH* has blessed" (*ibid.* 27:27).

Homelessness and Exile

Harmony is forged out of the raw materials provided by chaos. True harmony comes from dealing successfully with every kind of opposing force and, wherever possible, finding a way to integrate each one so as to make it work as part of the greater whole.

For Jacob to build his House it was therefore necessary for him to confront every kind of hardship and deal successfully with each challenge, transforming it into something that would actually contribute to the overall structure he sought to achieve. With consummate skill Jacob applied different *Chessed* or *Gevurah* traits according to specific need in each of the different situations he faced. The right balance in any given situation is called *Mishpat*: correct, fair judgment taking all factors into consideration. This is an aspect of *Emet*, truth. "You gave *truth* to Jacob" (Micah 7: 20). Nothing is more precious than knowing the true, just course to take in all situations, especially when dealing with conflicting aspects of one's very self.

For someone trying to build his House it is striking how much of Jacob's life was spent in bitter exile from home. According to tradition, after he received the blessings from Isaac instead of Esau, Jacob spent fourteen years unremitting study with Shem and Eiver. This was followed by Jacob's twenty-year stint with Laban. He then spent another two years on the road before finally coming home to Isaac. At the end of his life Jacob again went into exile, this time in Egypt, where he went to be reunited with his long-lost son Joseph. Only after Jacob's death was he carried back to the Land of Israel by his sons and finally brought to rest in his eternal home in the Cave of Machpelah in Hebron.

Building the Foundations

Yet Jacob's years in exile from home were themselves years of building. He started off studying with Shem and Eiver -- because the House he had to construct could only be built by going to the very roots of the Torah tradition, namely the wisdom that had been passed down from Adam to Noah and which Noah in turn handed on to his son Shem from whom it came to Shem's great-grandson Eiver.

"A man must leave his father and his mother and attach himself to his wife and they must become one flesh" (Genesis 2:24). After Jacob received the blessings instead of Esau, Rebecca and Isaac both counseled him to leave the Promised Land and go to Padan Aram to find a wife from among the "other side" of Abraham's family back in the land from which he had come. Laban was now their head. It was to Laban that Jacob headed immediately after his fourteen years with Shem and Eiver. It was to build his own family that Jacob went into exile from his parental home. For the first step in building his House was to gather together the *souls* who would be living in it.

Building his House was to turn into a protracted, hard and at times tormenting labor. To inspire himself as he first set off for Padan Aram, Jacob stopped at the holy spot where Abraham had built the altar to sacrifice Isaac. There was Jacob alone out on this Mountain-Field as the sun went down, leaving the world to darkness. Before bedding down for the night at this exposed spot, Jacob took stones to make a rough structure where he could lie down more safely, a first primitive "house". It was on that spot that he had his dream of the ladder with angels going up and down, and when he awoke he said, "This is none other than the House of God" (Genesis 28:17). This dream was Jacob's guiding vision until he completed his task (see next chapter).

Family Troubles

At Laban's, Jacob's work began in earnest. A house is far more than the mere building, the outward physical structure. The essence of the house is the souls living a meaningful, harmonious life together in it. To build his house, Jacob had to work hard to earn his wives Rachel and Leah, the amazing women who together with their two hand-maidens Bilhah and Zilpah were to mother his children. The holy rivalry between these women only added to Jacob's other trials during the years of child-bearing and early rearing, as their family of twelve totally different, highly individualistic boys and one girl took shape. Building houses means dealing with real live people the way they actually are, including cheats and liars like Laban.

When Jacob eventually left Laban to return home, the entire structure of his House was in peril of being razed down to the very foundation because of the raging fury of the jealous Esau. As Jacob entered the Land of Israel together with his long caravan of wives, little children and household, his camels, donkeys, cattle and flocks, Esau came out to meet them with four hundred armed warriors! The opposite of building is destruction. Jacob would only be able to create his amazing house of love and peace if he could first overcoming Esau, the extreme of Gevurah, harsh judgment, brute force and destruction.

With supreme wisdom and subtlety Jacob succeeded in establishing a modus vivendi with Esau, after which he immediately threw himself into the business of practical housebuilding. "And on that day Esau went back on his path to Seir. And Jacob journeyed to Succot and *built himself a house* and for his cattle he made huts (*Succot*), therefore he called the name of the place Succot" (Genesis 33:17-18). Jacob was not only worried about the humans. He also showed his practical concern for the animals. This is because the peace and harmony Jacob sought to construct must prevail throughout the entire creation.

Just when Jacob wanted to settle down and dwell peacefully in the land, disaster after disaster befell him. His daughter Dinah was seduced by a Canaanite prince. His beloved wife

Rachel died, after which his oldest son Reuven tried to force a major change in Jacob's private life. Afterwards, Jacob's favorite son Joseph was sold into slavery by his jealous brothers, who told Jacob that Joseph had been killed. Next Jacob's son Judah, having seen two sons die as a punishment for sexual crime, himself became involved in a major scandal with his daughter-in-law....

Issues involving sexual morality recur again and again in Jacob's life. This is because sexual purity is the vital foundation of a truly healthy, harmonious society, nowhere more so than in the home. Only through sexual purity are pure, holy souls born to people a world in which justice, kindness, courtesy, love and harmony prevail.

Another recurring theme in the story of Jacob even more prominent than that of sexuality is the theme of livelihood and eating. The very first Bible story about Jacob tells how he was preparing food for Isaac -- the pot of soup that he exchanged with Esau in return for Esau's birthright. Many of Jacob's years with Laban were taken up with building an economic support base by breeding herds of sheep with which to support himself. Joseph, having been sold into slavery in Egypt, ends up as Pharaoh's chief minister and comes up with a plan to save the whole country from seven years of famine, which is the opposite of livelihood. It is this famine that eventually leads to the denouement of the story of Joseph's disappearance, because the famine forces Jacob to send his sons to buy food in Egypt, where they are at last reunited with Joseph, who calls on Jacob to come to live in Egypt.

Life in all homes is bound up with the livelihood coming into those homes. Much of human consumption, whether of food or anything else, actually takes place within the house and home. This is why so much of the story of Jacob centers on the theme of livelihood. When Adam ate the fruit of the tree of knowledge, it was a sin of eating and consumption. To build the true House, Jacob had to rectify this flaw.

God is One

Jacob's moment of triumph came on his deathbed. After all his years of toil and trouble as he built his house step by step until everything was in place, he finally asked his sons what they believed in. All twelve replied with one accord: "Hear, Israel, *HaVaYaH* is our God, *HaVaYaH* is one!" (*Midrash*).

Preparing to pass on from this world, Jacob had the joy of seeing twelve fine, strong heirs determined to continue the tradition of his fathers with perfect loyalty and devotion. They were ready to build *their* houses and rear *their* children so as to multiply the House of Israel in order to bring the message of God's unity, harmony and love to all the world. Jacob had built his House and he could finally rest.

Jacob's Ladder

Jacob left Be'er Sheva and set off for Charan. And he reached the place and he stopped there for the night because the sun had gone down. He took from the stones of the place and made a pillow for his head, and he lay down in that place.

He dreamed: There was a ladder set on the ground and its top reached the heavens, and there were angels of God going up and down on it. There was HaVaYaH standing over him, and He said: "I am HaVaYaH God of Abraham your father and God of Isaac. The Land that you are lying on I will give to you and your seed. And your seed will be like the dust of the earth and you will break forth to the west, the east, the north and the south, and all the families of the Earth will be blessed through you and through your seed. See, I am with you and I will guard you wherever you go and I will bring you back to this land. For I will not abandon you until I have done what I have told you.

Jacob awoke from his sleep and he said, "Indeed HaVaYaH is in this place, but I did not know." He was filled with awe. He said: "How awesome is this place. This is none other than the House of God and this is the Gate to Heaven." Jacob rose early in the morning and took the stone he had placed under his head and set it up as a pillar and poured oil on its head. He called the name of that place Beit El, though Luz was the name of the city at first. Jacob took a vow, saying: "If God will be with me and guard me on this path I am traveling and will give me bread to eat and clothes to wear and I come home in peace to the house of my father, HaVaYaH will be my God. And this stone that I have set up as a pillar will be the House of God and from all that You give me I will set aside a tithe for You.

Genesis 28:10-22

"Jacob Left Be'er Sheva and Set Off for Charan"

After Jacob received the blessings instead of Esau, Isaac and Rebecca counseled him to leave the Land of Israel and go to Charan to find a wife from among the family of Rebecca's brother Laban.

According to tradition, when Jacob set off from Be'er Sheva, the raging Esau sent his son Eliphaz to kill him. However, Eliphaz had grown up on Isaac's lap. When he caught up with Jacob he could not bring himself to kill him. Eliphaz asked Jacob what he should do about his father's orders. The wise Jacob advised Eliphaz to take all his money since "a poor man is as good as dead". This way it would be as if Eliphaz had killed him (*Rashi* on Genesis 29:11).

Isaac had blessed Jacob with great prosperity. "God will give you from the dew of the heavens and from the fat of the earth and abundant corn and wine..." (Genesis 27:28). Isaac and Rebecca were themselves immensely wealthy. Yet as Jacob set off at the start of his life's journey, it was not as a wealthy heir with a bulging wallet. Jacob crossed the Jordan with nothing more than a stick in his hand (Genesis 32:11). His inheritance from Abraham and Isaac was not one of unearned wealth and privilege. It was to lead a life of toil and labor in the service of *HaVaYaH*, using his wits, his lips and his very hands.

"And He Reached the Place"

"Jacob left Be'er Sheva and set off for Charan. And he reached the place *and he stopped there for the night because the sun had gone down. He took from the stones of the place and made a pillow for his head and he lay down in that place"* (Genesis 28:10-11).

The Hebrew text of the Bible clearly states that Jacob reached not just "*a* place" but "*the* place", referring to a place whose identity is already known to the reader from having been mentioned earlier in the text. However, in the immediately preceding verses there is no mention of any place. Which place did Jacob reach?

The Hebrew word for "the place", *HaMakom*, alludes to God, Who created both the spiritual and physical space within which creation took place. God is thus "*The Place* of the world". Yet the world is not God's place in the sense that God cannot be said to be located within the world, though He is certainly present in the world. At the same time God is totally beyond the world.

The *place* that Jacob reached was the place of encounter with God, the very same *place* mentioned earlier in the Bible narrative in the account of Abraham's binding of Isaac. God had said to Abraham: "Take your son Isaac and go to the Land of Moriah and offer him up as an offering on one of the mountains that I will tell you... On the third day Abraham lifted up his eyes and he saw *the place* from afar... And they came to *the place* that God told him" (Genesis 22 vv. 2, 4 & 9).

The *place* that Jacob reached was none other than Abraham's mountain. Jacob arrived there a fugitive stripped of all material wealth. Poor, humbled, vulnerable, all Jacob had was his heart's longing and yearning for God and his willingness to serve Him. Having cast away the coin of this-worldliness from before his eyes, Jacob was ready to climb Abraham's Mountain.

Abraham's Mountain, Isaac's Field was more than a place of merely sentimental personal meaning for Jacob. It was from the dust of this spot that the body of Adam, father of all mankind, had been formed. This was the place where Noah sacrificed after the flood.

And it was more. According to tradition, this is the very spot that was the "growthpoint" from which the entire Earth emanated at the time of creation. The physical creation -- *Yesh*, Being -- came forth from *Ayin*, Nothingness, the higher, undefinable, untouchable spiritual reality. The Temple Mount in Jerusalem is thus the exact point at which the physical world intersects with the world of spirit.

The Foundation Stone

The holiest spot on the Temple Mount is the place where the Holy of Holies -- the inner sanctum of the Temple -- stood.

The floor of the Holy of Holies consisted of an immense natural stone called *Evven Shetiyah*, the "Foundation Stone". On it stood the golden Ark of the Covenant containing Moses' Tablets of Stone and covered by the golden *Kaporet* with its two cherubs or angels with outspread wings.

The significance of the Foundation Stone is explained in the following passage from *Mishkeney Elyon* ("Dwellings of the Most High") by Rabbi Moshe Chaim Luzzatto on the kabbalistic meaning of the Temple and its design.

When the Creator wanted to create this world, He included everything that was to come into being in ten great luminaries [the *Sefirot*] from which all created beings emerged like branches coming out of the trunk of the tree. Thus, there is nothing that does not have its place in the Supreme Chariot.

The last of these ten lights is called *Shechinah* ("The Indwelling Presence" [Sefirah of *Malchut*, Kingship]), and everything that exists is rooted there. Understand this well: besides the root that each thing which exists has in the other higher lights, it also has its root in the *Shechinah*, which is metaphorically called the Mother of Children.

Know that there is one particular *place* known to her in which all these roots are merged in unity. That place is the root of all things. There the Earth is rooted and all that is in it, the Heavens and the Heavens of the Heavens and all their hosts.

And at this meeting point where all the different roots come together in one place, in the middle can be seen a certain "stone". This stone is most precious. It includes every kind of charm and beauty. This is called *Evven Shetiyah*, the Foundation Stone. And thus, there actually is such a stone in our world here down below in the place of the Holy of Holies in the Temple.

From this stone tracks and pathways extend in all directions leading to all the individual things that exist. Where these paths and tracks start leading off from the stone in all directions they are major general paths. Every single item in creation knows its own path and from these general paths each item takes its specific share of nourishment given to it from the King. Further away from the stone, these major paths divide into countless numbers of smaller tracks, for here are the specific roots of all things from the greatest to the smallest, and every single item has its own track. But the ultimate root of all these tracks and pathways is to be found at the place I mentioned.

Where they all come together in the stone that is in the middle of this place, from there the Creator watches over them and examines all of them with a single glance. Of this it is written: "He fashions the hearts of them all *together* and discerns all their doings" (Psalms 33:15). For this stone is the very heart of the universe and there everything is joined together in unity under the watch of the King.

Mishkeney Elyon

Rebbe Nachman of Breslov sheds further light on the Foundation Stone:

The world has a foundation stone. Channels emanate from this stone, reaching every land. The Midrash teaches us that the wise King Solomon knew the details of these channels and was therefore able to plant all types of trees. If people knew the exact location of these subterranean channels, they would be able to grow fruit trees even in these lands. They could grow many trees that never grow here now. Each channel has the power to stimulate a particular species. Even if a particular channel does not pass through our land, all channels are intertwined and flow into each other. If one knew the exact place, he could plant any type of tree. If one knew the location of all channels, he could dig a well and know where to plant trees around it. He could then make any type of tree grow. The foundation stone of the world constantly rises and descends. If one knows its position then he knows what to plant at a particular time. All these things are concealed from the world, for some things may not be revealed. People say that the world is gaining knowledge. But earlier generations made the primary discoveries, and this took the greatest wisdom. Later generations make discoveries only because earlier ones prepared the way.

Rabbi Nachman's Wisdom #60

These teachings of Rabbi Moshe Chaim Luzzatto and Rebbe Nachman add a new dimension to the concept of energy lines around Earth as discussed in a number of contemporary scientific and spiritual works. The *place* that Jacob reached is the brain and nerve-center of the entire Earth, with nerves spreading out from it in every direction linking everywhere in creation.

Jacob's quest, then, was for the top, the brain, the "head" of creation. In the account of Jacob's dream, the Hebrew word *Rosh*, "head", appears no less than four times in eight verses. Jacob was in search of the centerpoint and source of all creation, *Bereishit* (Genesis 1:1). The universe is like a House, a *Bayit*, fashioned by God as a dwelling-place for His glorious Presence. Jacob was in search of the *Rosh Bayit*, Head of the House. The Hebrew letters of *Rosh Bayit* are an anagram of *Bereishit*, the first word of the Torah, from which all else emanates. Jacob was searching for the point at which the physical world connects with its source, the "Gate of Heaven".

"The Sun Had Gone Down"

Until now we have focused on the spatial significance of this *place*. It also has the utmost significance in relation to *time*.

Just as Jacob arrived there the sun set, ushering in the night. As we have seen, Abraham is associated with sunrise and Morning: "Abraham rose early in the morning" (Genesis 22:3 etc.). Isaac is associated with the declining sun, Afternoon: "Isaac went out to meditate in the field towards evening" (Genesis 24:63). Jacob's distinctive quality is that of Night, which can be not only a time of physical darkness but also one of spiritual darkness, doubt, uncertainty, insecurity, exile, trouble, torment.... Jacob's task was to take the teachings of his fathers Abraham and Isaac and apply them not just when times are good but even amidst darkness, hardship and difficulty: "Night". Jacob's mission would be to shine the combined light of Abraham and Isaac to light up the darkness through *faith* and *trust in God* even in the face of the worst negativity.

It is true that Jacob is also associated with the Sun (Genesis 32:32 and 37:9). This is because he always looked towards the "sun" of Wisdom for inspiration and guidance (see *Likutey Moharan* I, 1). But it was specifically after he was renamed Israel that Jacob became associated with the sun, which symbolizes Jacob as he will be revealed in all his glory in the future world when the dark side of creation will have been rectified. However, in our present benighted world of toil and pain Jacob is associated with night-time and darkness, a time of *searching* for God with the torchlight of faith.

Indeed, when the sun goes down, leaving the world to darkness and faith, something amazing happens. As the light fades from the skies, one by one tiny points of light can be seen twinkling in the sky. Gradually we see more and more... until eventually, on a dark night, countless thousands and thousands of stars and star clusters can be seen in every kind of evocative configuration. This glorious canopy could not be seen at all during the day because the stars are too faint to be visible when the skies are lit up by the sun. (Unfortunately for millions and millions of town- and even country-dwellers today, the night-time glow of our civilization simply hides all but the brightest stars, making it impossible ever to see the celestial canopy in anything resembling its true majesty as seen in deserts and other uninhabited areas.)

In a place where the skies can really be seen, the loss of daylight, far from signaling the final fading of perception, actually opens altogether new gates of perception, leading to deeper, subtler understanding. When we see the stars in all their magnificence and contemplate the mysteries of their configurations and the astronomic distances between them, we tiny earthlings can begin to get a faint inkling of the utter vastness of God's universe and the greatness of His works.

"Blessed are You, *HaVaYaH* our God, Ruler of the Universe: through His word He brings evening, in wisdom He opens the gates and with understanding changes the times and alters the seasons and arranges the stars and planets in their watches in the heavens according to His will" (from the Evening Service).

Renewal

The lights in the sky were given "to distinguish between the day and the night, and to be for signs and seasons and for days and years" (Genesis 1:14). From earliest times men have used the ever-repeated cycle of sunrise and sunset to measure "days", and they have used the sun's procession through the twelve celestial constellations every 365.25 days -- corresponding to the annual cycle of the seasons -- to measure "years".

A day passes very quickly. A year is quite a long time. People also need intermediary measures of time in order to plan their lives and see through their various current projects and activities. The weekly cycle of six working days followed by the Shabbat day of rest was divinely inbuilt in the very structure of creation, as we see from the first chapter of Genesis. But to measure the months God gave the Children of Israel a particular heavenly sign: the renewal of the moon.

Every twenty-nine and a half days the moon makes a complete orbit around the earth. Seen from earth the moon appears to go through different "phases" in the course of this orbital period owing to the its changing position relative to the earth and the sun. When the moon reaches its furthest point from the sun, the earth is directly aligned between the two of them. At night-time, we on earth then see the large round disk of the "full" moon. But as the moon continues its orbit, with every successive night a little more of it seems to have disappeared. Eventually all that's left is a thin crescent. Then, when the moon passes between the earth and the sun, it becomes totally invisible.

But immediately afterward this point the endlessly orbiting moon continues its journey and again starts moving away from the sun. And then, for a few brief moments after sunset on a clear evening, the thin crescent of the "new" moon can be seen on the western horizon before it too sets and disappears until the following evening.

"This renewal (*Chodesh*) will be for you the head of your months (*Rosh Chodoshim*)" (Exodus 12:2). In this first commandment given by God to the Jewish People, they were taught to measure their months by counting each one from the first sighting of the new moon at the very beginning of its waxing phase. The thin crescent of the new moon is a heavenly sign of renewal. The Hebrew word for month, *Chodesh*, means renewal!

In Temple times witnesses who had sighted the new moon had to come to Jerusalem to testify before the Beit Din (rabbinical court). Only then would the Beit Din announce that the new month had begun. This was called *Kiddush HaChodesh*, Sanctification of the Month. Time is more than a meaningless succession of moments. Time is holy if we make it so.

All the different Jewish holy days through the year fall on specific dates in their various months as laid down in the Torah. Since the beginning of the months in Temple times depends upon the sighting of the new moon, the exact timing of all the various holidays is thus determined by the sanctification of the new month by the Beit Din.

Each of the specific rituals associated with the various holidays has a particular effect on creation as a whole, playing a crucial role in its overall rectification. Understandably, all these effects can come about only if the holiday rituals are carried out at exactly the right heavenly time -- the "time of favor" -- in perfect alignment with the movements of the moon and other celestial bodies. The secret of the renewal of the moon (including the astronomical calculations made by the Beit Din to check that the witnesses could actually have seen it) was considered among the highest pinnacles of rabbinic wisdom.

In Temple times, the sanctification of the New Month by the Beit Din -- the key to the sanctification of time by man -- could take place only on the Temple Mount in Jerusalem. The Temple indeed was the central focus in all the rituals carried out on all the festivals throughout the year, the dates of which depended upon Rosh Chodesh, the New Moon.

The determination of Rosh Chodesh, the "Head of Renewal" which we use to measure time, thus depends upon the very place that is, as we have seen, the Rosh -- the "head" and brain-center -- of created space, the world. The *place* that Jacob reached is one where place and time are brought into perfect alignment through the commandment to sanctify the new month in the Temple after the new moon has been witnessed on the western horizon just after sunset. "The sun had gone down".

The Beginnings of a House

Jacob's arrival at the Temple Mount brought to this place where Space and Time come together the third division of creation: Spirit. For space, time and spirit are the three fundamental divisions of creation, as taught in Abraham's Sefer Yetzira where they are called Universe, Year and Soul.

That *place* on the Temple Mount is the *Rosh*, braincenter or "Head", of Space. It is at that very spot that *Rosh* Chodesh, the "Head" of Time, is declared. And now Jacob --a person,

Soul -- wanted to put down *his* head in that very spot in order to bring the three "heads" of Space, Time and Soul together.

"He took from the stones of the place and put them as *meRAASHotav*, a resting place for his head" (Genesis 28:11). The Hebrew word for "his head-rest", *meRAASHotav*, contains the letters of the word *ROSH*, Head.

By taking these stones and making a primitive structure where he could rest for the night on that exposed mountain-top, Jacob built his first rough house.

The house is the vital foundation for all human achievement. Most animals need some kind of home or nest that they either find or make for themselves. When Adam was expelled from the idyllic environment of Eden, his first need after food and clothing was for shelter from the elements, from predators and other threats to his existence. It was when men moved out of caves and started building residential and other structures for themselves that they began to develop the complex technical, economical, social, cultural and spiritual structures we call civilization.

Houses and buildings are the basic spatial units of human civilization. Throughout human history people have lavished resources in building every conceivable kind of structure for their convenience, comfort and glory, "like the glory of a man dwelling in a house" (Isaiah 44:13).

For Jacob, the purpose of the House is not to become a monument to its owner's greed for wealth and material self-indulgence. As creatures of flesh and blood, humans cannot do without a home base where they can rest, relax and attend to their various needs. It is indeed quite in order to aspire to a comfortable, pleasing home environment. "A beautiful home... and beautiful utensils expand a person's mind" (*Brachot* 57b). But as this very dictum implies, physical beautification of the home is not an end in itself. Its purpose is to serve a higher goal: expansion of the mind, *Daat*. It is through *Daat* that man becomes one with God.

For Jacob, the primary purpose of the physical house is to serve as our base for spiritual growth and connection with God. The house must be a fitting place for man to pursue *Daat*, the holy knowledge, insight and awareness that come through study, prayer, meditation, loving interaction with dear ones and friends, pursuit of the mitzvot and the application of God's teachings in all areas of our lives down to our most basic physical functions. Jacob's House, the Temple, is to serve as a model for all mankind of what our houses should be.

Daat

"With wisdom, *the house will be built and with* understanding *it will be established. And the rooms will be filled with* knowledge" (Proverbs 24:3-4)

In terms of the kabbalistic "tree" of the Sefirot, Jacob is the living embodiment of the sefirah of *Tiferet*, Harmony and Beauty. The place of *Tiferet* is in the center column of the central triad of sefirot, *Chessed-Gevurah-Tiferet*. *Tiferet* mediates between the sefirah of *Chessed* (Love and Kindness) on the right side of the tree and that of *Gevurah* (Power and Strength) on the left. The *Chessed-Gevurah-Tiferet* triad is at the center of the tree above the lower triad of *Netzach-Hod-Yesod* and below the upper triad of *Chokhmah-Binah-Daat*.

On the right-hand side, *Chessed* is aligned beneath *Chokhmah* (Wisdom); on the left side, *Gevurah* is aligned beneath *Binah* (Understanding), while in the center, *Tiferet* is aligned beneath *Daat* (Knowledge). *Tiferet* aspires to rise up to *Daat* and beyond it to *Keter*, the Crown, the Source of everything.

In the earlier parts of this book we have discussed how Abraham's quality of *Chessed* is rooted in *Chokhmah* while Isaac's quality of *Gevurah* is rooted in *Binah*. Jacob, having sat in the tents of his two masters Abraham (*Chessed/Chokhmah*) and Isaac (*Gevurah/Binah*), already possessed the qualities needed to build the House: *Chokhmah* and *Binah*. For "With *wisdom* (*Chokhmah*) the house will be built and with *understanding* (*Tevunot* = *Binah*) it will be established..." (Proverbs 24:3-4). Now that Jacob had reached this *place* of joining and union, his task was to actually build the House, to join *Chokhmah* and *Binah* in a perfect synthesis so as to create a fitting vessel for *Daat* to dwell in. "And the rooms will be filled with *knowledge* (*Daat*)" (*ibid.*)

Stripped to its barest essentials, a house (*Bayit*) consists of walls and a roof. The walls divide between the outside world and the private space created between them, while the roof affords protection against the open skies. In the halachah (Torah law), a house is the prime case of *Reshut HaYachid*, an "individual domain" as opposed to public space outside (the street, the wilderness, etc.) which is *Reshut HaRabim*, a "public domain" where no one person has any more rights than any other.

An individual domain enables the person or people who possess the rights to that domain to go about their activities safe from external dangers, free of outside interference. A house is a place where people can dwell in dignity. In Hebrew, to dwell is *leyshev* from the root *YaShaV*. Significantly, the Hebrew phrase for a settled mind is *Yishuv HaDaat*, literally "the dwelling of *Daat*". The House must be a place where *Daat* can dwell. It must be a place conducive to *Yishuv HaDaat*, clear, settled knowledge and awareness of the One God and of the unity that underlies the diversity of creation. In this sense too, the House is *Reshut HaYachid*, the domain in which unity dwells, as opposed to the outside, *Reshut HaRabim*, the realm of plurality, chaos and confusion.

Secure and calm within the walls of the House, the spiritual seeker can use his powers of *Chokhmah* and *Binah* to contemplate the creation and discern how beneath the apparent plurality of *Reshut HaRabim* outside lies the unity, harmony and order of God, the ultimate *Yachid*, the Only One. Thus "outside" actually becomes "inside", because the chaos and disorder "outside" are joined back to their unified source within God.

The knowledge of God is *Daat*. *Daat* is achieved through learning to join *Chokhmah*-thinking (holistic vision) with *Binah*-thinking (rational-analytic thought). The two become "joined" when one learns to oscillate constantly between them. For right-brain and left-brain thinking are both necessary. In the words of Abraham's *Sefer Yetzira* (1:4): "Understand with wisdom; be wise with understanding". We have to learn to see things whole yet understand their parts. We have to understand the parts in terms of the whole, and at the same time see the whole in terms of all its parts.

The combination of right- and left-brain thinking is indispensable in order to build the House. When a person wants to build a house, he has first to dream and envisage what it is he wants. Even before he can lay the first stone of the house he must already see in his mind's eye the completed, fully-furnished house with himself actually going about his life there together with his family.... This is right-brain *Chokhmah*-thinking. But dreaming will not build the house. It is necessary to define and analyze the individual details of the overall vision in order to plan how to execute the project. This is left-brain *Binah*-thinking. Yet each detail has to be planned and executed with its place in the context of the whole kept constantly in mind.

In order to actually build the physical house, it is necessary to take a plurality of stones, bricks and other materials and join them together one by one in order to construct a single whole: the house. Each individual item must be laid in its proper place as required by the plan of the overall structure. "Jacob took from the stones of the place and put a place for his head". The bricks and stones of mental or spiritual structures -- ideologies, philosophies, religious and spiritual pathways, etc. -- are the individual ideas and concepts upon which they are founded. The building-bricks of the words with which we express our ideas are the sounds and letters which make them up.

In the words of *Sefer Yetzira*:

Two stones build 2 houses. Three stones build 6 houses. Four stones build 24 houses. Five stones build 120 houses. Six stones build 720 houses. From here on go on and calculate that which the mouth cannot speak and the ear cannot hear" 4:16.

The stones of which *Sefer Yetzira* is speaking are the letters which we join in various permutations in order to make up words. The words themselves are "houses". Each of the particular permutations of letters that we call a word is a "house", a vessel or container that carries and communicates the meaning we attach to the word. The physical sounds make up the "house", and in the house dwells *Daat*, knowledge, namely the *meaning* of the word.

Jacob was undoubtedly a master of the methods of letter permutations, prayer and prophecy taught by his teachers Abraham and Isaac. Jacob's work of building his House on this holy spot was very much bound up with the building of spiritual structures through the letters and words of prayer and Torah. "And he slept in that place" (Genesis 28:11). The Hebrew word for "and he slept" -- *Vayishkav* -- contains an allusion to the 22 letters of the Hebrew alphabet. *Vayishkav* contains the words *Yesh KaV*, "there are *Kaph-Beit*". Numerically the letters *Kaph-Beit* = 22.

"And He Dreamed"

"There was a ladder set on the ground and its top reached the heavens, and there were angels of God going up and down on it. There was *HaVaYaH* standing over him..." (Genesis 28:12).

Jacob's dream was a state of supreme prophetic vision, for: "When prophets arise among you, I, *HaVaYaH*, make myself known to him in a vision, I speak with him in a *dream*" (Numbers 12:6).

The dream of the ladder with the angels going up and down was Jacob's prototype "Receiving of the Torah" for himself and all his descendants. Just as the Torah was later given to all the Children of Israel on a Mountain -- Sinai -- so their father Jacob received the Torah on this holy Mount Moriah, the place from which *Hora'ah*, Teaching, goes out to all the world. Just as Mount Sinai became a green field at the Giving of the Torah, so this spot where Jacob lay, Abraham's Mountain, was also Isaac's Field. And now, rising up above the House Jacob had started to build on this very spot was a "ladder" -- in Hebrew, *Sulam*. The numerical value of the letters of *SuLaM* is the same as that of the letters of *SINAI* (see Rabbi Nachman's Wisdom #86).

At the very heart of the Torah that Jacob received on this spot, his *Sinai*, is the concept of the *Sulam*, the *ladder* of ascent. Jacob was at the *Rosh*, the head and brain-center of the world, the point of interface, the "Gate", between this material creation -- "Earth" -- and the world of spirit --

"Heaven" -- from which it derives. This spot is the "House of God", the place where God "dwells", the place where holy spirit and prophecy are present and accessible to human beings. For this is the "Gate to Heaven", the point of connection between this lower world and the higher.

And the way to get up is on the "ladder"!

Earlier, we have examined how all creation is like a rotating wheel and that this is the primary concept of the Temple. In the words of Rebbe Nachman:

The Temple was in the category of "the superior below and the inferior above".... God is above every transcendental concept, and it is beyond all logic that He should constrict Himself into the vessels of the Temple... But God brought His presence into the Temple and thereby refuted philosophical logic. Philosophy cannot explain how man can have any influence on high. It cannot say how a mere animal can be sacrificed and rise as a sweet savor giving pleasure to God. They explain that this pleasure is the fulfillment of His will, but how can we even apply the concept of desire to God? But God placed His presence in the Temple and accepts the animal as a sweet savor. He made the fact contradict philosophical logic.

Rabbi Nachman's Wisdom #40

It is most significant that in Jacob's dream he first saw the divine angels going *up* and and then coming *down*. In essence, an angel -- in Hebrew a *Malach* -- is essentially an agent that performs some *Melachah*, an act of "work", whether physical or spiritual. A *Malach* is an energy sent by someone to affect someone (or some-thing) else.

Jacob's dream is of an "energy exchange" between Heaven and Earth. And it is the angels coming up from Earth who are initiating the exchange. When man makes the "arousal from below", stirring himself to prayer, sacrifice and other acts of devotion, his words and acts send *angels going up* the ladder to heaven. It is this that then elicits the *coming down* of other angels, these being God's agents bringing divine blessings and other favorable influences into this world in response to man's devotion.

In other words, our words and acts of devotion have the power to influence Heaven and bring back a flow of Heavenly influence in return. The lesson of Jacob's Ladder, the *Sulam*, is the very essence of the Torah and Mitzvot that God later gave at Sinai to all his descendants, "the *House* of Jacob, the Children of Israel" (Exodus 19:3).

"Jacob Took a Vow"

In the dream, God promised Jacob the Land of Israel. Jacob was just about to leave the Land of Israel to go to Charan, the home of Laban. His mission was to spread the blessings of the Land -- the tradition of Abraham -- outwards to all the people on earth, as God had told him: "You will break forth to the west, the east, the north and the south, and all the families of the Earth will be blessed through you and through your seed."

In the course of this mission Jacob and his seed would have to grapple with the worst forces of darkness and evil. But God promised Jacob His protection: "See, I am with you and I will guard you wherever you go and I will bring you back to this Land. For I will not abandon you until I have done what I have told you."

Jacob responded with his own act of commitment to God.

"Jacob rose early in the morning and took the stone he had placed under his head and set it up as a pillar and poured oil on its head.... Jacob took a vow, saying: If God will be with me and guard me on this path I am traveling and will give me bread to eat and clothes to wear and I come home in peace to the house of my father, HaVaYaH will be my God. And this stone that I have set up as a pillar will be the House of God and from all that You give me I will set aside a tithe for You" (Genesis 28:16-22).

Jacob's task was to go outwards: to teach not only outstanding prophets but ordinary men, women and children that God is not just in tall mountains and great plains. God is in all the little things of our lives as well, down to our very food and clothes.

Stripped of his wealth, in flight for his life, Jacob was like Adam all over again, cast out of the garden, facing the thorns and thistles of trying to make a living. Sheer physical survival is one of man's greatest trials. Jacob rectified the curse put on Adam by teaching us to put our trust in God and look to Him for everything we need.

One of the most important ways of looking to God is by devoting the first tithe (10%) of everything we "make" or "earn" to God in the form of gifts to charity and other good causes. Knowing that we are going to dedicate the very cream of our money-making efforts to God in this way actually sanctifies and elevates all of our efforts. Making a living can easily turn into a purely selfish, greedy pursuit. Tithing turns it into one that has a higher purpose.

The act of charity by man elicits a flow of charity, kindness and love from God. Jacob committed himself to charity and kindness. He took responsibility. And years later he returned to Beit El, the House of God, to fulfill his vow.

Breeding Souls

Jacob had laid the first stone of his House. Now he had to set about building it.

Far more important than the physical structure of the house is the community of *people* who must lead meaningful, fulfilling lives together in it. Jacob's first task was therefore to build his family and gather the souls who would form the eternal House of Israel.

God's first command to man in the Torah is to "be fruitful and multiply" (Genesis 1:28). This does not simply mean having many children. Parenting involves far more than conceiving and having babies! Not only do parents have to take care of their children's material needs for many years. They are also responsible for their spiritual development. They must do everything possible to see that their children turn into mature, responsible adults with a genuine commitment to lead lives based on true values. This responsibility devolves not only upon parents but also upon educators, those who control the mass media and anybody else who is in a position to influence the minds and souls of those who will form the next link in the chain of the human race.

The continuous increase in the world's already enormous human population arouses alarm in the minds of those who wonder how it is going to be possible to feed everyone. While so much attention is given to numbers, it is surprising that the ecologically conscious do not worry more about the *quality* of the upcoming generation, which will have no less profound an effect on the world our descendants will inherit.

What kind of global culture has been produced by the cynical mind-manipulators who determine the tone and content of TV and the other mass media, who obviously find that the best way to hold their audiences is with a steady diet of violence, blatant sexuality and anything else that panders to their lowest instincts? What has this diet done to the minds and souls of those brought up on it? The licentiousness, crime, violence, substance abuse and other ills sweeping today's "most advanced" societies does not bode well for the world's future.

Ensuring the *quality* of the world's population is everyone's responsibility. In the words of Rebbe Nachman:

Everyone must play their part in seeing that the world is populated with *Bney Adam* (Children of Adam, Man), people who are not just human but *humane*, as it is written, "And fill the earth" (Genesis 1:28). The world can only be a civilized place if it is filled with *Bney Adam*, namely people who possess *Daat*, spiritual sensitivity and understanding. Those who do not have this understanding cannot be considered human beings at all.

In other words, just as we are commanded to bring children into this world for the sake of its survival, so we are commanded to instill in our children and students spiritual understanding and reverence for God. This is the very essence of the commandment to procreate: to produce future generations of true humans, not wild beasts and animals who have nothing human about them except their outward physical appearance. As long as people lack true spiritual illumination and understanding and do not know and feel God and His power, they cannot be considered true humans since they do not have any knowledge of God. It is only this knowledge that makes a person worthy of being called human. Without this knowledge, the world is "chaos and desolation" (Genesis 1:2).

But "He did not create it to be desolate, He formed it to be *settled*" (Isaiah 45:18). For the world needs not merely to be populated but to be *settled* with *Bney Adam*, true human beings possessing spiritual wisdom and understanding, people who know God. This is the essence of the commandment to "fill the earth". It is necessary to fill the earth with *Bney Adam*, true human beings.

Everyone has an obligation to speak about God and spirituality to anyone they are in a position to influence in order to help them develop their spiritual awareness. For the foundation of civilization is when the world is inhabited by *Bney Adam*, people who know God.

Likutey Moharan II, 7:4

Jacob and Laban

To bring up a new generation to know God was the challenge facing Jacob. As the very embodiment of spiritual light, truth and harmony, Jacob had always to struggle against their very opposites, darkness, falsehood and discord, until he finally triumphed. All Jacob's achievements came only through hard work and effort.

His twenty years of work to build his family were years of protracted struggle, notably against his uncle Laban, the very archetype of the liar and swindler. *Lavan* means white. The gleaming white on Laban's exterior concealed the corruption and evil in his heart.

Laban was the brother of Rebecca, Jacob's mother. The match between Rebecca and Isaac had come about because Abraham did not want Isaac to take a wife from among the Canaanites. Their extreme moral degeneracy disqualified them from entering the ranks of the nation Abraham sought to build. He therefore sent for a wife for Isaac from among the family of his brother Nachor back in Aram Naharayim where Abraham himself had come from. Although this "other side" of Abraham's family had made nothing like the same radical break as Abraham from the corrupt, idolatrous civilization of the time, they did come from the line of Noah, Shem and Eiver, guardians of the monotheistic tradition prior to Abraham. All the finest qualities of this illustrious family came out in Betuel's daughter Rebecca, a fitting match for Isaac.

Following Abraham's lead, Isaac and Rebecca had no wish for Jacob to intermarry with the Canaanites, preferring to send him back to the "other side" of the family. Neither Isaac nor Rebecca (who actually came from there) had any illusions about the real character of Rebecca's brother Laban, a sorcerer-priest who was now the head of that side of the family. But it was precisely in the clutches of that "other side" -- the dark, unholy realm of evil, the *Sitra Achra* ("Other Side") of which the Kabbalah speaks -- that the holy sparks, the souls of the future Jewish people, were trapped. Jacob's task was to rescue these souls and bring them back into the fold of holiness.

While acting the kind, concerned, loving uncle, Laban did everything in his power to prevent those souls getting out of his clutches. For twenty years he mercilessly exploited Jacob and eventually tried to destroy him together with his whole family (Genesis ch's 29-31; see Deuteronomy 26:5 and *Rashi ad. loc.*). What greater challenge could there be than for the wise, canny Jacob -- recipient of God's gift of truth (Michah 7:20) -- to be pitted against the arch-deceiver Laban?

In Kabbalistic terms, Jacob's task as the embodiment of the sefirah of *Tiferet*, beauty, harmony and truth, was to rise up to *Daat*-Knowledge, which is the synthesis of *Chokhmah*-Wisdom and *Binah*-Understanding. But in order to attain holy *Chokhmah* and *Binah*, Jacob had to struggle with their unholy opposites: vision and intelligence harnessed to serve not love and creativity but selfishness and destruction. Laban is the counter of holy wisdom. Just as there are 32 (Lamed-Bet) Pathways of *Chokhmah*-Wisdom, so the first part of Laban's name is made up of the letters *Lamed Bet* (= 32). Just as there are 50 Gates of *Binah*-Understanding, so the last letter of Laban's name is *Nun* (= 50). The name Laban alludes to a level of divine wisdom known as *Loven Elyon,* the "Supreme Whiteness" (for the brain, the seat of wisdom, is white).

Ever since Adam fell from grace as a result of the serpent's deception, the only way to reclaim holy wisdom and understanding is by encountering the *Heichal HaTemurot*, the "Palace of Exchanges", where everything is confused and mixed up. Here evil masquerades as good while true good can even appear evil. Adam's eating the forbidden fruit of the tree of knowledge of good and evil caused a total mix-up of good and evil. The only way to sort them out is by first encountering the confusion and battling against the lies. This is why Jacob had to struggle against Laban.

The true goodness in Laban's house was to be found in his daughters Rachel and Leah and their half-sisters Bilhah and Zilpah. These four were to be the mothers of Jacob's destined twelve sons, founders of the Twelve Tribes of Israel, root souls of all the Jewish People. The souls are the true good in the universe. Jacob had to marry these women and with them birth the souls.

It was Laban's beautiful younger daughter Rachel who aroused Jacob's love from the moment he first caught sight of her on his arrival at Laban's. Laban saw that he only stood to gain by setting his penniless, fugitive nephew to work for him. Laban offered Jacob Rachel in exchange for seven years labor. At the end of the seven years Laban made a wedding party for his "little daughter Rachel", as stipulated by Jacob, but tricked him on the night by sending in her older, weak-eyed sister Leah to the marital chamber. Laban then made Jacob work for Rachel for another seven years. Rachel and Leah received Bilhah and Zilpah as their respective "hand-maidens". (Bilhah and Zilpah were Laban's daughters from concubines.)

Having Children

This is not the place to delve into the profound kabbalistic secrets embedded in the biblical account of Jacob and his four wives and the births of their twelve sons and daughter. Far closer to the surface of the story lie lessons that are of the greatest importance to us today as we face the surrounding moral decay in the world we live in and ask ourselves what we should do about it.

The simple, age-old craft of having children and bringing them up to be good citizens of God's earth is viewed today by enormous numbers of "progressive" and "enlightened" people as an irrelevant, boring and politically incorrect activity. As it is the world can barely support its teeming billions, so why -- they ask -- waste time and effort on something so tedious when there are far more interesting things to do in life? According to contemporary "orthodoxy", sexuality exists purely and simply for the gratification of the partners, who should be entitled to do whatever they want with whomever they want whenever they want -- as long as they use contraceptives, so as not to have to worry about inconvenient consequences.

This "orthodoxy" runs totally counter to the ethic of holy sexuality embodied in Jacob and his wives. For Jacob, sexuality is God's loving gift to husband and wife to seal their bond of love through joining together in utmost harmony in order to create new life. Jacob and his wives had something purest of pure to protect and develop: They came from the finest stock. Jacob possessed the soul of Adam. Jacob's fathers were Abraham and Isaac. Jacob and his wives now came to play their part in tending the holy Tree -- the Tree of Life -- by giving birth to living, vibrant children, souls through whose very lives and activities the divine attributes (*Sefirot*) of the kabbalistic Tree of Life would be revealed.

To conceive, give birth to and raise such children takes the utmost purity. In Kabbalah, the sexual act is sacred. It is a hidden garden of love enjoyed in purity by husband and wife as their ultimate expression of love for one another. They thereby join their seed and their innermost souls together in a single unity -- the unique new child, new soul, that they bring into being. When this soul is born, they must nurture it lovingly together, providing a secure, tender, caring environment in which this and all of their children can grow, mature and develop into the finest citizens of God's earth.

According to tradition, Jacob was 63 when he received the blessings from Isaac. He then spent fourteen years in the academy of Shem and Eiver, after which he spent another seven years working for Laban before getting married. Thus, Jacob was 84 at the time of his marriage. Later on, in his death-bed blessing to his first son Reuven, Jacob refers to him as "first of my strength" (Genesis 49:3). This means that Reuven was conceived from the very first drop of seed that ever left Jacob's body, which was not until he was 84, showing his perfect self-control throughout his life.

For Jacob, the holy act of impregnating his wife with seed was one that involved the utmost *Kavanah*, mental and spiritual *aiming* or *intention*. Kabbalah compares the ejaculation of sperm to shooting arrows. The art of archery is to have perfect *aim*. The *aim* of the sexual act is to bring a pure soul into the world. Husband and wife should have thoughts of supreme holiness and purity during intimacy.

The *Zohar* states that the seed comes from the brain. Students of anatomy may in that case wonder why there appears to be no duct from the brain to the sexual organs, whereas everyone surely knows that sperm is manufactured in the testes. (The brain obviously *influences* the production of sperm through hormones and other chemicals.)

However, with a little further thought we can easily see that modern anatomical knowledge does not contradict the wisdom of the holy *Zohar*. Every sperm contains a perfect genetic blueprint of the father. In union with the female ovum, the sperm is capable of replicating a perfect human being complete with his or her own unique blend of inherited and individual characteristics, with a totally unique soul and the potential not only to live an entire lifetime of activity and creativity but also to breed further generations from that same genetic heritage.

The entire design of the new human soul and body coming into being derives from *Chokhmah*-Wisdom and *Binah*-Understanding, represented respectively in the sperm (white) and the ovum (red). Conception means that the sperm and ovum fuse into a single nucleus (*Daat*-Knowledge). This single nucleus then begins to divide into two cells, they in turn divide, and so on and on, until finally the embryo is ready to be born and live its own life.

Thus, all the physical and spiritual genetic information required for this individual to live his or her life from birth to death is originally contained in that single nucleus ("brain") formed from the sperm and the ovum. Included among the other information in that "brain" is all the information needed to enable the person eventually to replicate sexually through his or her seed. In other words, that original nucleus containing all this age-old wisdom and information is the "brain" behind all the generations to come. This "brain" is obviously the source of all the seed of the person who will develop from it and that of all his or her generations to come.

The Twelve Tribes

Where did Jacob *aim* when he conceived his sons? He set his sights on the universal Soul of the whole creation, bringing down a part of that Soul in each of his sons.

The prophet Isaiah declares: "The moon will be disgraced and the sun will be ashamed, for *HaVaYaH* of Hosts will rule on Mount Zion and in Jerusalem" (Isaiah 24:23). The Rabbis said: "The sun refers to Abraham and the moon to Isaac. In the future, Abraham and Isaac will be ashamed [because of their bad sons Ishmael and Esau]. But not Jacob, for Jacob is associated with the stars [and Jacob's sons, corresponding to the twelve signs of the Zodiac, were all good]" (*Midrash Rabbah Bemidbar, Naso*).

The *Sefer Yetzira* discusses the creation in terms of the three basic categories of Space, Time and Soul. The entire creation is for the sake of man and is structured accordingly. Man has twelve fundamental soul-functions: speech, thought, motion, sight, hearing, action, coition, smell, sleep, anger, taste and laughter. There are twelve corresponding divisions of space and time. The twelve divisions of space are the twelve constellations of stars through which the sun "moves" in the course of the solar year. The twelve divisions of time are the twelve months of the year. Each sign of the Zodiac and its corresponding month of the year has a unique character bound up with the associated soul-function.

The twelve divisions in space, time and soul correspond to the twelve diagonals on the tree of the *Sefirot*. (When the sefirot are diagrammatically represented as a "tree" of ten points, there are twenty-two connecting lines, seven of which are vertical, three horizontal and twelve diagonal.) Jacob's twelve sons revealed to perfection all of the essential qualities of the inner Soul for whom God created the world of Time and Space.

Each of the twelve was unique according to his respective place on the tree. They were all personalities of tremendous power, as illustrated in the many Bible and midrashic stories about them and about their illustrious descendants in later generations. Each of the tribes received its own blessings from Jacob and later from Moses according to its unique trait. The tribes had their own emblems. Many of them are associated with animals (such as Judah with the Lion, Joseph with the Ox, Issachar with the Donkey, Dan with the Serpent, Naftali with the Deer and Benjamin with the Wolf.)

The House of Prayer

For Jacob, every soul that comes into the world is unique and precious and must be nurtured with the utmost love and understanding.

It is not only in building our families that we have the responsibility to love, care for and nurture souls. The same applies when we seek to build different kinds of "houses", whether circles of friends, organizations of various kinds or whole communities. All of human life is about joining with others and cooperating with them for every kind of different purpose.

The greatest "House" of all consists of people who gather for the specific purpose of communing together with God in prayer and meditation. Each new soul that joins this "House" is another brick in the edifice.

In the words of Rebbe Nachman:

Prayer reveals the glory of God, because prayer disperses the "clouds" of unholiness and impurity and makes them disappear. Abundant prayer brings about forgiveness of sin, and then the sun rises and shines, bringing healing....

The prayer that brings forgiveness and healing comes when a new "neighbor" joins the community of Israel. With every new neighbor who comes, the prayer is enormously enhanced and magnified. The greater the multitude of souls gathered together, the greater and more magnificent the House of Prayer. For "three stones build six houses, four stones build twenty-four houses, five build a hundred and twenty... until the mouth cannot utter it or the heart conceive it" (*Sefer Yetzira* 4:16). With every single stone that is added, the number of houses is multiplied exponentially out of all proportion. Now the "stones" are the souls -- "the holy stones have been poured out" (Lamentations 4:1) -- while the houses are "My house, the House of Prayer." Thus, with every single soul that joins the ingathering of the Community of Israel, the House of Prayer is vastly expanded and magnified. The addition of yet another soul creates an incalculable number of totally new and different combinations.

Every time a new neighbor joins an existing community of worshipers, the prayer is expanded and magnified amazingly, for one more soul has been added. And it is the abundance of prayer that brings forgiveness and healing...

Likutey Moharan II, 8:6

Breeding Livestock

*T*he sophisticated man-made environment of contemporary urban civilization interposes between ourselves and nature, which is mostly experienced through the windows of buildings, cars, trains and planes or filtered via TV and computer screens. The consumerist economy encourages people to take whatever they can for themselves without worrying about the Earth or the other living animals, birds, fish, insects, trees and plants with whom we share it.

But the House Jacob built is founded on peace and harmony not only within the human community but also between that community and the surrounding natural world. This will be the central theme of this and the coming chapters of this book.

To build this House required intimate knowledge of the world of nature and tender sensitivity towards its most vulnerable creatures. Jacob acquired this knowledge and sensitivity in the twenty years he worked as Laban's shepherd.

Tending Laban's Flocks.

At the end of the twenty years, Jacob summed up his time working for Laban:

"This twenty years that I have been with you, your sheep and your goats did not miscarry, and I did not eat the rams of your flocks. I never brought you a predator-savaged animal. If your animals were taken by predators, I bore the loss: you asked it from my hand. Whatever was stolen by day or by night I paid. By day the burning dryness consumed me and the bitter frost at night, and my sleep fled from my eyes. This is the story of my twenty years in your house. I served you for fourteen years for your two daughters and six years for your flocks, and you changed our agreed conditions for my wages ten times"

Genesis 31:38-41.

Laban played the good uncle who was showing his penniless nephew the greatest magnanimity and kindness in permitting him to work for him. In reality Laban stood only to gain. This was because of Jacob's scrupulous integrity: he was the exemplar of *Mishpat*, justice and fairness. Laban took full advantage of it.

When Jacob first arrived, Laban had only his daughter Rachel to take care of his sheep -- hardly the proper thing since most of the other shepherds were men. Jacob stepped in as manager of Laban's entire flock, caring for them most conscientiously. When his time was up Jacob could have simply handed Laban back the same number of sheep as he received. Instead he made sure that the flocks increased. "Your sheep and your goats did not miscarry."

According to the old shepherds' maxim, "The girls are for milk and the boys for meat." Out in the hills Jacob could easily have enjoyed barbecued lamb whenever he wished without Laban ever knowing. But Jacob would never take anything that was not his. "I did not eat the rams of your flocks".

Under Torah law Jacob was technically a *Shomer Sachar* ("paid guard"), who is liable for theft and loss (since these might result from his own negligence), but is exempt from liability for losses due to circumstances beyond his control such as an attack of predators. Even so, Jacob took it upon himself to pay for such losses: "I never brought you a predator-savaged animal. If your animals were taken by predators, I bore the loss...."

Jacob graphically depicted his far-from-romantic life outdoors: "By day the burning dryness consumed me and the bitter frost at night, and my sleep fled from my eyes." In the twenty years he worked as Laban's shepherd Jacob must have come to know every single nook and cranny and every grazing and watering spot in the surrounding hills. He must have become an expert in every aspect of nature, wildlife, climate, the skies and the stars. He also became an expert animal breeder.

Genetic Engineering

In his argument with Laban, Jacob says: "This is my twenty years in your house. I served you for fourteen years for your two daughters and six years for your flocks, and you changed our agreed conditions for my wages ten times."

Jacob was referring to the deal he made with Laban so that he should not return home completely empty-handed after all his work. It was after the birth of his eleventh son, Joseph, that Jacob asked Laban's leave to go home. Laban well understood Jacob's value to him and did not want to let him go so fast. Again, playing the magnanimous father-in-law, Laban said: "If I have found favor in your eyes, I have divined the truth: *HaVaYaH* has blessed me because of you." And he said, "Specify your reward from me, and I will give it." (Genesis 30:27-8).

Jacob did not wish to take anything from Laban. Whatever he took he wanted to earn through his own efforts. He therefore struck what he thought was a deal with Laban -- only Laban kept changing the conditions.

In essence, the deal was that Laban would remove all the spotted or patched sheep and goats from the flock. Jacob would continue tending the remainder, and from now on any spotted or patched lambs and goats that were born would be his (Genesis 30:31-2). Laban zealously removed from the flock every single animal that had any kind of spot or patch and took them well away from Jacob.

Jacob then carried out the most amazing feat of kabbalistic genetic engineering:

"Jacob took sticks of moist poplar, almond and plain and peeled white stripes in them, laying bare the white in the sticks. He set up the rods that he had peeled in the water-channels in the drinking troughs where the flocks came to drink. The rods were facing the flocks and they became heated when they came to drink. The flock were in heat facing the sticks and the flock gave birth to kids that were striped at the ankles, spotted and patched...." (Genesis 30:37ff.).

The deep kabbalistic mysteries involved in Jacob's choice of these particular species of trees and other aspects of his feat, are beyond the scope of this work. What is obvious is that he fully grasped the power of visual stimuli not simply to influence the mind but to evoke actual physical responses.

There is an old belief that striking features of a person seen by the man and/or woman prior to intimacy can come out in the child they conceive. Some may find it hard to accept this literally, yet no-one can deny the power of visual stimuli to affect people's behavior. It is precisely because of this that billions are spent on promotion and advertising to sell products and manipulate the public in other ways.

One of the greatest tragedies in today's sophisticated world is that those controlling the media know exactly how to exploit visual stimuli to make people keep buying and keep watching the TV and movies, yet they willfully blind themselves to the horrendous social and cultural effects of the constant diet of violence, unashamed sexuality and other negative images they provide. In the words of the Rabbis: "The eye sees, the heart desires and the body sins" (*Rashi* on Numbers 15:39).

A simple, practical lesson to be drawn from Jacob's breeding feat is the importance of surrounding ourselves with images and symbols that have the power to "breed" and evoke positive, constructive, creative, intelligent and sensitive behaviors. Judaism has a wealth of such symbols and images, including the Magen David (Star of David), Tablets of Stone, Torah Scroll, Shabbat lights, Chanukah Lamp, Tzitzit, Tefilin, the Temple building and its vessels (the Ark, Cherubs, Candelabrum, Incense Altar, Showbread Table, etc.) and the letters of the Aleph-Beit.

The Pipe-Playing Shepherd

The power of vision is associated with holistic Chokhmah-Wisdom. Hearing, on the other hand, is associated with Binah-Understanding. Not only was Jacob a supreme sage when it came to harnessing the power of vision. He was also a master musician.

He had to be. He was the father of Levi, whose descendants, the Levites, made up the magnificent choir that chanted daily during the Temple rituals to the accompaniment of a full orchestra. Jacob was also the ancestor of David, messianic king and "sweet singer of Israel", who composed the Book of Psalms, which sings the inner music of the soul and of all creation.

According to tradition, during the sleepless nights he spent working for Laban, Jacob kept himself awake by singing the fifteen "Songs of Ascent" -- Psalms 120-34 (*Bereishit Rabbah* 68:11). These fifteen Psalms correspond to the fifteen steps leading up to the main Temple Courtyard. This need not be taken to mean that Jacob sang the text of these Psalms exactly as we have it today, which is impossible since some of them are specifically ascribed to David and Solomon, while others refer to events in later Jewish history, such as the redemption from the Babylonian exile (Psalm 126).

What this Midrash suggests is that in these years of toil and struggle Jacob fortified himself with absolute faith and trust in God and with longing and yearning to ascend His holy mountain and build His House, as expressed repeatedly in these Psalms.

In the same way that visual images have awesome power to breed actual behavior, so sound and music have the power to move and stir the heart and inspire us to the highest levels of achievement.

Speaking of Jacob, the master musician, Rebbe Nachman writes:

Every shepherd has his own unique melody according to the herbs and grasses in the place where he pastures his sheep. Different animals eat different kinds of grasses. Shepherds do not always pasture their flocks in the same place. The shepherd's melody varies according to the place where he pastures his flocks and the herbs and grasses growing there. For every plant and every blade of grass has its own song. It is from the song of the grass that the shepherd gets his song.

This is why it says: "And Ada gave birth to Yaval: he was the father of those who dwell in tents and amidst herds. And the name of his brother was Yuval: he was the father of all who play the lyre and pipe" (Genesis 4:20-1). For as soon as people took up tending herds, musical instruments came into the world. In the same way, King David (peace be upon him), who was "skilled in music" (Samuel I, 16:18), was a shepherd. Indeed, we find that all the founding fathers had flocks.

"From the corner of the earth we hear songs" (Isaiah 24:16). Melodies and songs come from the "corner of the earth"! For it is from the herbs that grow in the earth that music is made. Indeed, it is the shepherd's musical skill that puts strength into the herbs and grasses, providing the animals with their food. This is why it says: "The blossoms have appeared in the land, the time of singing has come!" (Song of Songs 2:12). This means that the plants and flowers grow in the land because of the relevant songs and melodies. It is through his songs and melodies that the shepherd puts strength into the herbs and grasses, providing pasture for the animals.

These songs and melodies are of benefit to the shepherd himself. Being constantly surrounded by animals, the shepherd could easily descend from the human level to that of an animal. But his songs and melody save him from this. For song refines the soul, elevating the human being above animalistic tendencies. Music has the power to refine and elevate the human soul, and this is why the shepherd's melodies save him from falling to the level of an animal.

Likutey Moharan II:63

The Encounter with Esau

"When you make war against a city for many days to capture it, don't destroy its trees, wielding the ax against them. You may eat from the tree, but do not cut it down. For is the tree of the field a man that he should flee from you and suffer in the siege? Why should you destroy it?" (Deuteronomy 20:19-20)

*J*acob's phenomenal success at breeding flocks aroused the greedy Laban's ire. Sensing serious danger, Jacob hurriedly took all his family and possessions and fled. Laban chased after him, but God appeared to Laban in a dream and told him not to harm Jacob in any way.

Saved from Laban, Jacob made his way home to the Land of Israel together with his long, straggling caravan of wives, little children, camp-followers and thousands upon thousands of camels, donkeys, oxen, sheep and goats.

Rebecca had hoped that Jacob's extended absence from home would cool Esau's fury against him for taking the birthright and the blessings. However, Jacob knew that such a grudge would not easily be forgotten. True to character, Jacob sought to avoid conflict. He wanted to make peace with Esau, hoping to placate him with a massive gift of livestock representing the very material wealth Esau craved. But as Jacob arrived at the border of the Land of Israel, news came that Esau, vengeful as ever, was advancing with an army of four hundred warriors.

Jacob now faced the greatest challenge of his life. Against Laban his struggle had been to remain truthful and honest in the face of Laban's trickery and lies. But Esau's threat was of total physical annihilation. Laban's attack had been on the level of *Chokhmah*-Wisdom and *Binah*-Understanding. Esau's was on the level of sheer *Gevurah*: power and brute force.

For years Jacob had been laboring to build his House. Now Esau wanted to raze everything "down to the very foundations" (Psalms 137:7) for no other reason than that he was jealous because Jacob had shown himself the more worthy. Esau, embodiment of unholy *Gevurah*, is the archetypal killer and destroyer. Killing the innocent is stringently forbidden by the Torah. So is wanton destruction, as it says: "Do not destroy!" (Deuteronomy 20:19).

The prohibition of *Bal Tashchit*, "Do not destroy", is directly relevant to us today as we witness the waste and destruction of vital Earth resources by governments, businesses and private individuals. Our economy actually encourages unnecessary consumption and waste. The worldwide destruction of resources is a threat to our very survival.

The Torah prohibition of needless waste and destruction derives from a passage about proper conduct during military operations. Nobody with any sense wants to go to war, but even war is necessary and justified in self-defense against aggressive enemies who refuse to co-exist in peace and harmony. Yet even when campaigning against such enemies, it is forbidden to destroy valuable resources in their possession. The Torah gives as an example the fruit-trees surrounding a city that is under siege.

"When you make war against a city for many days to capture it, don't destroy its trees, wielding the ax against them. You may eat from the tree, but do not cut it down. For is the tree of the field a man that he should flee from you and suffer in the siege? Why should you destroy it?" (Deuteronomy 20:19-20)

Since the Torah prohibits the destruction of enemy property even at the height of war, it follows that the needless waste or destruction of property owned by those who are not enemies is certainly forbidden. A person is not even allowed to destroy his own property, let alone someone else's, and certainly not Earth resources that belong to everyone.

Man Against the Serpent

Advancing against Jacob, Esau was "wielding the ax" in order to "cut down the tree" to its very roots. The tree was the Tree of Life, as embodied in Jacob and his family. It was the Tree of the Souls going back to the first man, Adam. This Tree had been carefully nurtured and cultivated by Abraham, Isaac and now Jacob in order to bring forth its fruits, the future generations of Israel. "Do not cut the tree down. For *is the tree of the field a man...?*" The Hebrew words also mean: "For the Man (Adam) is the Tree of the field".

Jacob's struggle against Esau was the continuation of a very ancient struggle. It was the struggle of life and creation against the forces of death and destruction. In order for the creation to exist within God's infinite light, there had to be limits and boundaries. The entire creation came about through successive "contractions" of God's light, as discussed in the Kabbalah. The limiting boundary of creation is destruction. The limiting boundary of life is death. The forces of destruction and death are embodied in Esau.

Jacob's struggle against Esau was a replay of Adam's encounter with the Serpent. God's plan in creating Adam was that he should earn Godly perfection -- "good" -- through his own efforts. In order to confront man with a challenge requiring work and effort, God created a world containing evil as well as good. Man's work would be to reject evil and choose good. But in order to make the challenge real, evil had to be made to look good. This is why there had to be a Serpent, the lying Tempter who turns Accuser: Satan.

With deceit and lies the serpent tricked Adam and Eve into eating the fruit of the forbidden tree, leading to their fall from grace and expulsion from the Garden of Eden out into a world of struggle, pain and death. All Adam's subsequent generations had the task of rectifying his sin in order to return to grace and create a veritable Garden of Eden in this world.

Abraham and Isaac had begun the task. Now it was Jacob's turn. He had already spent twenty years of bitter exile outside the "Garden", the Land of Israel, "atoning", as it were, for Adam's sin. Jacob had survived Laban's onslaught of serpentine trickery and lies. Now he had to confront Esau, exemplar of the "Fallen Man" who lives only to gratify his own selfish lusts, unafraid to strike, wound, maim and kill all who dare cross his path, plundering, raping and grabbing whatever he wants.

What the Serpent had stolen from Adam through cunning was the Godly intelligence man needs in order to stand up against his own lower urges. This divine wisdom, reclaimed by Abraham and Isaac, was itself the birthright Jacob took from Esau -- also with "cunning". It was when Jacob and Esau had been fifteen that Esau on day came in from the field ravenously hungry and Jacob "gave him the soup" -- i.e. provided Esau with the material "food" he wanted to consume in exchange for the spiritual birthright that Esau spurned (Genesis 25:29-34).

It was also with "cunning" that Jacob later "stole" the blessings just as Isaac was about to give them to Esau. On Rebecca's insistence, Jacob dressed up in Esau's clothes and went in to Isaac first (*ibid.* 27:1-40). Only with holy "cunning" could Jacob outwit the subtle serpent incarnate in Esau.

"A Gift, Prayer and War"

As Esau advanced with his four hundred armed warriors, what was Jacob to do? The last thing he wanted was a violent confrontation that could only lead to bloodshed. Jacob was not a coward. Having sat in the tent of Isaac as well as Abraham, Jacob possessed holy *Gevurah*-strength as well as

Chessed-kindness. But Jacob's mission was not to prevail merely by destroying all opposition. It was to create synthesis and harmony among opposing forces, enabling them to co-exist in dynamic balance, each playing its proper role without overstepping its bounds and interfering with any other. Jacob's mission was the opposite of war and destruction: it was to let peace and justice prevail.

But how could Jacob make peace with an Esau who was nursing a venomous grudge? How could Jacob transmute this age-old conflict into a win/win situation in which Jacob and Esau could both survive and play their role in mankind's work of bringing the world back to God?

The key to Jacob's wisdom was simplicity. To create balance, he used balance. "Jacob prepared himself with three things: a gift, prayer and war" (*Rashi* on Genesis 32:40). On the one hand, he sought to placate Esau with a magnificent display of *Chessed*-kindness, sending him a fat gift of goats, sheep, cattle, oxen and donkeys, the material wealth Esau loved. At the same time Jacob prepared himself for war so as to be able to take on Esau directly if necessary with *Gevurah*-power.

But even as he took these practical steps, Jacob put his trust not in his own strategies and efforts but in God. True to his upward-looking center-column quality of *Tiferet*-harmony, Jacob turned to God for help through prayer. In the words of Jacob's descendant, David, as he faced Goliath: "You come against me with the sword, the spear and the javelin. But I come against you in the name of *HaVaYaH* of Hosts, the God of Israel" (Samuel I, 17:45).

Jacob's Prayer

"And Jacob said: God of my father Abraham and God of my father Isaac, *HaVaYaH*, who told me, Go to your land and your birthplace and I will deal well with you. I am too small for all the kindnesses and all the truth you have done for Your servant, for with my stick I crossed this Jordan and now I have become two camps. Please save me from the hand of my brother, from the hand of Esau, for I am afraid he might come and strike me and kill the mothers with the children...." (Genesis 32:10-12).

Jacob's prayer is simple and direct. God Himself had told Jacob to return home. Jacob was well aware that everything he had was God's gift. Before asking for anything, he first acknowledged all God's kindnesses until now. But with his caravan of mothers and little children, Jacob was most vulnerable, and he was afraid. He told God exactly what he felt and asked for precisely what he needed: *Help*! "Save me from the hand of Esau!"

In essence, Jacob's struggle against Esau is the struggle of the soul to come to its destiny by spiritualizing this material world of *Asiyah*, Action, in which we live. (The Hebrew letters of Esau spell out *Aso*, a root meaning "doing, acting".) The endless temptations and obstacles in this world are all a test for the soul, whose task is to elevate this refractory material world in the service of God. As long as we are in this world we have to function physically, eat, drink, make a living, reproduce and so on. The question is: do we allow our material needs and urges to dominate our lives, or can we find ways to transmute our very physical functions into avenues of ascent to God?

The mitzvot (commandments) of the Torah show us how to follow a Godly path in all the different situations we face in our lives in this world. But knowing what we ought to do is not enough. We have to get ourselves to do it. The dictates of the material world can be so powerful. The tests can be overwhelming. The material world has a degree of *Gevurah*-Power that the soul can only overcome with the help of God's superior strength. It is up to us to invoke that strength and power through prayer -- crying out to God for help -- in order to "save Jacob and redeem him from a hand too strong for him" (from the Evening Prayer).

When Jacob went into Isaac disguised as Esau in order to receive the blessings, the blind Isaac felt Jacob's skin-swathed arms and said, "The voice is the voice of Jacob but the hands are the hands of Esau" (Genesis 27:22). In this world the soul, "Jacob", is clothed in the skin and bones of the physical body: "Esau". For our mission here, is to act in the material world of *Asiyah* with our very hands: "The hands are the hands of Esau". But Esau's hands have the power to crush the soul unless "the voice is the voice of Jacob!" Only by using the faculty that distinguishes man from the animals, voice and speech -- Prayer -- can Jacob, the soul, prevail over Esau's materialism.

The material world of *Asiyah* is at the "feet", the bottom of the whole system of worlds upon worlds created by God as a means of ascent for the soul. In this world, the soul, Jacob,

Yaakov, is at the *EKeV*, "foot" of the universe. His mission is to find Godliness even at the lowest levels of creation. This he does by viewing all things in the radiant light of Chokhmah-Wisdom, represented in the letter *Yud*, root of all the twenty-two letters of the Aleph-Bet. Thus, Jacob's name is made up by joining the *Yud* to *EKeV* (the heel): *Ya-AKoV*.

When Jacob and Esau, the "twins", were born, "The first one came out all red like a hairy mantle all over, and they called his name Esau. And afterwards his brother came out, and his hand was holding the heel of Esau, and he called his name Jacob" (Genesis 25:25-6). From the very beginning Jacob had his "hand" (*YaD* = *Yud*, *Chokhmah*-Wisdom) at the heel (*EKeV*) of Esau, *Asiyah*, the heel and foot of all the worlds. That was why he was called *Ya-AKoV*.

Now, years later, as Jacob readied himself to confront Esau and his four hundred armed warriors, he again used his "hand", the *YaD* (= *YuD*) of *Chokhmah*-Wisdom -- Prayer (see Exodus 17:12 and *Targum Onkelos*).

Jacob's struggle was not with the physical Esau and his men but with Esau's spiritual root, the "Angel" that gives the material world its power over us. It was night -- the time of faith -- after Jacob took his family across into the Land of Israel, that he wrestled with the Angel:

"And he arose in the night and took his two wives and his two maid-servants and his eleven children and he passed over the crossing of the Jabok. He took them and brought them across the river and he brought over what he had. And Jacob was left

THE ENCOUNTER WITH ESAU

alone and a man struggled with him until the dawn came up. When he saw that he could not prevail against him, he wrenched Jacob's hip at its socket and Jacob's hip was strained as he wrestled with him. He said, "Send me away for the dawn has risen." But Jacob said, "I will not send you away unless you bless me." He said, "What is your name?" He said, "Jacob." He said, "Your name will no longer called Jacob but Israel, for you have struggled (*SaRita*) with angels and with men and you have prevailed" (Genesis 32:23-29).

"And Jacob was left alone". According to tradition, "he forgot some small jars and went back for them" (*Rashi ad loc.*). Jacob and his family were in mortal peril, yet Jacob went back across the river to fetch a few forgotten jars even though they were probably only earthenware pots, which for the ancients were like today's throwaway plastic. But Jacob stood for the very opposite of Esau's destructiveness and waste! "Do not destroy!" The physical world is not a lush smorgasbord laid on for us to plunder, waste and destroy as we please. Material property is precious. Even the smallest things should be treated with respect and care. Our very blood and sweat go into gaining our material needs in this world. If we destroy our property and resources, we are destroying ourselves. Our task in this world is to sanctify and elevate the material, for by doing so, we sanctify and elevate ourselves.

The "man" with whom Jacob wrestled was Esau's guardian angel (*Bereishit Rabbah* 77:3). Jacob's struggle is the unremitting struggle of the soul in a material world that constantly threatens to get out of hand and overwhelm us.

But Jacob would not give up even when the angel caught him at the hip. There are times when the material world locks us in its grip. People go under economically. They become weak, sick and disabled. They die. But regardless of the challenge, Jacob persists, holding his hand -- the *Yad* of *Chokhmah*-Wisdom -- to the heel, the *EKeV*, the world of *Asiyah*, in order to use it only for holiness and spiritual ascent. Jacob does not yield. He knows that all aspects of *Asiyah* can be elevated by turning to God in prayer.

Through his sheer persistence Jacob overcame the Angel. He would not let him go until he blessed him. The Angel acknowledged that Jacob had prevailed and gave him the name Israel, *YiSRa-EL*, for "you struggled with angels and with men and you have prevailed." Having defeated the angel, it was easy for Jacob to prevail over Esau, which he did not with military might but wisdom, humility, gifts, respect and honor, magnanimity and the spirit of reconciliation.

Succot

"Esau went back that day on his way to Seir. And Jacob journeyed to Succot and built himself a House, and for his cattle he built shelters, therefore he called the name of the place Succot" *(Genesis 33:16-17).*

Catching sight of Esau and his four hundred men advancing towards him, Jacob grouped his wives and their respective children and went out ahead of them to meet Esau.

"He prostrated on the earth seven times until he reached his brother. And Esau ran to meet him and embraced him and fell on his neck and kissed him, and they wept...."

(Genesis 33:3-4)

Jacob's display of humility aroused Esau's compassion. Jacob pressed him to accept his gifts, and Esau agreed. He even suggested that they join and travel together. But Jacob knew that their destinies were different and that to remain faithful to his own mission he must keep a respectful distance from Esau.

"And he said to him, my lord knows that the children are tender and the flocks and herds have their young, and one hard day's traveling could knock them out and all the flocks would die. Let my lord pass on in front of his servant and I will advance slowly at the pace of the cattle that are ahead of me and at the pace of the children...." (Genesis 33:13-14)

Jacob's reply reveals a down-to-earth practicality and a touching sensitivity to the needs of the weakest and tenderest. Jacob had the ability to take account of everyone's different needs and to orchestrate opposing forces into a dynamic harmony. With *Binah*-understanding he could pay attention to the tiniest details while at the same time using wide-angle *Chokhmah*-vision to see each detail in its proper place in the context of the wider whole.

By bringing even Esau -- representing the material world of *Asiyah* -- to make peace with him, Jacob showed that he had the power to harness the material world itself in service of his higher spiritual quest without letting its grosser aspects divert him from his path.

This was what qualified Jacob to build his House. It was not only to be a "house" in the metaphorical sense, a community of souls. There had to be an actual physical structure as well. The spiritual and physical had to be joined together. Immediately after his reconciliation with Esau -- *Asiyah* -- Jacob built a House:

"Esau went back that day on his way to Seir. And Jacob journeyed to Succot and built himself a *House*, and for his animals he built shelters, therefore he called the name of the place Succot" (Genesis 33:16-17).

When Jacob built his House he thought about everyone, not only the adults and children but even the animals. All have their different needs. Everything must have its just and proper place in the larger whole.

Jacob's domestic practicality comes to teach us that we have to bring even the smallest practical details of our material lives inside the "House" of our overall spiritual vision. If we merely think and talk about spiritual ideals without acting accordingly when we go about our daily business, our "spirituality" is an illusion.

The Torah teaches us how to bring all of life inside the "House" of spirituality by following the *halachot*, practical pathways that apply in all the various different situations we face as we go about our lives in the material world. The pathway that includes all others is that of personal prayer. This is the most powerful way to make the necessary connection between our spiritual goals and the details of our material lives. In the words of Rebbe Nachman:

"You must pray for everything. If your garment is torn and must be replaced, pray to God for a new one. Do this for everything. Make it a habit to pray for all your needs, large or small. Your main prayers should be for fundamentals, that God should help you in your devotion and bring you close to Him. Still, you should also pray even for trivial things. God may give you food and clothing and everything else you need even though you do not ask for them. But then you are like an animal. God gives every living thing its bread without being asked. He can also give it to you this way. But if you do not draw your life through prayer then it is like that of a beast. For a *man* must draw all the necessities of life from God only through prayer."

Rabbi Nachman's Wisdom #233

Ecological Significance of the Succah

To be true to his mission in this world, man must "draw all the necessities of life from God only through prayer". If he fails to do this, he is no better than an animal. Indeed, when man merely consumes and takes from this world the way animals do, not only does he fall below his own proper level, he brings the rest of the world down with him, causing the animals themselves to suffer.

Rabbi Nachman discusses this point in a teaching about the Succah (see below). During the annual autumn festival of Succot it is a mitzvah to dwell in a Succah, a temporary structure with a roof made of nothing but leaves, branches and similar natural vegetation. One should take one's best furniture and utensils out into the Succah and actually live there the way one normally lives in one's house, eating and drinking, studying, praying and meditating, relaxing, socializing and even sleeping in the Succah.

Succot, third of the major annual festivals, is particularly associated with Jacob, third of the founding fathers. Bringing all one's various activities down to the most material under the roof of the holy Succah symbolizes the need to bring all the details of our lives inside the "House" of spirituality. This is why when Jacob built his house, not only did he build for himself and his family. He also "made shelters [*succot*] for his animals."

Rebbe Nachman taught:

When animals die off before their proper time, the reason is because people fail to take care to observe the mitzvah of Succah properly. For the Succah, which is essentially a shelter, represents the sefirah of *Binah*, which is called a "Mother who *shelters* her children". [*Binah* is the mother, while the lower sefirot which emanate from Binah are her "children"].

It is man's *Binah*-intelligence and understanding that puts him above the animals. For this reason, in humans the breasts from which babies get their nourishment are higher up on the mother's body, whereas the udders from which young animals feed are lower down on the mother animal's body. In the same way on the spiritual level, man derives his sustenance from the sefirah of *Binah*, which is a very exalted level, whereas animals receive their sustenance from a lower level.

When a person fails to observe the mitzvah of Succah properly he falls from the level of *Binah* (= the Succah) and descends to a level where his nourishment comes from "animal udders". This means that he takes for himself the nourishment and energy that were intended for the animals.

By doing so, he takes away their very life-force, as a result of which the animals die. How far a person falls depends on his neglect of the mitzvah of Succah. The further he falls, the more he takes away the life-force belonging to the animals, causing their death. This is why it says that Jacob "made Succot for his animals". For the Succah is for the sake of the animals!

Building can be a very dangerous occupation, as our Rabbis said: "Everyone who engages in building becomes poor" (*Sotah* 11). For the house must be built with wisdom and intelligence, and then the person will come to no harm from building. When a person has wisdom and intelligence, it is fitting for him to build a house, as it is written: "The house will be built with wisdom and established with understanding. And with knowledge the rooms will be filled" (Proverbs 24:3-4). By building such a house, the person creates a space in which to draw blessing into the world. But when a person builds without intelligence, it is harmful to him and he becomes impoverished. This is his punishment for having failed to build the house with wisdom, for "the wisdom of the poor is despised" (Ecclesiastes 9:16). It is therefore through the Succah, which represents intelligence, *Binah*, that a person is able to build a house, as it says, "With wisdom the house will be built."

This is why "Jacob traveled to Succot and built himself a house" (Genesis 33:17).

Likutey Moharan I, 266

The Succah and the Temple

Rebbe Nachman's teaching about the Succah demonstrates man's pivotal role of responsibility for the welfare of the world as a whole. Our fulfilment of God's mitzvot with the proper care ensures a balanced flow of blessing and nourishment to all levels of creation. Failure to fulfill the mitzvot can cause the death of animals and other ecological disasters.

Rebbe Nachman explains that it was only through first "traveling to Succot" that Jacob was able to build his house. In other words, man's very ability to establish a sound material basis for his own life in his "house" depends upon his willingness to take responsibility for overall ecological balance. This he does through "Succah" -- bringing all the details of life under the *Binah*-intelligence of Torah, which provides specific pathways to be followed at all the different junctures in our lives. Fulfillment of the various mitzvot brings a flow of life and blessing to all creation, leading to the overall ecological balance upon on which man's own long-term welfare depends.

This is a vital lesson at a time when people all over the world have fallen under the spell of a mindless consumerism that is destroying the global environment at a rate which threatens our very survival. Mankind is doomed to destruction unless humanity can learn to regulate its consumption intelligently. This will only be possible with the *Binah*-intelligence of the Torah, weaning people from excess by showing them how to eat, drink and carry out their other material functions in a way that elevates them to the level of spiritual activities.

This is precisely what Jacob's House -- the Holy Temple -- is all about. The Temple is to serve as a powerful, vivid, concrete symbol of the idea of Succah for all mankind. The idea of Succah is to bring even the most mundane aspects of our material lives inside the "House" of spirituality, making them part of our spiritual quest. This is achieved first and foremost by praying about our everyday needs and activities. Thus, the Temple is the "House of Prayer for all mankind" (Isaiah 56:7).

This does not mean that the Temple is simply a large place of worship where people can come together to pray. Certainly, the Temple is a devotional center where people come to connect with God. But this is not merely because it provides a suitable physical space to accomodate the worshippers. Every single detail of the design of the Temple buildings and courtyards is itself part of the lesson about prayer. "The design of the Temple corresponds to the design of creation" (*Tikkuney Zohar*, Introduction). The various halls and courtyards of the Temple correspond to the various worlds discussed in the Kabbalah. These spiritual worlds receive vitality and blessing through man's service in this world. Not only do the Temple rituals bring about a flow of vitality into the spiritual worlds. Every detail of the daily services and other "household" activities in the Temple is a teaching to mankind about how to lead our lives in our own private homes and houses in a way that leads to harmony and ecological balance in this world.

The Temple is comprehensible to the human mind because it is similar to a human house. A human house has a place to prepare and cook food for the people living in it and a place to eat it. The Temple was a place to which various kinds of "food" were constantly being brought in the form of animals, birds, corn, wine and oil for the various sacrifices. These were "consumed" on the altar, which is compared to the human table, or in some cases eaten by the priests and their families or by those who brought the sacrifices in an exercise of holy eating.

The human house provides space for us to rest and enjoy privacy and intimacy with our dear ones. Corresponding to this in the Temple is the "Holy of Holies", which is sometimes called *Cheder HaMitot*, the "room of the beds" or "bedroom"! The Holy of Holies, which is the place of ultimate union of the Holy One and His Indwelling Presence, is a teaching about the purity and holiness of the love between husband and wife in the intimacy of their own private chamber.

When Jacob had his dream of the ladder at the spot where this House of God was to be built, he saw angels ascending and descending. The various physical rituals in the Temple send expanding waves of influence to all the higher worlds: "angels ascending". This in turn elicits a response of blessing and life-force flowing from the higher worlds back into this world: "angels descending". The Temple rituals are vivid teachings about the holiness to which we should aspire when we eat and drink and go about our other activities in our own private homes and houses. Through sanctifying our mundane activities, we too send "angels" to the higher worlds and elicit the flow of blessing and vitality into this world.

"Rise, Go Up to the House of God"

It was after Jacob's triumph over Esau -- *Asiyah* -- that God told him to go up to Beit El, "The House of God", so that he could fulfill the vow made years earlier after his dream of the ladder.

And God said to Jacob: "Rise, Go up to Beit El and dwell there and make there an altar to El, the God who appeared to you when you fled from Esau your brother." And Jacob said to his house and to all who were with him, "Remove the foreign gods that are in you and purify yourselves and change your clothes. And let us rise up and go up to the House of God, and I will make there an altar to *El*, the God who answers me on my day of trouble and Who was with me on the path I have traveled" (Genesis 35:1-3).

Jacob's journey to Beit El turned into a great pilgrimage of men, women and children in a joint act of self-purification, repentance and self-dedication to God. This is symbolic of the destined future repentance of mankind as foretold by the prophets:

"And it will be at the end of days that the *Mountain* of the *House* of *HaVaYaH* will be established at the head of the mountains and it will be lifted up above the hills and all the nations will stream to it. And many nations will go and say, Come and let us go up to the Mountain of *HaVaYaH*, to the House of the God of Jacob, and He will teach us His ways and we will go on His pathways. For from Zion the Torah will go forth and the word of God from Jerusalem. And He will judge between the nations and reprove many peoples and they will break their swords into plow-shares and their spears into pruning-hooks and nation will not lift up sword against nation and they will no longer learn war" (Isaiah 2:1-4).

Said Rabbi Elazar: What does Isaiah mean when he says, "And many peoples will go and say, 'Come let us go up to the Mountain of God to the House of the God of Jacob!'"? Why the God of Jacob and not the God of Abraham and Isaac? The answer is: Not like Abraham, who saw it as a Mountain ("as it is said this day, On the *mountain HaVaYaH* is seen" -- Genesis 22:14). And not like Isaac, for whom it was a Field ("And Isaac went out to meditate in the *field*" -- Genesis 24:63). But like Jacob, who called it a House: "And he called the name of that place Beth El, the *House* of God" (Genesis 28:19).

Pesachim 88a

Jacob built the House of Prayer for all mankind. Abraham saw spirituality as a lofty Mountain, but this made it forbidding and inaccessible to all but a few, because "Who can ascend the mountain of *HaVaYaH*?" (Psalms 24:3). Isaac made it more attainable by turning it into a Field that can be tilled and cultivated through sustained work and effort. Yet this too requires a level of discipline that cannot be maintained by everyone.

However, Jacob "called it a House". Everyone understands what a house is. The teaching exemplified in Jacob's life is to bring even the smallest practical details of our lives within the "House" of spirituality. First and foremost, this is done by praying about them simply and directly in our own words. The world of *Asiyah* can be an obstacle to spirituality, but prayer turns it into a chariot of ascent to God.

When Jacob's House is established on the Temple Mount, the nations "will break their swords into plow-shares and their spears into pruning-hooks and nation will not lift up sword against nation and they will no longer learn war".

This magnificent vision of future peace and harmony can be attained if each one of us will learn to play his or her part in building the House by pursuing the highest spiritual goals in and through the practical details of our lives down to our very eating and drinking, working, socializing, etc. Only if we can succeed in attaining harmony between the spiritual and material in the domains where we have influence in conjunction with the people we actually live with can we hope for harmony to spread through the world as a whole.

Jacob's Heritage

"Moses charged us with the Torah as the heritage of the congregation of Jacob" (Deuteronomy 33:4).

Jacob's return to his ancestral land and pilgrimage to Beit El are far from being the end of the story. The foundations of Jacob's House were laid but the laborious, multi-generational task of actually building it was yet to come. The story of the building of the House is the on-going history of Jacob and those who go by his name until today, his descendants, the Children of Israel.

"And Jacob dwelled in the land where his father dwelled" (Genesis 37:1). "All Jacob wanted was to live contentedly, but the trouble over Joseph burst out. The tzaddikim just want to live contentedly, but the Holy One blessed-be-He says: Isn't it enough for the tzaddikim that they have so much prepared for them in the World to Come but they want peace and contentment in this world also?" (*Rashi ad loc.*).

The very essence of Jacob is peace. His mission is to forge harmony out of opposites in order to bring true peace in this and all the worlds. But for that very reason Jacob had to grapple all his life with conflict and the clash of opposites. In addition to his troubles with Esau and Laban, he endured soul-rending jealousy and strife within his own family, especially when his other sons ganged up against Joseph, first-born of Jacob's favorite Rachel, selling him into slavery while telling Jacob he was killed by a wild animal.

Jacob's twelve sons express different aspects of the sefirot, all of which must be brought into an overall dynamic balance in order to rectify the creation. The unfolding tale of the rivalries between the brothers, especially that between Joseph and Judah, was programmatic for all of later Jewish history, which is the story of the rivalry between the House of David and Kingdom of Judah against the Kingdom of Israel (the Ten Tribes) under the leadership of the tribe of Ephraim (who was one of Joseph's sons). It is through the twisting-turning outplay of this rivalry on the stage of world history that God will be revealed to all the world with the coming of Mashiach the son of Joseph and Mashiach the son of David.

Having been sold into slavery in Egypt, Joseph rose to become Pharaoh's Viceroy, saving the country from famine through his plan to consume intelligently during the good years in order to conserve food for the bad years. Egypt being the only place where food was available, Jacob sent his sons there to buy grain, which eventually led to their dramatic reconciliation with Joseph. Jacob and his family of seventy souls now moved to Egypt, becoming within a few generations a nation numbering more than six hundred thousand.

Just as Adam had been expelled from Eden into a world of pain and toil, so the Children of Israel found themselves exiled from their ancestral land enduring bitter servitude to Pharaoh. Instead of building the House of God in the Land of

Israel, they were sunk in the degenerate culture of what was then the most "sophisticated" of all countries, building store-cities for Pharaoh. The cycle of history had swung to the opposite extreme from when Abraham boldly rejected the idolatrous city-culture of his time and went off alone in quest of the Land.

Yet the purpose of the downswing was to lead to the upswing, when with heavenly signs and miracles Moses led the six hundred thousand Children of Israel out of the cities of Egypt into the stark, awesome majesty of the desert, where at the foot of Mount Sinai they heard the voice of *HaVaYaH* for themselves and accepted the Torah.

"Moses charged us with the Torah as the heritage of the congregation of Jacob" (Deuteronomy 33:4). It is through the Torah that Jacob's descendants in all the generations work to complete his task of building the House of God. For the Torah provides the pathways and guidelines through which all the details of our lives in the material world of *Asiyah* can be brought inside the spiritual "House" to serve as a means of ascent and connection with God. This is the heritage of Jacob.

The following chapters will focus on those aspects of the Torah pathway that enhance our awareness of the world of nature and the environment and bring harmony and balance into the way we interact with them. In an age when much of humanity's interaction with nature and the environment is almost pathological, it is more necessary than ever to turn to the Torah, for "all her pathways are peace", and they alone can bring peace and harmony within human society, between man and the natural environment, and between man and God.

Day by Day

"Know today and take into your heart that HaVaYaH *is the only God in the heavens above and on the earth below, there is none other" (Deuteronomy 4:39)*

*E*ating the fruit of the tree of knowledge has left mankind in a state of distorted consciousness.

True knowledge -- holy *Daat* -- is a state of consciousness in which we are aware of the truth: that all that exists is from *HaVaYaH*, and He alone rules over the entire creation -- "in the heavens above and on earth below". It is not enough to know this intellectually. We have to work to bring this knowledge from our heads down into our hearts until it is something we *feel* and are constantly aware of even as we go about our mundane activities. God is not only somewhere "out there" -- "in the heavens above". God is with us here and now -- "on the earth below" and in all the details of our lives!

This is a level of knowledge and awareness that many people rarely if ever experience, though it is embedded deep within everyone's soul. Most of the time, however, the dictates of everyday life keep our conscious minds so preoccupied with our immediate needs and interests that it takes a positive effort to make ourselves aware of God's presence and see the Godly wisdom contained in all things. The difficulty in maintaining this awareness amidst all the

THE HOUSE ON THE MOUNTAIN

distractions from the surrounding world and from our own worldly egos is one of the consequences of Adam's eating of the fruit of the tree of knowledge.

Prayer: An Exercise in Awareness

The mission of the founding fathers Abraham, Isaac and Jacob was to forge a path of ascent so that mankind could return to Adam's spiritual level before the sin. Our heritage from the fathers is the rich treasury of Jewish practice, many aspects of which are bound up with elevating ourselves above ego-consciousness to the level of *Daat*, spiritual knowledge and awareness.

This is especially true in the case of the prayers and blessings recited at various points through the day. Abraham instituted the morning prayer and the blessing after eating. Isaac and Jacob instituted the afternoon and evening prayers. Over the generations the daily prayer ritual was expanded and embellished until it took its present form as found in the classic *Siddur* -- the "Order" of prayers -- shared (with minor differences) by Jewish communities all over the world. The main blessings and prayers were composed by the Men of the Great Assembly in the early Second Temple period (3rd century B.C.E.). All of them were prophets who had received the mystical tradition of the Torah via a direct line of transmission stretching back to Moses and the Patriarchs.

Having been composed by mystics who were masters of the Hebrew letters and their secrets, the very words of the Hebrew prayers are power-combinations of letters that transmit spiritual influence upwards into the higher worlds in order to channel a flow of divine goodness and blessing back down into this world. At the same time, the blessings and prayers in the Siddur have a simple, readily understandable meaning as affirmations of faith, expressions of gratitude, praise, prayerful invocations and requests.

Prayer is an act of service. In order to channel divine blessing, it is necessary to speak out the actual letters and words of the prayers with our very mouths, causing the air of this world of *Asiyah* to vibrate so as to send fanning ripples of influence to all the higher worlds. Yet prayer is called the "service of the *heart*". This is because although the words must actually be spoken, the essence of the work of prayer is in the mind and heart. It is to know and *feel* the meaning and significance of the words we are saying. It is this focusing of attention that elevates our minds above ego-consciousness to *Daat*. Prayer is an exercise in awareness.

The "simple meaning" of the prayers can differ from person to person, and indeed it may change and develop as a person advances on the spiritual pathway. Our purpose here is to offer some suggestions about how the daily blessings and prayers can be used to focus our awareness on God's creative power as manifested in the world of nature around us and to help us cultivate attitudes of thankfulness, humility and social and environmental responsibility.

The Morning Blessings

On waking up in the morning, the first act of the day is to pour water over our hands in order to cleanse them of the unholy physicality that overtakes the body during sleep. The hands are the instruments with which we act in this material world of *Asiyah*. By pouring the pure waters of *Chessed*-kindness over our hands, we elevate them from being the "hands of Esau" serving only the self, and dedicate them to holy action in God's service throughout the day.

After getting up, the first instinct of the worldly ego may be to satisfy the body's cravings for food and then get busy attending to its other needs. It is a training in self-control to break this instinct and instead make time first thing in the morning to attend to our spiritual needs through a period of meditation and prayer.

The morning prayers begin with a series of blessings of thanksgiving for some of the most basic kindnesses God shows us every single day.

First is the blessing over the human body, *Asher Yatzar*: "Blessed are You, God, King of the Universe, Who fashioned man with wisdom and created within him many openings and many cavities...." This is one of many blessings that are associated with a specific physical function. It is recited after relieving ourselves. The blessing elevates the physical function by turning it into an occasion for inner meditation and thanksgiving for the marvels of

God's creation as manifested in the subtle wisdom of the body's design and functioning. Only through the body can the soul exist in and interact with the physical world. Recognizing the divine wisdom in the body itself is the first step in grasping the spiritual meaning of our existence in the physical world. Only with this awareness is it possible to bring balance and harmony into our interactions with the surrounding world.

The blessing of *Asher Yatzar* is followed by a blessing of thanks for the soul and its return to the body after sleep, and blessings over God's gift of the Torah, which guides us in every aspect and detail of our life in this world.

Then come *Birkhot HaShachar*, the "Morning Blessings", expressing our gratitude for specific benefits that we enjoy in this world, such as our ability to see, the fact that we have clothes, we can move our limbs, stand up, walk around, etc. Each blessing helps us make a connection between the general idea of God, King of the Universe, and the specific aspect of life to which the blessing refers.

The Sacrificial Readings

The purpose of the prayer service is to bind this world and our lives within it to the higher spiritual worlds. What the synagogue prayer services are intended to accomplish for the individual and the community, the daily Temple rituals accomplish for the whole world, bringing harmony into mankind's interaction with the natural environment.

In the absence of the Temple, the most we can do is to re-enact these rituals in our minds and on our lips. One of the ways this is done is through the customary reading of certain Biblical and Talmudic passages relating to the daily sacrifices, kindling of the *Menorah* (candelabrum), burning of the incense, and other aspects of the Temple rituals.

Lack of familiarity with these rituals may make them seem strange at first or even primitive. This may be because they involve such primal elements, such as the water with which the priests washed their hands and feet, the blood of the sacrificial lambs, the fire on the altar, the salt, the corn and wine, the pure olive oil of the *Menorah* and the eleven herbs and spices in the incense.

In fact, the Temple rituals with their music, song and prayer brought the mineral, vegetable and animal and human worlds together in acts of joyous worship that elevated all of them, drawing sustenance and blessing to each on its proper level and forging harmony between them all.

In the present state of imbalance between mankind and the natural environment, daily reading of the sacrificial portions is an act of faith in the power of our thoughts, our words and the yearning of our hearts to initiate a new order in which the Temple will be rebuilt and the Torah of peace and harmony will go out from Jerusalem to all the world.

Psukey Dezimra: Verses of Song

The Kabbalah teaches that the morning prayer service is a ladder of ascent leading the spiritual devotee upwards step by step from this physical world of *Asiyah* to the higher spiritual worlds. The Morning Blessings relating to our daily physical needs and the Sacrificial Readings about the animal offerings and other Temple rituals are obviously very much bound up with this world.

The next section of the prayer service, known as *Psukey deZimra*, "Verses of Song", consists of various psalms (or extracts from psalms) together with other scriptural passages of praise and song. This section of the service corresponds to the spiritual World of *Yetzirah* ("Formation"), which is the world of the lower angels, the spiritual forces (*Tzurot*) underlying and supervising all the various material and physical processes in the world of *Asiyah*.

The "Verses of Song" includes several vivid depictions of the world of nature:

"Call out to God with thanks, with the harp sing to our God -- Who covers the heavens with clouds, Who prepares rain for the earth, Who makes mountains sprout with grass. He gives to an animal its food, to the young ravens that cry out...." (Psalms 147:7-9).

"Halleluyah! Praise *HaVaYaH* from the heavens, praise Him in the heights! Praise Him, all His angels; praise Him all His legions. Praise Him, sun and moon; praise Him, all bright stars. Praise Him, the most exalted of the heavens and the waters that are above the heavens. Let them praise the Name of *HaVaYaH*, for He commanded and they were created. And He established them forever and ever; He issued a decree that will not change. Praise *HaVaYaH* from the earth, sea giants and all watery depths. Fire and hail, snow and vapor, stormy wind fulfilling His word. Mountains and all hills, fruitful trees and all cedars. Beasts and all cattle, crawling things and winged fowl. Kings of the earth and all governments, princes and all judges on earth. Young men and also maidens, old men together with youths. Let them praise the Name of *HaVaYaH*, for His Name alone is exalted; His glory is above earth and heaven...." (ibid. 148:1-13).

Even if our lives are centered mainly in today's man-made urban environment, daily mindful recital of these magnificent passages cannot but expand our horizons and enhance our consciousness of the awesomely wondrous natural environment within which our self-obsessed culture pursues its frenetic course. The "Verses of Song" instill a joyous faith and trust that within and behind all the different phenomena around us lies the hand of the One Creator, Whose tender kindnesses and mercies are to be discerned in all the workings of the universe.

The *Shema* and *Amidah* Prayer

This faith reaches its fullest expression in the recital of the Shema, our affirmation of the unity of God: "Hear, Israel,

HaVaYaH is our God, *HaVaYaH* is one!" The Shema is recited in the morning and the evening. The timing is thus related to one of the most basic cycles of creation: day and night, two opposites. It is necessary to recite the Shema at the beginning of both, in order to instill within us the faith that God's unity transcends opposites. The timing of the morning Shema is related to the time of sunrise. The morning prayer thus keeps us aware of this most basic natural phenomenon and helps us tap into the spiritual potential at this moment of renewal, growth and divine love.

The recital of the morning Shema is preceded by the blessing of *Yotzer Or*, "He forms the light and creates darkness...." This blessing takes us from contemplation of the visible light of the sun and other heavenly luminaries to the invisible "angels" or spiritual forces that give them their energy and determine their orbits and influence. The lower angels in the World of *Yetzirah* receive their power from the higher angels in the World of *Beriyah*, "Creation". All these angels are part of a magnificent, orchestrated whole singing the praises of the One God.

The Shema and its blessings is followed by the Amidah, the "Standing Prayer" of nineteen blessings recited in a whisper of rapt devotion to God. The Amidah prayer -- corresponding to the highest "world", that of *Atzilut*, is the climax of the entire service. Having affirmed in the Shema our faith in God's total power over all creation and His involvement in every detail, we now have the courage to step forward with reverence and humility in a private, intimate audience with the King and prayerfully put our own requests.

The nineteen blessings of the weekday Amidah prayer include prayers for all our needs individually and collectively. Praying to God for our various needs implants in us the trust that even as we ourselves take whatever active steps we deem necessary in order to satisfy them, this can be achieved only with the help of God and in obedience to His laws. This certainly applies to rectifying the world and bringing about a new order in which peace and harmony will reign. To pray to God daily not only for our own needs but for the welfare of the community and the whole world is to take responsibility.

Afternoon and Evening Services

Being in and of this material world, we have no option but to pursue our daily business, each one according to his or her vocation. Even trying to satisfy our most basic physical needs can become very time- and energy-consuming. It is easy to become so mentally absorbed in the mundane that we lose our higher *Daat*-consciousness and spiritual sensitivity. In order to "re-energize" spiritually, it is necessary periodically to step back from the mundane world and take a more holistic view of our lives in God's kingdom by making special times for prayer and contemplation.

The timing of the afternoon and evening prayers is related to the decline and setting of the sun, which again keeps us spiritually aligned in rhythm with this most basic natural cycle. In particular the first blessing before the evening Shema, *HaMaariv Aravim*, provides an opportunity to lift our inner eye to the heavens and contemplate the wonder and glory of the natural creation:

"Blessed are You, *HaVaYaH*, our God, King of the universe, who by His word brings on evenings, with wisdom opens gates, with understanding alters periods, changes the seasons and orders the stars in their heavenly constellations as He wills. He creates day and night, removing light before darkness and darkness before light. He causes day to pass and brings night, and separates between day and night...."

The Amidah prayer is recited in both the afternoon and evening services just as it is in the morning service. Since it is a prayer not only for all our individual needs but for those of the wider community and the rectification of the entire world, our constant recital of the Amidah with renewed longing and yearning three times a day is an act of the highest commitment and service.

Eating

Our bodily survival in the physical world depends upon eating, a function that necessarily puts us in direct contact with the natural environment. For many people, the interaction has the character of a battle, which is why the Hebrew word for man's most basic food, bread -- *Lechem* -- is related to the word *miLChaMah*, which means war.

"Because you ate from the tree from which I ordered you not to eat, the ground is cursed for you. You will have to toil to eat from it all the days of your life.... By the sweat of your brow you will eat bread...." (Genesis 3:17-19).

Throughout human history, making a living has been a struggle for most people, and so it still is today. Ironically, in an age when technology has brought so many to hitherto undreamed of levels of prosperity, the war to secure mankind's needs and desires has turned into a war of assault on the natural environment. Untrammeled consumerism, extravagance and waste are ravaging and despoiling the natural environment in a way that threatens our future survival.

The many mitzvot, blessings and prayers surrounding the earning, preparation and ingestion of our food turn what would otherwise be a purely physical, material process of self-gratification into an exalted service that deepens our understanding and appreciation of the wonder and mystery of creation.

Man's interaction with the material world to make a living is fraught with danger because of the power of the material world to suck us in and make us forget our spiritual mission. Whether we produce our food directly from the earth through agriculture and raising animals or earn it through some other economic activity, there are mitzvot relating to every different kind of activity. In agriculture, business or any other field, the relevant mitzvot provide us with ways of transforming the physical act into a pathway of connection with God. The discipline of the mitzvot enables to keep our involvement in the physical world within its proper limits so that it serves us in our spiritual goals rather than deflecting us from them.

The actual preparation of food is surrounded with many mitzvot: avoidance of all forbidden foods, including forbidden species; separation of tithes from agricultural produce of Israel; inspection of food to avoid worms and bugs, etc.; separation of the priestly *Chalah* from dough; proper slaughter of animals and birds; not cooking or eating meat and milk together, and so on. Such mitzvot directly govern the way we interact with the natural world, helping us maintain our spiritual alignment when taking from it what we need. Before eating, the table should be arranged with dignity and honor. Food should be treated with great reverence. Prior to eating bread, the hands should be ritually washed with the waters of *Chessed*-kindness to elevate them from being the "hands of Esau" to instruments of holy service.

When at last we put the food into our mouths this can easily turn into a moment of selfish greed and lust. Judaism transmutes it into one of spiritual devotion and divine connection through the blessings recited over various different kinds of food. It is our recital of the blessing that elevates us from the animal level to that of a human. Through the words of our lips and the meditation in our hearts we connect the specific fruit or other food we are about to eat with its Creator, the Source of all life and sustenance, thereby enabling the divine sparks within the food to enter our system so as to nourish our souls as well as our bodies.

Having satisfied our physical hunger, the natural tendency is to leave the body to its work of digesting and assimilating the food while we get up and move on to whatever we want to do next. But the Torah teaches us to control this tendency and take a few moments after eating to focus on the divine system of nutrition and sustenance through the recital of *Birkhat HaMazon* after eating bread or the appropriate after-blessing for other foods. Acknowledging how God provides us with all our needs is a powerful training in faith and trust, and helps curb greed and selfishness.

Other Blessings

Besides the blessings over food, there are many other blessings to be recited at other junctures. These include blessings over fragrant smells, striking natural phenomena such as comets, great mountains and rivers, the ocean, thunder and lightning, rainbows, and exceptionally beautiful trees and animals. Each of these blessings provides an opportunity to deepen the moment by enabling us to connect the specific experience with God, Creator of the Universe.

Shabbat

"Remember the Sabbath day to keep it holy. For six days, you may labor and do all your work. But the seventh day is Shabbat for HaVaYaH *Your God. You may do no work -- you, your son and your daughter, your slave and your maidservant, your animal and the stranger who is in your gates. For in six days* HaVaYaH *made the heaven and the earth, the sea and all that is in them, and He rested on the seventh day. Therefore,* HaVaYaH *blessed the Sabbath day and sanctified it"* (Exodus 20:8-11).

It is a strange irony that many people dislike work intensely and do it only if they have to, yet they find it hard to accept the idea of taking a complete holiday from all work once a week in order to experience Shabbat.

When Adam was in Eden he did not have to struggle to make a living. With all his needs provided, he was free to soar to supreme spiritual heights. But because of the sin of eating the forbidden fruit, mankind has to bear the scourge of having to sweat to earn a living. Many people are enslaved bodily and mentally to their work: that is how they live and that is how they die.

It was out of love and compassion that God "gave" the weekly Shabbat to release us from this slavery and comfort us during our exile in this world of labor. Once every seven days we can have a foretaste of the great bliss of the eternal Shabbat awaiting us when we finally complete our service in this world and our souls will return to the Garden of Eden.

Shabbat is a time to let our souls take the wings of *Daat*-consciousness and reunite with God in joy and delight. But the complete holiday experience of Shabbat can be attained only by forgetting about work and struggle and abstaining for the entire day from even the tiniest act of productive labor and physical manipulation of this world for our own ends. "For six days, you may labor and do all your work. But the seventh day is Shabbat for *HaVaYaH* Your God. You may do no work..."

The gift of Shabbat can be enjoyed only by fulfilling the necessary preconditions. Only by abstaining from all work is it possible to enter the state of perfect "rest" from the mundane world that enables us to ascend to the exalted spiritual levels accessible through this unique weekly celebration.

Melechet Machshevet

The Hebrew word for work is *Melachah*. The specific kinds of labor that are incompatible with Shabbat are those that fall into the category of *Melechet Machshevet*, actions that have the dimension of *Machshavah* -- "thought" or "intention". A labor that is *Melechet Machshevet* is one that is carried out with a thought or intention in mind, namely to manipulate something in the material world in a particular way with the purpose of bringing about a new state from which we hope to benefit.

The rabbis listed thirty-nine types of labor that may not be performed on Shabbat. These correspond to the thirty-nine types of labor that were involved in the building of the Sanctuary in the wilderness by the Children of Israel. These thirty-nine types of labor are generic categories encompassing every conceivable kind of productive labor in the world -- plowing and harvesting, processing and cooking food, weaving and sewing clothes, building, repairing, writing, lighting a fire, turning on a light or appliance, driving a car, producing a computer chip, piloting a spaceship and countless others.

Productive labor to provide for our material needs is a necessary and honorable activity, but it is not the primary purpose of our existence in this world. Nor indeed is our purpose here merely to consume the material fruits of our labors and live off the fat of the land. Our true mission is to use the material things of this world as aids in pursuit of our spiritual destiny. This transforms the thirty-nine labors with which we provide for our needs from being a bitter scourge into holy acts that turn this material world into God's Sanctuary in which everything reveals and declares His glory.

Only when we are not slaves to our work activities do we have the power to focus and direct them to holy ends and thereby sanctify them. There is something very compulsive about work. Even when people have more than they need for today, they still worry about what they will have when tomorrow comes. Fear and anxiety about future consumption drives people to keep doing and doing without a break, as if this will somehow keep them in control and give them what they desire.

Wanting to be in control was what made Adam take the fruit of the tree of knowledge. He was punished by having to toil and struggle in this world -- and even then, he is not in control! As long as man wants total control, refusing to work in partnership with the greater power of God, he turns himself into his own taskmaster, beating himself with the scourge of work.

The prohibition of all work on Shabbat comes to free man from slavery to his own compulsiveness. People find it hard to understand why Shabbat is incompatible with all kinds of favorite leisure-time activities from TV, driving, sports, concerts, theater, cinema and the like to gardening, writing, painting, playing with computers and many more. These restrictions seem to turn what is supposed to be a holiday into a tedious, forced rest.

It should not surprise us that so many people have no idea about what Shabbat really is since the true Shabbat experience is virtually unknown in our contemporary urban-technological culture. Big cities know no Shabbat. They never ever stop. Twenty-four hours a day, seven days a week people are shopping, TV's, radios, and videos jabber away, phones ring, lights flash on and off, cars flow endlessly along the highways, planes fly to and fro....

Unaware of the degree to which they are swept up in this energy, many people have simply lost the ability to relax and just BE without doing, doing, doing. It is as if they fear what might come into their minds if they were to stop, leave go of all gadgets and appliances and simply let things be without having to keep busy, be entertained or otherwise distracted for a while.

One reason why meditation has had such an impact in advanced technological societies over the past half century is because the practice of simply sitting and exploring the spiritual possibilities of the state of not-doing appeals to such a deep-seated craving in sensitive souls trapped amidst the tensions of contemporary "civilization".

The word Shabbat is related to the Hebrew root *SheVeT*, "sitting". This does not mean that the twenty-five hours of Shabbat from just before sunset on Friday until after dark on Saturday night have to be spent literally sitting doing nothing. The purpose of this weekly rest from all physical labor is to enable us to enter the world of spirit in a way that is not possible when we are preoccupied with our normal weekday activities.

The keynote of Shabbat is *Oneg*, the pleasure and delight that come from joyous prayer, the pursuit of knowledge and wisdom, strolling around enjoying the wonder of God's world, relaxing with dear ones and friends over festive meals, conversing, story-telling, singing together....

"If you restrain your feet because of the Shabbat, refrain from pursuing your own needs on My holy day and proclaim the Shabbat a delight, giving honor to God's holy honored one, and if you honor it by not doing your own ways, seeking your needs or discussing the forbidden. Then you shall take delight in *HaVaYaH* and I will let you ride on the heights of the earth and let you eat the heritage of your father Jacob, for the mouth of *HaVaYaH* has spoken" (Isaiah 58:13-14).

Shabbat Practise and Awareness of Nature

Many of the positive practices of Shabbat are bound up with appreciating the wonders of creation and heightening our awareness of the surrounding natural environment (see below). This is of the greatest importance at a time when our "advanced" civilization is causing irreparable damage to the natural Earth environment through its mindless, compulsive consumer extravagance and waste. One of the main reasons why humanity is standing by and letting this happen is because our urban-technological environment cuts people off from direct contact with nature, leaving them insensitive to the effects of consumerism on the natural environment.

If people had the courage to turn off their TV's, computers and other gadgetry in order to look with new eyes at the skies, the trees and plants, the birds and other living creatures, it would have a profound effect on their outlook and awareness. The detailed laws of Shabbat observance apply specifically to the Jewish People and not to gentiles. But the Shabbat mode of relating to the world may prove to be of universal significance. When man stops trying to manipulate the world for his own ends he can sit back and see it for what it is: God's most amazing creation. Only when he sees it as such can he indeed really enjoy it -- savoring its wonder and beauty with love, deep reverence and gratitude.

Shabbat Eve Prayers

Awareness of *Maaseh Bereishit*, the "Work of Creation" is one of the principle themes of Shabbat, and many of the prayers in the traditional Shabbat liturgy help us enhance this awareness.

There is a custom to read the Song of Songs on arrival in the synagogue on Friday afternoon prior to the Shabbat eve services, or alternatively at some other point during Shabbat. This exquisite love song of a shepherd and his beloved (God and the Soul, or God and the Jewish People) is set amidst fields, meadows, orchards, vineyards, gardens, hills and mountains covered with fragrant herbs, aside the freshest, purest untouched springs, with sheep and goats grazing peacefully and trailing down the hillsides. There are references to all kinds of trees, plants, herbs, spices, various animals, the sun and the moon, etc.

Recital of the Song of Songs is a guided meditation that lifts us out of our everyday mentality and brings us into Shabbat consciousness, taking us to an idyllic, faraway, pure, simple, innocent world of artless natural beauty, grace, love and joy.

The Friday afternoon *Minchah*-service is followed by *Kabbalat Shabbat*, "Receiving the Shabbat". This starts with a series of Psalms 95-99 and 29, followed by the *Lecha Dodi* ("Come my beloved") and Psalm 92, "A Psalm for the Shabbat Day") and Psalm 93.

Mystical texts refer to the Friday night Shabbat spirit as "the field of holy apples". Receiving the Shabbat is like going out into a field. The kabbalistic practice of going out literally into the fields on Friday and chanting the prayers while facing the setting sun has already been discussed. The various Psalms in the *Kabbalat Shabbat* service are full of references to the grandeur and glory of nature:

"The heavens will be glad and the earth will rejoice, the sea and its fullness will roar; the field and everything in it will exult, then all the trees of the forest will sing with joy." (Psalms 96:11-12).

"*HaVaYaH* rules, let the earth exult, let many islands rejoice. Cloud and thick darkness are around Him; righteousness and justice are His throne's foundation. Fire goes before Him and consumes his enemies all around. His lightning bolts light up the world; the earth saw and trembled. The mountains melted like wax from *HaVaYaH*, before the Lord of all the earth..." (*ibid.* 97:1-5).

"The sea and its fullness will roar, the world and those who dwell therein. Rivers will clap hands, mountains will exult together..." (*ibid.* 98:7-8).

"The voice of *HaVaYaH* is upon the waters, the God of Glory thunders, *HaVaYaH* over many waters. The voice of *HaVaYaH* is in power; the voice of *HaVaYaH* is in splendor. The voice of *HaVaYaH* breaks the cedars, and *HaVaYaH* will break the cedars of Lebanon. He will make them dance like a calf, Lebanon and Siryon like young buffalos. The voice of

HaVaYaH cleaves with shafts of fire. The voice of *HaVaYaH* convulses the wilderness, *HaVaYaH* convulses the wilderness of Kadesh. The voice of *HaVaYaH* frightens the hinds and strips the forests bare, and in His Temple everything proclaims `Glory'!" (*ibid.* 29:3-9).

"More than the roar of many waters, mightier than the waves of the sea -- You are mighty on high, HaShem." (*ibid.* 93:4).

Kiddush and the Shabbat Meals

"Thus, the heavens and earth were finished and all their hosts. On the seventh day God completed His work which He had done, and He rested on the seventh day from all His work which He had done. And God blessed the seventh day and sanctified it, for on it he rested from all His work which God created to make" (Genesis 2:1-3).

This passage is recited three times on Friday night, twice in the course of the Synagogue evening service and once after returning home for the Friday night meal, when it is recited over a cup of wine as part of the *Kiddush*, Sanctification of the Shabbat over a cup of wine.

Recital of this passage is bound up with the aspect of Shabbat that has to do with *awareness*. This aspect is expressed in the Biblical command, "*Remember* the Shabbat day to keep it holy... for in six days God made the heavens and the earth, the sea and all that is in them, and He rested on the seventh day" (Exodus 20:8 & 10). To remember something is to keep it in the forefront of one's mind, to be conscious and aware of it.

One of the purposes of Shabbat is to help us keep ourselves aware of the fact that God created everything. Awareness of this fact decisively affects everything we do in this world.

Those schooled in modern philosophy and science often have difficulty relating to the Biblical account of creation in six days and God "resting" on the Shabbat. This problem could be eased if they would seek out the kabbalistic meaning of the Hebrew text rather than depending on misleading literal translations.

The Friday evening prayers and meal are times for giving special attention to *Maaseh Bereishit*, the "Work of Creation". The full cup of wine over which the passage "Thus the heavens and earth were finished" is recited at the *Kiddush* at the beginning of the meal symbolizes the blessing that flows from this awareness.

This is not the place for a detailed discussion of the deep significance of the three Shabbat meals (Friday night, Saturday morning and Saturday afternoon) collectively or individually. Suffice it to say that we adorn the Shabbat table with flowers and bring to it the choicest possible variety of produce of God's creation, the finest bread and wine, fish, meat, salads, fruits, desserts, nuts, cakes and dainties, etc. each according to their taste. The purpose is not pure gastronomy. It is to treat the soul to every kind of delight in order to enhance the joy of experiencing God everywhere, in everything.

Some have the custom of bringing fragrant herbs to the table in order bring the scents of the field inside the home and make blessings over them. The variety of different kinds of foods provides an opportunity to offer many different blessings of praise and thanks.

More than any other time during the week the home on Shabbat becomes a mini-Temple, with the table as the altar where we partake of sacrifices of thanksgiving, thereby accomplishing something of the fixing of creation that came about through the Temple rituals.

Offerings in the Temple are brought to the accompaniment of the Levitical chants and songs. Parallel to these in the home are the special Shabbat *Zemirot*, "songs" for the Shabbat meals. Many different Jewish communities around the world have added their own contributions to the rich treasury of Shabbat *Zemirot* that poetically express the many different themes of Shabbat. Prominent among these themes is awareness of the nature order:

"In six days, all was created and still endures, the most exalted heavens, earth, and seas, all the hosts of above, high and exalted, sea giant and man and mighty beasts -- that the creator, Hashem, is the Rock of the Universe" (from *Menuchah veSimchah*).

"Praises shall I prepare morning and evening to You, O Holy God, Who created all life, holy angels and sons of man, beasts of the field and birds of the sky" (from *Yah Ribon*).

The Shabbat Day Liturgy

The theme of awareness of nature is also prominent in the Shabbat day liturgy. Being a day of rest, Shabbat gives us more time for prayer and contemplation than the weekdays. One of the main difference between the Shabbat and weekday morning liturgies is the addition of many extra Psalms and praises on Shabbat.

In the morning service, the first of the additional Psalms is Psalm 19, "The heavens declare the glory of God and the expanse of the sky tells of His handiwork...." (v. 2). This psalm is an invitation to lift our eyes up to the skies, stars and planets. It gives graphic expression to the might of the sun and its daily journey across the sky. The magnificence of the natural creation is also a theme in the other additional Psalms in the morning service, such as Psalms 33, 90, 97, 135 and 136, and in the prayer of *Nishmat*, "The soul of every living being shall bless Your Name..." *Yotzer Or*, the first blessing before the morning *Shema*, speaks about the sun and the moon and other celestial bodies and the angels above them.

During the wintertime on Shabbat afternoon it is customary to recite Psalm 104, which is all about the elemental natural forces of air, fire, water and earth, the sun and the moon, and all the different trees, plants, animals, birds and creatures of the sea.

From Month to Month

"And God said: Let there be luminaries in the firmament of the heavens to distinguish between the day and the night, and they will be for signs and for seasons, for days and years" (Genesis 1:14).

"So long as the earth endures, seed-time and harvest, cold and heat, summer and winter, day and night shall not cease" (ibid. 8:22).

*O*ne of the best ways of maintaining one's connection with God through nature is by keeping aware of the changing times and seasons through the year.

The seasons are governed by the circuiting of the heavenly luminaries around the earth, especially the sun. The eccentricities of the sun's annual journeyings around our skies cause the days to lengthen or shorten according to the time of year, resulting in spring, summer, autumn and winter.

Each night the sun drops below the horizon, leaving the world to darkness. Without the sun to outshine it, the heavenly canopy of stars now comes into view. In fact, the stars were there the whole time, but they simply were not visible to us because of the brightness of the sun-lit daytime skies.

The Twelve Signs of the Zodiac

If you watch the night sky carefully through the course of the year, you notice that while the stars and constellations always remain in the same positions relative to one another, they all rise and set a little earlier every night, until after three hundred and sixty-five days they rise and set at exactly the same times as they did a year before.

According to post-Copernican astronomy, this is because the earth is in orbit around the sun. The sun and the stars are relatively fixed in space, whereas the earth not only spins on its axis once every twenty-four hours, causing day and night, but also makes a complete orbit around the sun every three hundred and sixty-five and a quarter days. Day by day we are moving forward in our orbit, which means that as each day gives way to night, the stars towards which the earth is traveling come into view slightly earlier than the preceding night. At the end of one complete orbit of the sun, we are back in the position where we started a year earlier, and as a result our view of the stars and the times at which they rise and set are exactly the same again.

Each morning, therefore, as the sun comes up above our horizon, it does so against a slightly different backdrop of stars from that of the previous day. Of course, the stars themselves become invisible to us as the day dawns and the sun rises, but they are all still there. If we were somehow still able to see the stars despite the brightness of day, we would see that with each successive day the sun appears to have advanced slightly against the backdrop of the stars.

Einsteinian relativity shows that it is actually impossible to determine if it is the earth that is moving around the sun or vice versa. Either way, it makes no difference to what is actually visible in our skies from here on earth. Pre-

Copernican astronomy held that the sun moves around the earth, while post-Copernican astronomy holds the opposite. Both are models attempting to explain one and the same fact: that from our point of view on earth, as the year progresses, the sun appears to move through a succession of different constellations -- if only they were visible to us behind the glare of the sun itself.

This fact was well-known to sky-watchers thousands of years ago. In the days before electric lighting and night-time urban glow, it was unnecessary to go to desert mountain observatories in order to see the stars in all their glory. The ancient sages knew the paths of the stars and planets as well as they knew the streets of their own towns and villages.

They realized that these august luminaries and their fascinating and evocative configurations are more than a massive accident. Observing how the movements of the sun and the stars through the year correlate with the changing seasons and other conditions on earth, they understood that the orbiting heavenly luminaries actually influence what happens on earth, thereby laying the foundations of astrology.

Observing that the sun in its annual journey through the heavens moves against a backdrop of twelve successive constellations of stars, the ancient sages discerned twelve forms suggested by these constellations, the Ram, Ox, Twins, Crab, Lion, Virgin, Scales, Scorpion, Bow, Goat, Bucket and Fish, the twelve "Signs of the Zodiac". To these they ascribed special significance.

So impressed were they with the power and influence of the stars and planets that most of the ancients actually worshipped them, none more so than the Egyptians, who excelled in every form of idolatry. They especially worshipped Aries, the Ram, first of the twelve signs of the Zodiac, coinciding with spring, time of rebirth and regeneration.

Above the Stars

Abraham with his holistic *Chokhmah*-vision grasped that the entire system of stars and planets is itself part of a far greater unified spiritual/physical system that is infinitely vast, unfathomable in its wisdom and intelligence, and all under the complete control of a single, perfect Creator: *HaVaYaH*. Abraham handed on his wisdom to Isaac, and Isaac to Jacob. But in Egypt Jacob's descendants, the Children of Israel, fell prey to the sophistication of Egyptian astro-theology and mostly forgot about their heritage.

When the time came for the Children of Israel to be freed from their slavery in Egypt, God overturned the entire system of celestial government through stars and planets, intervening to bring about a series of catastrophic ecological disasters that hit Egypt in a totally supernatural way. The Egyptians' water-supply turned into blood, after which they suffered horrendous infestations of frogs, lice and wild animals, plague, boils, hail, locusts and darkness, all of which flew in the face of the entire system of ancient idol-worship. Finally, in one night all the Egyptian first-born -- the priests of the system -- died. The dramatic departure of the Children of

Israel from Egypt showed that the stars and planets have no power or influence whatsoever except if *HaVaYaH* wills it.

The Exodus from Egypt took place under the spring-time astrological sign of Aries, the Ram. In flagrant defiance of Egyptian worship of the Ram, the Children of Israel took their paschal lambs and slaughtered them as a sacrifice to *HaVaYaH*, showing that God alone rules in heaven and on earth.

While the Egyptians and all the other ancient idolaters gave pride of place to the Sun in their astrological systems, God revealed to the Children of Israel that the key to understanding the mysteries of the heavens lies with another astrological phenomenon: the phases of the moon. The moon is the archetype of humility. She has no light of her own. All her light is "borrowed", reflected from the sun. Only with humility is it possible to know anything of God and to shine His light into the world. Acknowledging that nothing we have is our own and that all we have comes only from God is the key to true power, strength and regeneration. The monthly renewal of the moon is a sign of life and rebirth.

Rosh Chodesh

Just prior to the Exodus from Egypt God commanded the Children of Israel to count time according to the phases of moon (Exodus 12:2). Sighting of the "New Moon", the slender crescent of the moon visible briefly on the western horizon just after sunset at the very start of a new waxing phase, would inaugurate a new month. The Hebrew word for

THE HOUSE ON THE MOUNTAIN

month, *Chodesh*, means "renewal". The beginning of the month is called *Rosh Chodesh*, the "Head of the Renewal".

In the course of three hundred and fifty-four days the moon waxes and wanes twelve times. These twelve lunar cycles or "months" correspond to the twelve signs of the Zodiac, (though not exactly, because of the eleven-day discrepancy between the 354-day lunar year and the 365-day solar year. To keep the lunar and solar years in sync, the Jewish calendar adds an extra "leap month" seven years out of every nineteen. Discussion of the mysteries of *Sod Ha-Ibbur*, the "Secret of Intercalation", is beyond the scope of the present work.)

To attribute to the moon a power of its own over the world would be to exchange one idolatry for another. While the astrological influences in each lunar month depend on the changing positions of the stars and planets, the ultimate source of all these influences is *HaVaYaH* alone. The four Hebrew letters of *HaVaYaH* have twelve possible permutations. It is through these twelve different permutations that God creates time -- for changes and differences are what time is all about: "The times they are a-changing!" This is why the root meaning of the kabbalistic expression for time, *Shanah* (usually translated as "a year") is *change*.

The twelve permutations of *HaVaYaH* send correspondingly different kinds of influence and blessing into the creation at different times of the year via the angels, stars and planets making up the divine system of providence. Each permutation is ascendant in one of the twelve months of the year. The

376

special qualities of the corresponding sign of the Zodiac are an expression of the power of the ruling permutation. Thus, it is not the astrological sign that rules but *HaVaYaH*.

The renewal of the moon is a *sign*. It signifies that a new permutation is "taking over" from the permutation ascendant in the previous month. Rosh Chodesh, marking the renewal of the moon and the celestial "change of guards", is a *Moed*, an "appointed time" of special closeness between God and the Children of Israel -- a *festival* (Leviticus 23:4 and *Rashi ad loc.*; Numbers 10:10).

Since Rosh Chodesh is a time of renewal of creation, one of the main devotional themes of the day is *Maaseh Bereishit*, the "Work of Creation". This is present in the *Hallel* (Psalms 113-118) sung communally in the Synagogue in the Rosh Chodesh morning service. "From the rising of the sun until its going down, praised is the name of *HaVaYaH*" (Psalms 113:3) .... "The sea saw and fled, the Jordan turned backwards. the mountains danced like rams and the hills like the young of the flock" (*ibid.* 114:3-4). The theme of nature is especially prominent in Psalm 104, which forms part of the Rosh Chodesh service and is all about the wonders of creation, as discussed in Shabbat.

In Temple times, after the ceremony of Sanctifying the Month by the Beit Din (rabbinical court, Rosh Chodesh was marked with the offering of additional sacrifices of two oxen, a ram, seven lambs and their respective libations of wine, flour and oil (Numbers 28:11-15). These sacrifices help rectify creation through sending influences from below upwards as commanded by God so as to elicit positive, benign influences from above to below.

In the absence of the Temple, this fixing is accomplished through the recital of the corresponding Rosh Chodesh *Mussaf* or "Additional" Prayer, which includes an account of the Rosh Chodesh Temple sacrifices. At the climax of the central blessing of this prayer, "blessed are You, *HaVaYaH*, Who sanctifies Israel and the heads of the months", those familiar with the kabbalistic intentions of the prayers focus on the permutation of *HaVaYaH* ascendant in the month now beginning.

The Rosh Chodesh liturgy thus affords opportunities for deep connection with God through *Maaseh Bereishit*, the "Work of Creation". The connection is one that can be made both by the individual in his/her own personal devotions and jointly with other dear ones, friends and fellow seekers. From Biblical times onwards, it has been customary to celebrate Rosh Chodesh with a special festive meal (Samuel 1, 20:24) and by visiting spiritual guides and teachers (Kings II, 4:23).

With the scattering of the Jewish population across the sprawling conurbations of the contemporary world, the kind of close-knit spiritual community that assembles three times daily, on Shabbat and festivals for joyous prayer and mutual support is not feasible for the great majority of people. This leaves many spiritual seekers feeling isolated and lonely. It is hard to travel long distances daily in order to join with like-minded others for prayer and support, and on Shabbat traveling is actually forbidden.

This gives the Rosh Chodesh gathering a special significance in our times, as it provides an excellent opportunity for friends and dear ones to gather together for prayer, study, meditation, song, socializing etc. Today's phone, internet and satellite technology makes it possible for like-minded people in far-flung places all over the world to join in international hook-ups so as to experience a sense of togetherness in their spiritual quest.

Kiddush Levanah - - Sanctification of the Moon

One of the most beautiful occasions for connecting with God through the wonders of nature is at the ceremony of *Kiddush Levanah*, "Sanctification of the Moon", held each month a few days after Rosh Chodesh, or at the latest at some point before the full moon in the middle of the month. Where possible it is recited at the conclusion of Shabbat after the Saturday night *Maariv* service when we are dressed in our fine Shabbat clothes and are in a mood of great joy.

The custom is to go outside under the open skies at night, look up at the moon and then face the place of the Temple while reciting a blessing of praise and thanks to God:

"Blessed are you HaShem our God, King of the Universe, Who with His utterance created the heavens and with the breath of His mouth all their hosts. He gave them a decree and a time so that they should not alter their assigned task. They are joyous and glad to perform the will of their Owner -- the Worker of truth, Whose work is truth. To the moon He said that she should renew herself as a crown of splendor for those borne [by Him] from the womb, those who are destined to renew themselves like it and to glorify their Creator for the name of His glorious kingdom. Blessed are you HaShem, Who renews the months".

Recital of the blessing is accompanied by psalms and other passages. See the *Siddur* for the full text and further details about when and how *Kiddush Levanah* is recited.

Following *Kiddush Levanah* it is customary for the participants to join together in a dance-circle (alluding to the circle of the twelve constellations of the Zodiac) and dance while singing the words from *El Adon* in the Shabbat morning liturgy:

"Good are the luminaries that our God has created, He has fashioned them with knowledge, with insight and discernment. Strength and power, has He granted them to be dominant within the world. Filled with luster and radiating brightness, their luster is beautiful throughout the world. Glad as they go forth and exultant as they return, they do with awe their Creator's will. Splendor and glory they bestow upon His Name, jubilation and glad song upon the mention of His reign. He called out to the sun and it glowed with light, He saw and fashioned the form of the moon. All the host above bestows praise on Him, splendor and greatness -- the Seraphim, Chayot and holy Ophanim."

The Festivals

Each of the different months of the Jewish year has its own unique character and feel. There is hardly a single month that does not have a festival or special observance of some kind. In most cases these are closely linked with the season of the year in which they fall.

The Jewish People is eternally and inseparably attached to the Land promised to Abraham, Isaac and Jacob, and the various festivals are intimately bound up with the agriculture of Israel and the ecology in general. Both for the Jews in Israel and for those presently living elsewhere, the festivals provide a wealth of opportunities for spiritual connection through ecology and nature.

The ecological dimension of the Jewish festivals and other seasonal observances deserves an entire study by itself. Within the confines of the present work it is possible only to provide a few brief notes and suggestions, leaving further investigation of this subject to the student.

Nissan

"This month will be for you the head of the months" (Exodus 12:2). Nissan, the month of redemption for the Children of Israel in all ages, is the first of the months. It is also called *Aviv*, Springtime, for in Israel the rains and clouds of winter are mostly gone, the hills are green and flowering, the fruit trees are in blossom, and the wheat and barley in the fields are reaching full ripeness.

The mild sunny spring days are ideal for walks in the country to reconnect with nature after being closed up at home during the winter. Release and joy are the themes of the Pesach (Passover) festival that takes place on the night of the full moon of the month of Nissan. In preparation for the festival, Chassidim would go out into the woods and meadows for lengthy periods of prayer and meditation. Those who are unable to go out into nature before or during Pesach can experience the natural beauty of spring through the customary reading of Song of Songs after the Pesach *Seder* and on the Shabbat that falls during the festival (*Shabbat Chol HaMoed*).

Because of the requirement for our homes to be free of all *Chametz* (leaven) during Pesach, people tend to be preoccupied with home cleaning in preparation for the festival. While the autumn Rosh Hashanah and Yom Kippur season of awe is associated with looking *inside* ourselves with introspection and self-examination, the spring-time pre-Pesach cleaning of our closets and drawers, houses and yards puts the focus on the *outer* home and surrounding environment. Pesach cleaning is a good opportunity to think carefully about our lifestyle how to bring it into greater harmony with God and nature.

The Festival of Pesach

The seven-day festival of Pesach is the first of the three annual pilgrim festivals. In Temple times Jews would flock to

Jerusalem to enter the awesome, sacred courtyards of the Temple and offer the Pesach and other festival sacrifices, after which they would join with their families, friends and the poor and needy for ritual meals where they would eat of the sacrificial meat and joyously partake of *Maaser Sheini*, the special tithe of all the different kinds of produce of the land which they would bring to eat in Jerusalem in holiness and purity. The streets of Jerusalem were bedecked with produce and filled with excited crowds together with their sacrificial sheep, goats and cows.

At present, we can only imagine all this and think ourselves into the spirit of the festival using the *Machzor*, the Festival Prayer Book, with its many references to Temple practice. Thus, on the afternoon of the fourteenth of Nissan, eve of the Pesach Seder Night, it is customary to recite passages about the Pesach sacrifice that was brought on that day. Reference has already been made to the connection between the paschal lamb and the Ram or Aries, the astrological sign of Nissan.

In our time when we do not have the Pesach sacrifice, the main focus of the festival celebration is the Seder Night ritual, when we recite the *Haggadah* telling the story of the Exodus from Egypt, drink four cups of wine, and eat *Matzah*, unleavened bread, and bitter herbs (*Maror*). Sitting at our tables bedecked with the Pesach plate and its colorful greens, vegetables and the shankbone and egg symbolizing the Pesach sacrifices, our homes are once again a mini-Temple and our tables an altar.

At the heart of the idea of redemption from Egypt is that of spiritual redemption from distorted, restrictive worldviews and mindsets. Egypt represents the ultimate in sophisticated city decadence and corruption, from which the Children of Israel had to escape in order to build a new way of life founded on a simple, pure truth that could be learned only amidst the stark natural grandeur of the wilderness. The Exodus teaches that God rules over everything. The Haggadah can be understood on a multitude of levels. For the ecologically-minded, the account of the ten ecological catastrophes or "Plagues" with which God smote the Egyptians should provide plentiful material for thought.

In Temple times, the sixteenth of Nissan was the time of the *Omer*, a national offering of a portion of the finest barley flour from the new crop specially harvested the previous evening and brought to the Temple together with special animal sacrifices. The weeks following Pesach are in Israel the time of the grain harvest, and the Omer offering was the first from the new grain. Before the sixteenth of Nissan it is not permitted to eat from the new crop, for man may only partake of the fruits of this world after first giving thanks and acknowledgment to God. The humble offering of barley (which is primarily an animal food) brings us into the harvest season with the proper attitude of respect and gratitude. According to the Talmud (*Rosh Hashanah* 16a), Pesach is the time when God judges the world for grain, determining the success of the harvest. The Omer offering brought at this time of judgment has obvious ecological implications.

The second major climax of the Pesach celebrations comes on the seventh day of the festival, recalling the splitting of the Red Sea, which the Children of Israel crossed on dry land while the Egyptians were finally destroyed. The timely parting of the waters was one of the most striking historical exceptions to the normal workings of nature, showing that God is in total control of every part of creation, making and suspending the laws of nature at will. The Seventh day of Pesach is an appropriate time for reflection on God's control of natural processes and the concept of miracles. It is also a time for looking *forward* to the messianic redemption that we are now awaiting, hailing the restoration of the Holy Temple and bringing the world to be filled with the knowledge of God as the waters cover the seas.

Counting the Omer

The Omer offering on the sixteenth of Nissan inaugurates a period of counting forty-nine days ("Counting the Omer") until the festival of Shavuot, second of the main festivals, recalling the Giving of the Torah by God to the Children of Israel at Sinai, which was the purpose of their redemption from Egypt.

The period of the Omer count is one of steady spiritual work, day by day and step by step internalizing the lessons of Pesach in preparation for the culminating experience of "Receiving the Torah" on Shavuot. Fields and meadows are good places for this work, as discussed in the writings of Rebbe Nachman:

"When summer begins to approach it is very good to meditate in the fields. This is a time when you can pray to God with longing and yearning. When every bush of the field begins to return to life and grow, they all yearn to be included in prayer and meditation." (Rabbi Nachman's Wisdom #98).

Most of the Omer period falls during the month of Iyar. Rebbe Nachman specifically discusses this "season when the earth gives forth her bounty and puts strength into all the trees and plants. Now that the fruits are ripening, all medicinal plants have greater power, because the earth then puts strength into them.... The Hebrew letters making up the name of Iyar are thus the initial letters in the verse (Exodus 15:26) *Ani YHVH Rofecha*, "I, *HaVaYaH*, am your healer" (*Likutey Moharan* I, 277). The month of Iyar is thus an appropriate time for healing amidst nature.

The eighteenth day of Iyar, *Lag BaOmer* (thirty-third day of the Omer count), is the memorial day for Rabbi Shimon bar Yochai (3rd century C.E.), author of the *Zohar*. Crown of all the kabbalistic writings, the *Zohar* contains the keys to the Jewish mystical view of this world and the place of nature within it. In Israel, large numbers of people visit Rabbi Shimon's gravesite amidst the hills of the Galilee in Meron, and many camp out for days in the surrounding woods and fields. Throughout the world people celebrate Lag BaOmer by lighting bonfires, joining together for an outdoor *kumsitz*, and taking hikes and rambles in the countryside.

Shavuot

The festival of Shavuot on the sixth of Sivan commemorates the giving of the Torah at Mount Sinai. When the Torah was given, the mountain burst forth with a carpet of lush verdure. In memory of this, it is customary on Shavuot to decorate the synagogue with flowers and foliage. Thus, we surround ourselves with natural beauty as we stand in the synagogue to "receive the Torah" anew each year.

Shavuot is called "the harvest festival" (Exodus 23:15). It falls at the climax of the grain harvesting season in Israel. In the Temple two loaves of the finest leavened wheat bread were presented on Shavuot as a thanksgiving offering. Shavuot is also called the "day of the first-fruits" (Numbers 28:26), and in Temple times it inaugurated the season when farmers would bring their choicest first-fruits of wheat, barley, grapes, pomegranates, figs, olives and dates to the Temple court-yard. There they would present the fruits to the priest and make a declaration of acknowledgment and thanksgiving to God. The Talmud states that on Shavuot God judges the world for the fruits of the trees, which in Israel mostly ripen in the ensuing summer months.

The ecological significance of the two loaves and first-fruits is obvious. Ecology and agriculture are also prominent themes in the Book of Ruth, which is read in the Synagogue on Shavuot morning. Ruth, the outstanding Moabitess convert to Judaism, was the great-grandmother of David, the messianic king. The Book of Ruth begins with famine in the land of Israel and goes on to tell the moving story of Ruth's encounter with Boaz in the course of the grain harvest. Boaz teaches his workers about the mitzvot of gifts to the poor. Caring for the poor and needy is the very essence of the Torah that was given on Shavuot.

Tammuz and Av

During these hot, arid summer months in Israel much of the spring vegetation dries up. The three weeks from the seventeenth of Tammuz are a period of semi-mourning culminating in the fast of the 9th of Av, *Tisha B'Av*, commemorating the destruction of the first and second Temples.

As discussed throughout this book, the Temple promotes peace in the world and harmony between man and the natural environment. The destruction of the Temple signifies the driving of the Divine Presence from the world because of human folly and excess, leading to discord in the world and imbalance between man and nature. As we witness the destruction and abuse of the natural environment in the present day through human greed and waste, we would do well to use this period of the year to think carefully about the lessons taught by Jewish history and to contemplate the meaning of the Temple and its importance for the world.

After *Tisha B'Av*, the mood changes from mourning to one of repair, regeneration and renewal. This is the summer vacation period, and many people take the opportunity to refresh and inspire themselves by touring and hiking in the countryside.

Elul

The month of Elul corresponds to the astrological sign of Virgo, the maiden, symbolizing the unspoiled purity of the relationship between God and the Jewish People. The Elul period is one of self-examination and return to God in preparation for the Days of Awe -- *Rosh HaShanah* (New Year) and *Yom Kippur* (Day of Atonement). With the summer days now beginning to cool, Chassidim endeavor to spend time in the woods and meadows for meditation and prayer.

The Days of Awe

The month of Tishri corresponds to the astrological sign of Libra, the Scales. The first of Tishri is Rosh HaShanah, the New Year, the day of judgment for the whole world, when "all who come into the world pass before Him like sheep being numbered" (*Rosh HaShana*h 16a). While much of the emphasis on Rosh HaShanah and the ensuing Ten Days of Repentance is on individual self-correction, a central focus of the Rosh HaShanah prayers is on universal repair and fixing, for the judgment that is made on this day is one that takes in "all who come into the world" -- which means not only all humanity but all other creatures and even the very angels. Our prayers on this day should be not only for ourselves but for the whole world.

The days of awe culminate in Yom Kippur, the Day of Atonement. The high point of the Yom Kippur prayers is during the additional Mussaf service, in which we recount step by step the special Yom Kippur service of the High

Priest in the Holy Temple, which is replete with mysteries relating to the rectification of all creation. The climax of the service was the high priest's entry into the Holy of Holies. As he left, he would offer a prayer for a year of blessings and goodness. We too should pray on Yom Kippur for a year of blessing and success for ourselves, for the House of Israel, and for the entire world.

Succot

Five days after Yom Kippur on the fifteenth of Tishri, the night of the full moon, the seven-day festival of Succot begins. The ecological significance of Succot is more apparent than that of any other festival.

The first major mitzva of the festival is that of dwelling in the Succah. As mentioned previously, the human home is the ultimate in the man-made. It is the homes, houses and buildings that make up our contemporary urban civilization that are the main focus of the human consumption that is presently causing such destruction to the earth environment. The festival of Succot challenges us to think about the real meaning and purpose of a home, which is to serve as a mini-Temple in which the Divine Presence may dwell with us as we go about our lives, sanctifying our consumption through moderation and with blessings of gratitude.

The mitzva of Succah is to take our daily eating, drinking and other activities including our very sleeping out into a temporary structure whose roof may be made of nothing but natural cut branches and leaves, etc. According to the halachah, the roof of the Succah may be made only of materials that are specifically not man-made in any way. Wood and other vegetation that have been turned into even the most primitive kind of utensil or instrument are invalid. The stars should be visible through the Succah roof at night.

The Succah comes to instill in us the trust that what protects us in this life is not the man-made world of tools and trappings we construct around ourselves but rather the divine providence that is with us and cares for us every moment of every day for ever and ever.

The Succah that each Jew builds corresponds to the Sanctuary built in the wilderness. In our Succot we become priests in the Sanctuary, and the blessings and prayers we offer over the festival foods and dainties turn our eating and drinking into the partaking of sacrificial portions.

The Four Kinds

The foremost ecological theme of Succot is that of the water cycle. Succot is called the "festival of ingathering" (Exodus 23:16), for in Israel, after drying their grapes and figs under the hot summer sun, people would now take them inside their houses before the onset of the rainy season.

Eating our ingathered produce naturally arouses thoughts and worries about how the next year's produce will turn out. In Israel, these thoughts center on whether it will be a rainy winter, since agriculture there is totally dependent on rainfall. The Torah tells us that the rainfall depends on man's behavior

(Deuteronomy 11:13-14) and teaches us to look trustingly to God, turning our concerns and worries into prayers and acts of service.

The second main mitzva on Succot is thus to take in our hands the Four Kinds -- the *Lulav* (palm branch), *Etrog* (citron), *Hadassim* (myrtle branches) and *Aravot* (willow branches) and shake them together in the six directions of created space: south, north, east, west, up and down.

Each of the Four Kinds exemplifies dependence on water. The presence of palms in a desert testifies to the presence of an oasis. The Etrog tree is notorious for its need for abundant watering in order to produce good fruits. The fragrant myrtle bush needs plenty of water to grow and stay fresh, while willow leaves dry and shrivel after only the shortest period without water.

The Talmud states that on Succot the world is judged for water (*Rosh Hashana*h 16a). The mitzva of the Four Kinds is our way of seeking to sweeten the judgment. We wave them in all six directions, manifesting God's power and kingship over every part of creation. Every day of Succot it is customary for the congregants to circuit the Reader's Desk with the four kinds in their hands while reciting special prayers. In the Temple, the theme of water was also present in the special daily libation of purest spring-water to the accompaniment of music, singing and dancing -- *Simchat Beit HaSho-eva*, "the Joy of the Water-Drawing". In our time, this is recalled during Succot by singing and dancing in the synagogues and study halls.

The prayers for water become more and more explicit as the festival proceeds. On the seventh day of Succot, *Hoshanah Rabbah*, the congregants circuit the Reader's Desk seven times with the Four Kinds, after which special prayers alluding to rain and water are recited. Finally, the congregants take bundles of willow branches and beat them on the ground. The shape of the willow leaf resembles that of the human lips, alluding to the power of prayer, even that of the weakest and most vulnerable. "Let him put his mouth in the earth, perhaps there is hope" (Lamentations 3:29).

Hoshanah Rabbah is thus followed by *Shemini Atzeret*, the "Eighth day of Solemn Assembly", conclusion of the Tishri Days of Awe, when we specifically pray for rain.

Cheshvan and Kislev

The onset of rain and colder weather tends to keep people inside their homes. The winter months are a time to work steadily to internalize the many lessons learned during the festival season.

Chanukah, the festival of lights, which starts on the twenty-fifth of Kislev and lasts for eight days, celebrates the victory of the Hasmonean priests over Greek hegemony and culture in the Second Temple period (circa 275 B.C.E.).

The Greek philosophers could not accept that the Creation may contain secrets that lie beyond the capacity of the human intellect to fathom, and they could not tolerate Jewish belief and practice, which are founded on faith alone. Three Jewish practices in particular they tried to obliterate: Shabbat, which testifies to God's creation of the world; Rosh Chodesh, the sign of rebirth and regeneration; and Milah, circumcision, which is a sign of our dedication to God and acceptance of His covenant.

The eight-day festival of Chanukah always contains one Shabbat and sometimes two. Rosh Chodesh of the month of Tevet always falls during Chanukah. And a baby boy born on the first day of Chanukah is circumcised on the eighth day of Chanukah.

Chanukah thus testifies to the Torah's victory over skeptics and atheists. The pure light of holy spirituality shines triumphant from the Chanukah lamp which is lit all eight nights of the festival. Starting with one light on the first night, we add an extra light on each successive night until on the last night we end up with eight, symbolizing infinity (for Judaism counts time in base-seven, as "the world was created in seven days", and eight is beyond seven). The Chanukah lamp is positioned either by the doors of our houses or in our windows, to signify that, having drawn down the light of faith in God inside our very homes, we can now shine this faith outwards to all the world.

The Chanukah lights symbolize the negation of the Greek philosophical approach to the world, (which alienates man from creation by separating the knower from that which he knows), and the vindication of the Torah faith in a loving Creator who rules the world with kindness and justice. Only when we cleanse our minds of the influence of false and distorted world-views can we see the world around us for what it is: God's creation.

Shevat

In Israel, most of the winter rains have fallen by the time of the month of Shevat, corresponding to the astrological sign of Aquarius, the Bucket. After their winter sleep, the trees now draw new strength through their roots from the water-soaked earth. The fifteenth of Shevat, *Tu BiShvat*, is the "New Year of Trees". It is customary to eat many different kinds of fruit and make many blessings on this day, as the words of our blessings give strength and power to the angels appointed over the trees, sending blessing into the produce of the new year. The ecological importance of *Tu BiShvat* is quite obvious.

Adar

Adar is the last month of the year counting from Nissan. If the keynote of Nissan is birth and vitality, that of Adar might be thought to be the opposite. Indeed, Moses our Teacher left the world on the seventh of Adar. Haman, descendant of Esau's atheistic grandson Amalek and the very archetype of Jew-hatred, thought that the month of Adar would be a propitious time to destroy the Jewish People and wipe out all knowledge of God from the world. Haman tried to exterminate the Jews and plotted to have their leader, the tzaddik Mordechai, hanged. But his plans were thwarted by Mordechai's niece, Queen Esther. Haman was hung on his own gallows, while the Jews went on to rebuild the Temple and keep the Torah alive for all generations.

The festival of Purim on the 14th and 15th of Adar celebrates the miraculous fall of Haman, symbolizing the ultimate destruction of Esau, the unholy counterpart of Jacob. Esau is the archetypal glutton, selfishly consuming and destroying the world. The Purim observances signify the opposite of Esau.

The first mitzva of Purim is to hear twice over the story of the miracle as recounted in *Megillat Esther*, the Scroll of Esther. It is read publicly in the Synagogue in the evening and the morning. Thus, before we even start thinking about eating and drinking to gratify our bodies, we first go to the level of mind and spirit and listen to a story the entire plot of which develops out of banqueting and wine-drinking. Throughout Purim it is a mitzva to give charity to all who ask. Taking one's money and giving it as charity to needy others is the opposite of selfish greed. The theme of consideration and compassion for others is central in the other two main mitzvot of the day: sending portions of cooked food to friends and giving gifts to the poor.

The Purim celebrations culminate with the Purim feast and drinking party on Purim afternoon. Having risen to the level of soul and spirit through the reading of the Megillah, and having sent portions to our friends and gifts to the poor, we are finally ready to eat and drink in holiness. The carnival spirit of Purim causes the supreme sanctity of the Purim feast to remain concealed from many revelers. In fact, it is a thanksgiving offering to God for all his miracles and blessings, and it signifies man's triumph over the serpent who tricked Adam into eating the fruit of the tree of knowledge of good and evil. We now drink wine and rise to a level that is beyond *Daat*-knowledge, a level that lies beyond the knowable and cannot be expressed in words: *Keter*, the Crown.

If Adam's sin was to consume the fruit of the tree of knowledge selfishly, the fixing is to learn to eat, drink and consume in holiness. As humanity learns to do this, balance and harmony will return to the world and the earth will again become a garden in which all will sing the praise of God.

The Earth is the Lord's

"The earth is HaVaYaH's *and all that it holds" (Psalms 24:1)*

*T*he earth and everything in it belongs to God, as the Psalm says: "The earth is *HaVaYaH*'s and all that it holds" (Psalms 24:1). On the other hand: "He gave the earth to the sons of man" (Psalms 115:16). This means that the earth is entrusted to us. We are entitled to eat of its goodness -- but only if we remember that ultimately everything belongs to God, and as His trustees, we are obliged to follow the laws of the land.

The Sabbatical Year

The whole creation is founded on the principle of six days of work followed by the Shabbat day of rest. The Torah law of the land is based on the related principle of six years of agricultural work followed by a year of Shabbat release, the *Shemittah* or Sabbatical year.

"Six years you may sow your field and six years you may prune your vineyard and gather in its produce. But in the seventh year the land shall have a Shabbat of complete rest for *HaVaYaH*" (Leviticus 25:3-4).

During the six years of work the farmer is full owner of his field. He is entitled to work the land as he desires. After giving his gifts to the poor and tithes, the owner may eat or otherwise use the produce as he pleases. But in the seventh year, ownership of the land returns to the Lord of the Land,

and the farmer is no longer free to treat it as his own personal property.

In the Land of Israel during the Sabbatical year most kinds of agricultural work are forbidden. Ground-crops that grow by themselves may neither be harvested nor eaten, while the fruits of the trees must be left for anyone to take. Even the wild animals are entitled to their share of the Sabbatical produce. The fruit of the Sabbatical year has a holiness of its own. It may not be sold commercially. The produce must be treated with respect and not be wasted.

The Sabbatical year is a teaching about our true situation as guests on this earth and the proper respect with which its produce must be used.

The seven year Sabbatical cycle has a bearing on the tithing of produce. During the six years of agricultural work, the gifts of *Terumah* to the priests and of *Maaser Rishon*, the Levitical tithe, remain constant. But there is a second tithe that is used differently in different years of the sabbatical cycle. In the first and second years of the cycle, this second tithe would in Temple times be eaten in purity by the farmer himself with his family and friends in Jerusalem. However, in the third year this tithe must be given to the poor. In the fourth and fifth years of the cycle, the second tithe would be eaten by the farmer himself, while in the sixth year it is given to the poor.

A farmer who had faithfully observed all the laws of the land could come to the Temple on Pesach of the fourth and seventh years of the cycle and declare:

"I have removed the holy portion from the house and I have given it to the Levite and the stranger, to the fatherless and the widow in accordance with all Your commandments that You commanded me. I have not transgressed Your commandments and I have not forgotten.... Look down from Your holy abode from Heaven and bless Your people Israel and the land that You have given us as you swore to our fathers, a land flowing with milk and honey" (Deuteronomy 26:13 & 15).

Many of the land laws do not apply directly to today's city-dwellers. But we all depend on fruits, vegetables and other produce, and we must remember that the bounty of the land comes from God. Besides blessing God for all that we eat, we must check that all the necessary tithes etc. are taken from produce before we consume it. A good way to remember our position as God's guests in this world is by familiarizing ourselves with the Torah land laws. It is also good to keep track of the years of the cycle and be aware of where we are standing. The last Shemittah year was in the year 5775 (2014-2015), and the next will be in the year 5782 (2021-22).

The Jubilee Year

Just as in the forty-nine day Omer count we count seven times seven days so the Torah commands us to count seven Sabbatical cycles of seven years each, making a total of forty-nine years, after which we celebrate the fiftieth year as the *Yovel* or Jubilee year:

"And you shall count seven weeks of years -- seven times seven years.... And you shall sanctify the fiftieth year and proclaim release throughout the land for all its inhabitants: it shall be a jubilee year for you" (Leviticus 25:8-9).

According to Torah land law, if a person sold inherited ancestral land in Israel and failed to buy it back, the land would automatically revert to the original owner in the Jubilee year. In addition, all Israelite slaves were set free. These laws do not apply today, but the redemption and freedom of the Jubilee are precisely what we are awaiting as we look forward to the coming of Mashiach, the rebuilding of the Temple and the return of all the Children of Israel to our land. When the laws of the land are observed by all, true peace and prosperity will come to the world:

"If you will go in My statutes and keep My commandments and practice them, I will give your rains in their time and the earth will give its produce and the tree of the field will give its fruit. Your threshing will overtake the vintage and your vintage shall overtake the sowing. You shall eat your fill of bread and dwell securely in your land. I will grant peace to the land and you will lie down untroubled by anyone...." (Leviticus 26:3-6).

* 9 7 8 0 9 9 5 6 5 6 0 1 7 *